Canada and International Affairs

Palgrave's Canada and International Affairs is a timely and rigorous series for showcasing scholarship by Canadian scholars of international affairs and foreign scholars who study Canada's place in the world. The series will be of interest to students and academics studying and teaching Canadian foreign, security, development and economic policy. By focusing on policy matters, the series will be of use to policy makers in the public and private sectors who want access to rigorous, timely, informed and independent analysis. As the anchor, Canada Among Nations is the series' most recognisable annual contribution. In addition, the series showcases work by scholars from Canadian universities featuring structured analyses of Canadian foreign policy and international affairs. The series also features work by international scholars and practitioners working in key thematic areas that provides an international context against which Canada's performance can be compared and understood.

Anessa L. Kimball

Beyond 2%—NATO Partners, Institutions & Burden Management

Concepts, Risks & Models

palgrave
macmillan

Anessa L. Kimball
Department of Political Science
Université Laval
Quebec, QC, Canada

ISSN 2523-7187 ISSN 2523-7195 (electronic)
Canada and International Affairs
ISBN 978-3-031-22157-6 ISBN 978-3-031-22158-3 (eBook)
https://doi.org/10.1007/978-3-031-22158-3

This Palgrave Macmillan imprint is published by the registered company Springer Nature Switzerland AG
The registered company address is: Gewerbestrasse 11, 6330 Cham, Switzerland

To the versions of me who did not believe this was possible.

Acknowledgments

/Those who know me confirm I am not deterred once passionate about a puzzle or convinced by an argument./ This project on NATO burden sharing, bargaining, and enlargement ruminated since post-cold war enlargement debates appeared on NATO agendas in the late 1990s. In 1998, the threads of the arguments in this research began while Kimball represented Kent State University in the Defense Planning Group at the National Model NATO Simulation, Howard University, Washington, DC. In Ohio, the Lyman Lemnitzer Center for NATO and EU studies at KSU was where their study of NATO began with an undergraduate specialization in North Atlantic Security Studies benefiting from a course by Lawrence Kaplan, renowned historian, at that time in his 60s and living in Washington, DC. They met last when Kimball interned at the Atlantic Council of the US in spring 2000 reminiscing about a shared intellectual passion for NATO. Kimball spent weekends that term at the US Library of Congress reading and listening to De Gaulle's speeches on defense 'commitments' to NATO and the 'cultural policy of grandeur' as a guiding doctrine for foreign policy. Those efforts culminated in an interdisciplinary Honor's BA in International Relations. Their BA thesis was approved by faculty affiliated with political science, French, and history in 2000. Said research attracted support for graduate studies and Kimball completed M.A. and Ph.D. studies at SUNY Binghamton under the mentorship of D. Clark (2006). Training at SUNY-Binghamton in the department of political science focused on the fundamentals of quantitative and formal institutional analysis of IR and comparative politics. Kimball's publications appear at this intersection. Prof. Kimball was hired as regular faculty, assistant professor, in the department of political science, at l'Université Laval June 2006; since June 2021 Kimball is a full professor.

This book was not possible without the support of the Canadian Defense and Security Network and, particularly, Professor S. Saideman whose counsel and comments were essential. Professor S. Vucetic offered suggestions and data. Professor A. Lanoszka sent insightful comments on a selected chapter. Earlier versions were presented at the Canadian Political Science Association annual meetings, 2021 & 2022, as well as the 2021 & 2022 Canadian Defence Economics & Security Workshop and the American University Transatlantic Policy Center's 2022 annual NATO Conference; comments made by discussants and participants improved multiple parts of the project. I thank the team of graduate students supporting data collection and more—F. Chaves Correa, E. Douguet and M. Philaire. C. Picard provided invaluable effort in the literature compilation, manuscript copyediting, as well as supporting my sanity. L. Birch, N. Gadway, B. Sprague, A. Merlin and C. D'Angelo reminded me to never give up. MEM benefited from the intense writing period resulting in newly granted independence to explore our corner of the city with friends and learned to cook several meals as a means to survive while I wrote. I am grateful for a well-established collaborative co-parenting environment with CEM. I invested money and time in this proposal starting March 2021 retreating from Québec city to write with a view of beautiful Lac-Etchemin. Over several weekend retreats to the same chalet, the core of the proposal came together. It was submitted in November 2021. Finally, I started a book-length project due to social pressure from the 'idea one cannot be promoted to full professor on articles and chapters.' I thank myself for requesting and obtaining full professorship retroactively before signing a book contract at the end of April 2022. Those not otherwise mentioned supporting my promotion with letters include: B. Falk, S. Bell, C. Leprince, B. Toubol and P. Colautti along with L. Brisson and V. Joseph from SPUL. To the next step towards impossible obtentions, a solo-authored book on NATO defense burdens; a call for action to contemporize burden research and allocation contributions.

Contents

List of Figures

List of Tables

List of Policy Pop Out

Acronyms

(S)ACT	(Supreme) Allied Command Transformation
ASEAN	Association of Southeast Asian Nations
COE	Centre of Excellence
DSA	(US bilateral) Defense and Security Agreements
EFP	Enhanced Forward Presence
EU	European Union
FN	Framework Nation (COE)
GDP	Gross Domestic Product
HQ	Headquarters
II	International Institution
IO	International Organization
IR	International Relations
ISAF	International Security Assistance Force
JAPCC	Joint Air Power Competence COE
JCBRN	Joint Chemical, Biological, Radiological, Nuclear Defense COE
KFOR	Kosovo Force
MC	Military Committee
MILMED	Military Medicine COE
MOU	Memorandum of Understanding
MP	Middle Power
NATO	North Atlantic Treaty Organization
NOJ	Notice of Joining (COE)
OSCE	Organization for Security and Cooperation in Europe
PFP	Partnership For Peace
POW	Program of Work (COE)
PR	Public Relations

RIT	Rational Institutionalist Theory
SC	Steering Committee (COE)
STRATCOM	Strategic Communications COE
UK	United Kingdom of Great Britain and Northern Ireland
UN	United Nations
US	United States

CHAPTER 1

Introduction

NATO's next round of enlargement to Finland and Sweden, the sixth, is unlike previous post-cold war rounds; negotiation was shorter, accession approvals from partners are expected in less than 6 months (half the average), and this is in the midst of a Russian war in Ukraine. To answer the question why? One must examine national politics, shifting security risks, and political will.

> Public support for NATO accession, and the added security of NATO's 'Article V' mutual defense clause, has skyrocketed in both countries since Russia's invasion of Ukraine; recent polls indicate support at 76% in Finland and 59% in Sweden. U.S. officials from the Departments of State and Defense concur with Finnish and Swedish assertions that the two countries would be 'security providers,' strengthening NATO's defense posture in the Baltic region in particular. Finland is expected to *exceed NATO's 2% GDP* defense spending target in 2022, and Sweden has *committed to meet the 2% goal* as soon as possible.—Updated 14 July 2022 (Archik et al., 2022)

This book is not about Finland and Sweden entering NATO; however, their impending entry supports the arguments herein. First, NATO burden sharing research lacks multiple measures about shifting security risks to partners as the alliance expanded geographically. It also does

A. L. Kimball, *Beyond 2%—NATO Partners, Institutions & Burden Management*, Canada and International Affairs,
https://doi.org/10.1007/978-3-031-22158-3_1

not consider how security threats diversified in the post-cold war era. Second, in the late 1990s, NATO enlargement was 'sold' to publics to reduce burdens on all partners; one study rejects said claim employing NATO civilian budget share data comparisons (Kimball, 2019). Enlargement considered security risks to the alliance and partners while trying to avoid political risks. This was done by bundling the riskiest states in the 2004 round to distribute externalities across the alliance with some underwriting by US defense and security agreements (Kimball, 2021b). Those agreements provided information about the defense 'quality' of entrants and facilitated enlargement because a majority of post-cold war entrants did not meet the 2% target, but were admitted. Third, since 2003, NATO Centres of Excellence (COE) are a way partners share alliance transformation burdens to meet future defense and security needs. The observation so few studies examine risks to partners and the alliance alongside the observed paucity of research considering how NATO developed extra-club institutions, i.e., COE, at zero cost to itself, to reduce future uncertainties, taken together are a call for modernizing associated research programs. The result is a research gap where risks and threats lack multiple measures, the geostrategic and political risks of enlargement remain absent from models and impending enlargement ensures negotiations on burdens are forthcoming—this is a moment to revisit 2% (Becker, 2017; Dvorak & Pernica, 2021; Oma, 2012) and go beyond.

Cooperation, the emergence of institutions and collaboration are tools states use to reduce uncertainty about the future (i.e., create mutual expectations about future behavior). States, as partners in NATO, have internal political constraints and differing defense and security capacities to contribute to the club's core goods. The risk management model of burden sharing accounts for shifting territorial threats to the club, and partners, due to enlargement along with increasing risks to cohesion from diversity in capacities and practices to integrate operationally. Burden sharing beyond a military spending target includes the complexity of the institutions' partners support to make NATO function daily as well as in its deployed operations. This book offers multiple approaches and theoretical perspectives examining burden sharing in three ways: military spending, participation in a new NATO operation and the establishment, elaboration, and participation by partners in NATO Centres of Excellence. The quantitative models offer two periods of study from 1949 to present and from 1993, i.e., the creation of the Partnership for Peace. The book advances our understanding of burden sharing through added measures, new modeling specifications and institutional analysis while comparing the effects of factors from a risk management perspective. It makes the case for reconceptualizing and reconsidering burdens and allocations to the Atlantic Alliance; this is when new partners are in accession and NATO is in a defensive posture with multiple members perceiving increased threats from Russia.

Explaining Arrangements Among Sovereign States Providing Collective Goods

Institutional arrangements contracted among sovereign states producing collective goods are the subject of theoretical and empirical study by political scientists, economists, legal scholars and historians. Traditional international relations (hereafter, IR) theories seek to understand why institutions emerge, their design and the characteristics shaping their tenure. Differences over the perception of relative (i.e., individual) versus absolute (i.e., total) gains in the context of the underlying strategic game constrained realism and liberalism to concentrate on institutional emergence and tenure in cooperative or conflictual strategic environments (Kimball,). Realists anticipate alliances endure as long as states receive benefits exceeding costs indicating a perception of relative gains. Liberals will cooperate for absolute gains, a smaller amount. Others suggest cooperation emerged due to intergovernmental social historical forces under favorable leadership conditions (Moravcsik, 1997). Finally, social theorists shifted focus to factors such as the convergence or divergence of identities (Wendt, 1992; Zehfuss, 2001) explaining international cooperation. However, realism, liberalism, constructivism and other approaches cannot explain how states allocate/bargain over burdens across time, due to a focus on 'if states cooperate.' If states cooperate, then most theories are silent on 'how it be designed.'

Cooperation contract designers must solve fundamental problems about paying for and distributing collective goods within the institution. When institutions provide semi-private goods, club arrangements arise forcing partners pay a 'fee' to participate and receive the good at a better level of access or quality. Despite the emergence of clubs providing public goods (Sandler & Hartley, 2001), partners facing different threats may not perceive all threats equally salient and/or face capacity constraints influencing allocations; partner differences produce frictions within the club affecting cohesion. This occurs from a failure to distinguish partner threats from club threats influencing national decisions about resource allocations. Finally, IR approaches differ on the management of diverse risks while sharing burdens across differently capable partners. Institutionalist/delegation arguments on how institutions reduce risks, influence burdens, and manage strategic problems contribute an improved model for studying burden sharing, whereas power-based theories focus on the tools deployed by stronger partners to obtain leadership and manage risks (bilaterally). The *risk management model* proposes NATO mitigates risks to the club and then to partner security while producing collective goods. As a result, club risks are considered alongside those arising from internal environments for partners. This link is essential because decisions on contributing to NATO operations and defense spending are taken at the national level. The US reduced uncertainty about states through contracting defense and security agreements, this facilitated enlargement; its relationship with spending is examined herein. This book aligns itself to contribute a risk management burden sharing model examining new factors along with classic measures while making data available for future study.

NATO—Studying the Burden of Providing Collective Goods for a Club

With seven decades of existence, NATO burden sharing has attracted substantial research (Hartley & Sandler, 1999). NATO burden analysis is organized along three dimensions according to a study of 153 *articles* published from 1966 to 2020 (Bogers et al., 2020). The first category, accounting for 99 of the articles (65%), examined the distribution of burdens across partners, 42 articles studied determinants of behavior (28%), whereas only 5% examine how partner allocations are merged to produce the overall level of the good for consumption (Bogers et al., 2020). They identified the emergence of waves of scholarship starting with Sandler's (1977) joint-product model which underwent renewed interest at the end of the cold war (Bogers et al., 2020). Interest in the second paradigm, that is the determinants of state burden sharing behavior, emerged with Kupchan (1988) and underwent a revival with studies of mission mandates and burdens (Saideman & Auerswald, 2012). Finally, economists, Hirshleifer (1983) and then Sandler and Hartley (2001), explored the last paradigm (i.e., how contributions aggregate to provide the collective defense good) accounting for the smallest percent.

The authors point out research fails to account for **multiple theoretical perspectives and omits intra-alliance factors and space remains to contribute to the third paradigm qualitatively and quantitatively with alternative measures** (Bogers et al., 2020). This book contributes on all points to scholarship.

As a research program, *Beyond 2%* expands NATO burden analysis through a decomposition of the political, financial, social and defense burdens partners take on for the institution. The emphasis of a 2% GDP on military spending for partners serving as a proxy defense capability indicator to the alliance does not reflect how said goal reduces risk should Article V be invoked through attack (2% is a political target). Considering defense burdens multi-dimensionally explains why some overcontribute to NATO and why burden sharing arguments cause friction when there are 30 diverse partners with differing threats and risks. In creating a burden management model focusing on risks to partners, *Beyond 2%* explores the weaknesses of major theories regarding alliance burdens. It argues partner risks and threats are essential to understanding how burdens are distributed across a set of overlapping institutions within NATO's structure. The research takes on the complexity of burdens in NATO while focusing on aspects other than the '2%' including political, social and military, along with economic burdens—presenting a balanced synthesis of the complex concept while identifying measures. Burden is measured across multiple categories: economic ('2%' of GDP on military spending); military (fixed assets, personnel versus mission deployments); political (civilian contributions to leadership, HQ management)[1]; and social (leading missions, training partners, educating defense personnel at NATO Defense College in Rome, COE). NATO partners differ in their sensitives to defense and security risks due to geography, capabilities and threats affecting willingness to shoulder the different burdens associated with collective defense. The delegation of power internally regarding defense policy and allocations differs across partners with individual constraints. Those differences influence partner decisions concerning defense budget allocations (recalling the distance between what a partner allocates at home and the club 'target' is called the compliance gap concerning 2% [Heinen-Bogers, 2022, p. 13]) and contributions to alliance operations; both are examined.

The management of uncertainty associated with risks and threats differs across partners having divergent perspectives on shouldering all of NATO burdens. A nuanced view of burden sharing explains why Canada remains unhappy with criticisms of its under 2% contribution, since it omits mission activities to which it overcontributes compared to allies with larger militaries (Kimball, 2019). A nuanced analysis demonstrates states collaborate to manage the strategic problems of defense credibility and uncertainty about the future state of the world differently within NATO due to threat perceptions and institutional opportunities. Powerful partners may be defense underwriters for newer partners (and through arms transfers); but one state dominates defense and security agreements bilaterally, the US (Kavanagh, 2014). This project presents a set of factors that influence military spending accounting for the role of the US as a defense endorser. An external endorser reduces uncertainty and moves the equilibrium closer to an actor's preferred position in Milner's (1997) model of Congress as an endorser of US executive agreements. In NATO, the US serves the role of endorser reducing uncertainty through contracting bilateral defense and security agreements (DSA) with partners, and, as such, it may leverage its position with partners having more agreements despite consensus rules at NATO.

This research serves as the foundation for a model of risk management burden sharing accounting for how risks and partner heterogeneity affect the acceptance of burdens other than '*the 2%*' target. It presents new data, examines threat perception and improves on research considering the effects of NATO Centres of Excellence (COE) and enlargement on burdens. This book offers several methods studying two quantitative measures (one used in the literature and another original) with a comparative case study of COE mobilizing rational institutionalist and constructivist approaches.

It explores why theories do not examine institutional burden management across different partners. Classic approaches are anchored, historically, in perceptions of gains or losses, as well as the aggregation of contributions (Morrow, 1991; Sandler, 2004). Simply, the 2% minimum threshold does not account for partner diversity and must be revised, as a club target for a credible defense partner (Becker, 2017; Dvorak & Pernica, 2021; Oma, 2012; Zyla, 2018). The complexity of burden sharing is opened to aspects beyond military expenditures.

Most research excludes risk management and partner distinctions combined with incomplete theoretical approaches resulting in a snapshot of burden management due to a limited time period/event examined. As a result, a unique discourse, a gambling double down behavior emerged from those seeking to confirm overcontributions (Canada,

Turkey, Poland) compared to those seeking to defend under contributions (UK, France, Germany, Netherlands) in the post-cold war—an unstated cleavage. Turkish support of Syria in 2019; it "fac[es] strategic regional pressures related, in part to US activities in its neighborhood. Reminding that Turkey is tacitly 'marginalized' by the EU's frustrating approach to its membership" (Kimball, 2021a, p. 349), NATO faces a challenge concerning Turkey evidenced by its attempt to block Finnish and Swedish membership requests in the summer 2022. Turkey and Poland illustrate states with increasing power capacities since 2000 yet different linkages to the US (Kimball, 2022).

Despite concerns major powers dominate international organizations (Beardsley & Schmidt, 2012), the deconstructed data indicate some NATO partners design bilateral relations with the US to signal defense and security capacity, and then contribute to the club's collective defense. For example, while Poland obtained US arms imports before NATO entry, Hungary and Czechia imported more from NATO partners from 1993 to 2019.[2] This project examines arguments about US overcontributions through supporting partners with smaller capacities. Disaggregated data clarified some received US arms transfers, but others were supported by NATO global partners. This research provides analyses of burden sharing and mission contributions and considers how NATO, as an agent of partner states, contributes to sharing the global burden of crisis management. NATO's essential club good of crisis management extended beyond the '1949' NATO region when it accepted mandates increasingly from others to act in extra-regional crisis and undertook enlargement. Crisis management is examined, as well, in studying how NATO Centres of Excellence ensure club transformation to meet future cooperative security threats. This book's offerings cut across theory, methodology, research design and international security with a contribution to classroom learning and statistical modeling using supplementary materials.

Book Structure

Using an eight-chapter structure, this book offers a synthesis of cooperation, sharing defense burdens, and alliance institutions in Chapter 2. From a policy goods perspective, it discusses the management of economic and political risks to retain political power alongside defense threats given individual geographic perspectives. It reviews how cooperation manages the distributional dilemma. Defense/security and political liberalization stakeholders differ over policy modifications and the defense spending required to ensure a partner's defense 'credibility.' The final portion of the second chapter focuses on burden sharing research identifying gaps this book rectifies and contends analysis must go beyond debates around a number, more symbolic than significant at, operationalizing the concept of 'credible defense contribution capacity.' Research must account for enlargement and the emergence of extra-alliance institutions shifting burdens in novel ways creating opportunities to advance understanding.

Chapter 3 presents a balanced synthesis of the complex concept of burden sharing. NATO members differ in sensitivities to defense and security risks due to geography, capabilities, and threats affecting willingness to shoulder the burdens associated with collective defense. Chapter 4 examines the data employed by extant research, identifying how it fails to account for how actions functionally collaborate to produce the club's goods (collective defense, cooperative security and crisis management). NATO members face trade-offs ensuring credible commitments to NATO budgets while participating in operations—newly collected measures with a comparative study of distinct brick and mortar assets, e.g., Centres of Excellence, advance knowledge.

Chapter 5 contends realism, liberalism, constructivism, and other approaches face difficulty explaining how states allocate cooperative burdens as the focus was on 'if states cooperate' under perceived threats and risks. If states credibly cooperate, the main theoretical approaches remain silent on 'how it will be organized.' This occurs from a failure to consider member variation and distinguish member threats, affecting national allocation decisions from club threats. Approaches diverge about risk management while negotiating collective burdens. Institutionalist/delegation approaches examine how institutions reduce risks and manage strategic problems offering another research contribution.

Chapter 6 discusses the risk management institutional burden sharing model. Drawing from the rational choice bargaining literature and a set of state preferences, for example, members want to maximize individual security and benefits compared to club benefits, members monitor to prevent stronger members from engaging in cartel behavior to the detriment of club cohesion. Richer members should invest in less capable members to reduce club, and partner, uncertainty. The essence of *Beyond 2%* argues determining state threats and risks relative to alliance risks influences military spending, defense/security procurement, investments in training and troop allocations to regular and punctual missions; these are complementary methods of measuring burdens *Beyond 2%* GDP as a percent of total budget spending on the military. These remain arguments untested in most literature and original contributions.

Chapter 7 presents analyses using several methods. The first set of analyses examines the factors influencing military spending by NATO partners from 1949 to 2019 with an emphasis on being as inclusive as possible in terms of partners and years included. This model compares nicely with previous research using the same dependent variable but also offers support for the risk management and informational advantage arguments proposed. A novel measure of threat captures inter-capital distance to Moscow is also significantly related to spending. The second set of models offers multiple contributions. First, it contributes to middle power burden sharing research through a novel theoretical linkage using an expected utility model of foreign policy accounting for how partner differences affect the consistency around the probability a partner contributes to a new NATO operation following 1990. Second, this book presents original data on IO activities since 1949 and examines the subset of operations NATO under way and completed along with partner contribution. It offers a different measure of burden sharing—a dependent variable accounting for participation in a new NATO operation since 1990. This research includes states that became partners in the next 15 years. The influence of enlargement on burden sharing is absent from most studies with some exceptions (Kimball, 2019, 2021a, 2021b) and this despite reducing burdens being an enlargement 'selling point' combined with more than two decades of time and a dozen entrants.

Focusing on the post-cold war offers an opportunity to examine the effects of hosting/sponsoring NATO Centres of Excellence (COE) on the chances it contributes to a new operation. NATO COE are funded by partner states, but remain outside of the NATO structure, operating explicitly at no cost to NATO and offer a sample of the cooperative security, defense threats/risks partners foresee, agree to collaborate upon and are willing to invest financial, personnel, and equipment expertise to develop. Results indicate a strong negative and significant influence on new NATO operation participation and COE hosting. Another contribution is a brief case study of two NATO COE (JCBRN & MILMED)[3] using constructivist and rational institutionalist approaches in an examination of primary texts, Memoranda of Understanding: the first with Allied Command Transformation (on Establishment) and the second with each other (on Functional Operation) and the host state. COE contribute to three of four pillars of alliance transformation—each speaking to constructing a collective knowledge, training, practices, and functional interoperability; the social interactions create a community and orienting partners as to how to collaborate. The Centres call upon diverse expertise drawn from partners in legitimization practices, e.g., operating in theater if a threat is located there is a 'reach back' capacity for expertise—as the JCBRN has done. COE developed doctrine and procedures implemented in the field (MILMED) and offered in strategic messaging for NATO partners, e.g., Canada's police and army training mission in Ukraine, UNIFIER starting in 2015 and suspended in February 2022 in the fortnight previous to the Russian invasion of Ukraine.[4] Studies on COE (Lobo, 2012; Simion, 2016) do not examine institutional bargaining aspects nor compare multiple theories. The final chapter offers a closing discussion along with policy implications and suggestions for extending the research (including projects in progress).

This book includes four policy pop outs for civil servants, negotiators and scholars retracting the lens to offer general comments. There is public access to the book's digital appendices including raw data in several formats (Excel, STATA) for the researcher, complied datasets for analysis with replication with code for model estimation and explanations of technical concepts. Another contribution is the centralization of data for future research.

Notes

1. This study does not examine aspects of the political staffing/personnel.
2. See Fig. 3.2.
3. Joint Chemical, Biological, Radiological, Nuclear Defense; Military Medicine.
4. https://www.cbc.ca/news/politics/canada-ukraine-military-training-1.6350186, last access 11 July 2022.

References

Archik, K., Bowen, A., & Belkin, P. (2022). *NATO: Finland and Sweden Seek Membership* (No. IN11949; Congressional Research Service). US Congress. https://crsreports.congress.gov/product/pdf/IN/IN11949

Beardsley, K., & Schmidt, H. (2012). Following the flag or following the charter? Examining the determinants of UN involvement in international crises, 1945–2021: Following the flag or following the charter? *International Studies Quarterly, 56*(1), 33–49. https://doi.org/10.1111/j.1468-2478.2011.00696.x

Becker, J. (2017). The correlates of transatlantic burden sharing: Revising the agenda for theoretical and policy analysis. *Defense & Security Analysis, 33*(2), 131–157. https://doi.org/10.1080/14751798.2017.1311039

Bogers, M., Beeres, R., & Bollen, M. (2020). NATO burden sharing research along three paradigms. *Defence and Peace Economics*, 1–14. https://doi.org/10.1080/10242694.2020.1819135

Dvorak, J., & Pernica, B. (2021). To free or not to free (ride): A comparative analysis of the NATO burden-sharing in the Czech Republic and Lithuania—Another insight into the issues of military performance in the Central and Eastern Europe. *Defense & Security Analysis, 37*(2), 164–176. https://doi.org/10.1080/14751798.2021.1919345

Hartley, K., & Sandler, T. (1999). NATO burden-sharing: Past and future. *Journal of Peace Research, 36*(6), 665–680. https://doi.org/10.1177/0022343399036006004

Heinen-Bogers, M. (2022). *Burden sharing in security organizations: Broadening the burden sharing debate*. Tilburg University.

Hirshleifer, J. (1983). From weakest-link to best-shot: The voluntary provision of public goods. *Public Choice, 41*(3), 371–386. https://doi.org/10.1007/BF00141070

Kavanagh, J. (2014). *U.S. security-related agreements in force since 1955: Introducing a new database*. RAND Corporation.

Kimball, A. (2019). Knocking on NATO: Strategic and institutional challenges risk the future of Europe's seven-decade long cold peace. *The School of Public Policy Publications, 12*. https://doi.org/10.11575/SPPP.V12I0.68129

Kimball, A. (2021a). L'OTAN peut-elle encore avoir un rôle multilatéral? In *L'après COVID-19: Quel multilatéralisme face aux enjeux globaux? Regards croisés: Union européenne – Amérique du nord – Chine* (pp. 343–356). Bruylant-Larcier.

Kimball, A. (2021b). Managing risks, side payments, and multi-institutional enlargement: The role of US defence, big four investment agreements and candidate risks on NATO and EU enlargement. *European Politics and Society, 22*(5), 696–715. https://doi.org/10.1080/23745118.2020.1820152

Kimball, A. (2022). Deliberative institutional design & U.S. defense and security agreements: Comparing Canadian agreements to those with partners and competitors. *Journal of Transatlantic Studies, 22*(2), 230–250. https://doi.org/10.1057/s42738-022-00098-1

Kupchan, C. (1988). NATO and the Persian Gulf: Examining intra-alliance behavior. *International Organization, 42*(2), 317–346. https://doi.org/10.1017/S0020818300032835

Lobo, S. (2012). *NATO transformation and centers of excellence: Analyzing rationale and roles.* University of Oslo. http://urn.nb.no/URN:NBN:no-32044

Milner, H. (1997). *Interests, institutions, and information: Domestic politics and international relations.* Princeton University Press.

Moravcsik, A. (1997). Taking preferences seriously: A liberal theory of international politics. *International Organization, 51*(4), 513–553. https://doi.org/10.1162/002081897550447

Morrow, J. (1991). Alliances and asymmetry: An alternative to the capability aggregation model of alliances. *American Journal of Political Science, 35*(4), 904. https://doi.org/10.2307/2111499

Oma, I. M. (2012). Explaining states' burden-sharing behaviour within NATO. *Cooperation and Conflict, 47*(4), 562–573.

Saideman, S., & Auerswald, D. (2012). Comparing caveats: Understanding the sources of national restrictions upon NATO's mission in Afghanistan: Comparing caveats. *International Studies Quarterly, 56*(1), 67–84. https://doi.org/10.1111/j.1468-2478.2011.00700.x

Sandler, T. (1977). Impurity of defense: An application to the economics of alliances. *Kyklos, 30*(3), 443–460. https://doi.org/10.1111/j.1467-6435.1977.tb02203.x

Sandler, T. (2004). *Global collective action* (1st ed.). Cambridge University Press. https://doi.org/10.1017/CBO9780511617119

Sandler, T., & Hartley, K. (2001). Economics of alliances: The lessons for collective action. *Journal of Economic Literature, 39*(3), 869–896. https://doi.org/10.1257/jel.39.3.869

Simion, E. (2016). *NATO centres of excellence and the transformation of the North-Atlantic alliance.* University of Oradea. https://nbn-resolving.org/urn:nbn:de:0168-ssoar-73403-8

Wendt, A. (1992). Anarchy is what states make of it: The social construction of power politics. *International Organization, 46*(2), 391–425. https://doi.org/10.1017/S0020818300027764

Zehfuss, M. (2001). Constructivism and identity: A dangerous liaison. *European Journal of International Relations, 7*(3), 315–348. https://doi.org/10.1177/1354066101007003002

Zyla, B. (2018). Transatlantic burden sharing: Suggesting a new research agenda. *European Security, 27*(4), 515–535. https://doi.org/10.1080/09662839.2018.1552142

CHAPTER 2

Cooperation, Sharing Defense Burdens and Defense Institutions

Introduction

States contract joint defense burdens because of fundamental issues associated with internal defense production (Kimball, 2010; Palmer & Morgan, 2006). Not all states have equal capacity to produce arms to secure themselves, as realists note. If states cannot increase security internally by arming, then a combination of alliances, conflict and/or conquest is predicted by realists (Kimball, 2006). Rational bargaining models focus on conflict, though cooperation emerges under similar conditions; therefore, conflict and cooperation are seen as a continuum on which states bargain concerning the distribution of resources, influence, burdens, etc. Recasting burden studies using the rational bargaining and institutionalist approaches permits scholars to escape some traps of realism, e.g., ignoring national factors, and improve upon liberalism's positive but ambiguous propositions for cooperation because rational institutionalist scholars link strategic bargaining problems to institutional solutions. This book builds from concepts of non-conflictual interactions to guide novice scholars; readers with a solid base in the fundamentals of interstate cooperation and institutions are invited to advance to the section on NATO, as a case study, the literature compilation or pressures from Russia.

A. L. Kimball, *Beyond 2%—NATO Partners, Institutions & Burden Management*, Canada and International Affairs,
https://doi.org/10.1007/978-3-031-22158-3_2

Cooperation, Coordination, Collaboration—Contracting Institutions

Scholars distinguish cooperation, coordination and collaboration based on the duration of the expected interaction. One scholar focused on aspects of cooperation improving participants' well-being relative to the status quo ex ante, but such cooperation is not necessarily mutually beneficial, i.e., pareto optimality improving for the community, at large (Martin, 2000, p. 13). Another identified cooperation as, actors adjusting to the actual or anticipated preferences of others, using a process of policy coordination. Interstate cooperation occurs if the policies followed of a government are regarded by its partners as facilitating realization of their own objectives, as the result of a process of policy coordination (Keohane, 2005).[1]

Milner examined coordination and cooperation in a multimethod book tackling how reducing uncertainty affects international agreement ratification in national legislatures (1997).

> Policy coordination in turn implies that each state's policies have been adjusted to that their negative consequences for the other states are reduced. This conception of cooperation ... has two important elements. First, it assumes that an **actor's behavior is directed toward some goal(s).** It need not be the same for all actors involved... Second, the definition implies that **actors receive gains or rewards from cooperation**. The gains acquired by each need not be the same in magnitude or kind, but there are gains for each. Each actor helps the others to realize their goals by adjusting its policies in the anticipation of its own reward. Cooperation can thus be conceived as a process of exchange. Both involve the pursuit of 'want-satisfaction' through behavior that is contingent on the expected response of another. (Milner, 1997, p. 7)

Coordination is thus a longer-term form of cooperation, "imply[ing] mutual policy adjustment among countries intended to reduce the negative (or enhance the positive) effects of one country's policy choices on the others. Crucially, this means that in the absence of 'coordination' countries' policies would have been different" (Milner, 1997, p. 9). Coordination is the alignment of expectations (reciprocal predictability of actions) across interdependent actors, whereas cooperation is the alignment of interests (Camerer, 2003; Heath & Staudenmayer, 2000). Collaboration is the continuation of coordination within a regularized framework of interactions, i.e., an institution structuring the repeated interactions. For example, the development among NATO partners of joint defense doctrine across a variety of issues/challenges is a long-term policy collaboration club output/collective good. In game theoretic terms, coordination refers to situations where gains are achieved only through consistent choice with communication across players; Chicken, Stag Hunt, and Battle of the Sexes serve as examples. In cooperation games, players make enforceable contracts with third parties, i.e., leader–follower, chain-store paradox. In non-cooperative games, actors' independent decisions are taken without enforceable contracts, e.g., prisoner's dilemma, so egoistic behavior is expected to dominate in equilibrium preventing cooperation. Cooperation can emerge under such conditions if actors understand the 'shadow of the future' is long, i.e., the chances for reiterated interactions over a temporal period are high.

States contract to reduce uncertainty creating institutions with discrete mandates and obligations bargained by the partners (Koremenos, 2005). These institutions serve to induce patterns of behavior and, when properly designed, are self-enforcing (Koremenos & Nau, 2010; Lipson, 1991). An institution determines the motivations of the actors by structuring the situation in order to avoid defection (Drake & McCubbins, 1998, p. 21).

> Institutions are the rules of the game in society or, more formally, are the humanly devised constraints that shape human interaction. In consequence they structure incentives in human exchange, whether political, social, or economic. Institutional change shapes the way societies evolve through time and hence is the key to understanding historical change. [Their major role is to] reduce uncertainty by establishing a stable (but not necessarily efficient) structure to human interaction. (North, 1990, p. 3)

The emergence of political liberalization/democratization in Europe is traced to a need to constrain the spending of the state and increase the leader's credibility (Drake & McCubbins, 1998; Root, 1989). Monarchs/autocrats care about retaining political power and economic welfare, so they should liberalize economically and politically, if it favors retaining personal political power and economically benefits the state. Exogenous crises can advance liberalization by changing expected future costs of maintaining empire/control encouraging autocrats to offer liberties in exchange for future secured economic benefits (Drake & McCubbins, 1998). Economic liberalism and political liberalism are considered common NATO and EU club criteria (Katchanovski, 2011; Wiarda, 2001). Eastern states joining in 1999 benefited from internal political structures granting increased executive control to advance aspects of civilian-military relations, military force socialization and operational collaboration while still in the Partnership for Peace (Kimball, 2021b). "The political arrangements and institutions that help leaders stay in office are not necessarily the ones that promote growth and prosperity… the increased chances of an economic crisis are the acceptable price to pay if it means avoiding a political crisis which challenges a leader's hold on power" (Snider, 2005, p. 206). The security aspects in Eastern Europe post-cold war enlargement produced a pattern where states entered NATO before the EU.

The political survival literature (Bueno de Mesquita et al., 1999) contends leaders increasingly provide public goods, as the size of the winning coalition required to retain office increases. As such, democracies provide more public goods, and, moreover, there is an efficient mix between satisfying essential domestic demands for social goods relative to the provision of national security goods (Kimball, 2010; Powell, 1999); the distributional dilemma, also known as the trade-off between 'guns and butter'. Leaders must demonstrate foreign and domestic policy competence to increase chances of public re-endorsement, i.e., another political mandate for themselves or their party.

Uncertainty about the future is a strategic problem states resolve through contracts/institutions. States contract out security to ensure the availability of resources for domestic demands (i.e., the guns versus butter dilemma) and formal defense pacts are created in response to demands for social goods (Kimball, 2010). Those claims contrast realist arguments for allying as a capacity aggregator against shared threats (Altfeld, 1984; Morrow, 1991) though a long shadow of the future promotes cooperation among egoist actors under certain conditions (Powell, 1991). Reconciling rationalist claims, mobilizing political survival arguments and managing the provision of public demands point to internal sources of security contracting for understanding partner behavior.

Club partners strike a balance between providing national security at home and contributing assets to collective defense, cooperative security and crisis management. Partner risks vary with geographic location relative to the foci of a crisis/threat/risk and its differential effects on partners. Research omitting why partner differences influence allocations is a partial examination. As institutions grow in scope and expand in membership, multiple bargaining problems arise ranging from disputes over the allocation of power, resources and benefits to about the credibility of collective defense commitments. For example, NATO's air policing mission serves as a reassurance to Baltic partners of the protection of the common airspace. Defense cooperation helps partners manage the distributional dilemma of retaining political power while ensuring the configuration of the state's (national) defense and security needs are met.

70 Years of a Transatlantic Defense Pact—NATO, a Critical Case for Multimethod Study

The transatlantic pact secured North American commitment to Europe in the post-Second World War period. "NATO's sui generis partnering of the U.S., Canada and major European allies was a product of the historical conjuncture when uncertainty about the political environment generated substantial willingness to cooperate in providing a collective defense (from Soviet attack)" (Kimball, 2019, p. 7). NATO undertook the other essential tasks of cooperative security and crisis management within the NATO area; however, this evolved over time. It was essential to secure US commitment to maintain the emerging balance of power. Canadian participation served to symbolize and formalize the indivisibility of continental security. Across the multitude of institutions emerging, NATO maintained a capacity for crisis reaction and collective defense exceeding that of the EU (Smith & Timmins, 2000, p. 85). It is more adept to efficiently react to crises than the UN due to the time required to generate a peacekeeping force from participants with varying capabilities. "The UN is a central actor in crises, but few interventions are carried out under a joint command with another international organization, and [appear] in Africa" (Kimball, 2021a, p. 344). As a public treaty organization, NATO attracts scholarly and media attention. As an international commitment for 30 partners, the obligations to the institution serve as leverage in national budgeting and defense discussions. The institution enlarged to more than double the number of original signatories in the last decades while not reducing the level of collective goods provision by the club. However, this is not without frictions, debates, and doubts. In 2019, the French President, Macron, declared NATO brain dead (Kimball, 2021a) due to Turkish unwillingness to follow NATO's decision about Syria. The 2022 invasion of Ukraine forced Slovakia, Poland, Czechia, and others to donate available defense resources to Ukraine under the public quid pro quo NATO assets be provided in the interim.[2] NATO burden sharing research is partitioned into different methodological approaches with minimal theoretical overlap. For example, the subset of research concerning second-tier or middle power partners free-riding draws from perspectives (Zyla, 2016, 2018) beyond collective action and international political economy (Hartley, 2020; Kim & Sandler, 2020; Sandler & Hartley, 2001) but has not embraced methodological plurality with analytical statistical modeling to identify middle powers. Some research is motivated by questions of spending justice/fairness and concerns about 'free-riding,' that is exploitation (Heinen-Bogers, 2022; Sandler, 2004; Sandler & Hartley, 2001) where states have incentives to benefit from the club good without equitably contributing creating inefficiencies. Yet, enlargement redistributes burdens but may exacerbate bargaining by increasing costs.

Even with many studies of NATO burden sharing, lacunae are described in the next section. Some gaps include a lack of mixed method studies, an absence of multiple theoretical approaches and little consideration for how differences influence state decisions concerning allocations and burden management. There is an omission of the extra-NATO institutions in post-enlargement burden sharing and how they are linked to its capacity to meet alliance transformation in the future.

Synthesizing Seven Decades of NATO Burden Sharing Research

One published survey of NATO burden sharing journal articles identified three research content trends (Bogers et al., 2020). The compilation here does not attempt to regroup *their sample of articles*; the focus of this review is on the methodologies used by researchers. This review considers how scholars studied burden sharing, across what years, how many cases/missions, etc.[3] It includes over 105 *articles, books, and policy papers*; 31% published before 2000 including those identified as foundational with the most citations (Bogers et al., 2020).

Across the publications examined, 47% of analyses were quantitative and 23% qualitative; therefore, research combining multiple methods accounts for 16% of the sample[4]; this research offers a mixed method approach. In addition, 32% of NATO burden sharing research examines a majority of the partners, while a subset of partners is explored in 14% and another 14% offer single or comparative case studies of 3 or fewer partners. Only 5% of research examines the institution, as an actor, in comparison with 'other groups' of states. The decentralization of the literature, along dependent variables and examining subsets of states, is overcome here with a theoretical model accounting for partner risks and benefits to explain how states distribute the institution's burdens in alliance-level extensions. This book inserts itself in the 36% of research examining most (at least 20) NATO partners. Though over one-third of burden sharing research focuses on all states, only 15% cover NATO's entire history (1950 onwards), where this contribution offers analyses covering its entire tenure. Nearly three out of five studies examine a limited time period, mission, event, etc. As a result, the burden sharing literature cannot offer a generalized model as less than 10% of publications examined included all/most partners and eligible years. This research contributes in the categories representing the smallest portion of the existant literature.

NATO Under Pressure: Considering Russian Aggression in Ukraine Since February 2022

This book was written during an historic convergence, spring and summer 2022, when Russian aggression in Ukraine reinforced the commitment of NATO partners to the institution's key mandates. In months of Russian fighting in Ukraine, not only was there a massive mobilization from Europe and North America donating arms, military equipment and other items, but several partners made commitments to increase military spending including Germany.[5] The period witnessed some partners increasing dependence on NATO; for example, Slovakia sent anti-missile equipment to Ukraine under the public commitment NATO step in and fulfill its defense needs.[6] Enhanced Forward Presence, four battlegroups in Poland, Latvia, Lithuania, and Estonia, grew from less than 3,500 troops to a maximum of nearly 5,000 troops and extended to Romania. The US increased troop presence in bilateral commitments to Poland and Germany by 2,000 troops while shifting a thousand troops stationed already in Germany to Romania.[7]

Ukraine is not a member of NATO, but EU and NATO partners are supporting its defense because it lies along the fault line with Russia. The destabilization of Ukraine's territorial integrity and internal security along with the invasion created an active refugee crisis with implications for European neighbors in the short to medium term. Moreover, political and economic risks negatively affect the stability of internal and external markets notwithstanding the collective defense and cooperative security risks of an emboldened Russia. For an institution whose hands are fundamentally tied because Ukraine is not a member, due to the risks of provoking Russia, NATO worked diligently to avoid directly escalating the conflict. The Russian incursion into Ukraine and connected bombings indicate a level of respect for the areas of Ukraine connected to NATO members. Recalling in January 2022, Russia and Belarus signed enhanced defense cooperation follow-on agreements to the 1999 Union State of Belarus and Russia exposing another 1,084 km of Ukraine's borders to Russian invasion.[8] Ukraine, otherwise, shares about 1,300 km of land border with Russia. Its Black Sea border is 1,050 km. Ukraine defends nearly 7,000 km of borders and over half are exposed to threat/unstable. The 'firmest' are with Romania (613 km of split border including 292 km fluvial), Poland (535 km), Hungary (137 km), and Slovakia (97 km) for 1,382 km of combined 'NATO' border followed by Moldova (1,222 km including 955 of land, the remainder fluvial). Moldova's border is fragile with 454 km of Transnistrian border shared with Ukraine while Russia is actively supporting separatists in the region. Effectively, 20% of its borders with NATO partners plus Moldova still expose 63% of Ukraine's borders. Its internal and external security in the next years demands NATO's conflict management and cooperative security toolkits while maintaining collective defense for club partners most exposed to risk.

Finland and Sweden—Joining NATO: Balancing Contributions with Risks

Another externality of Russian activities in Ukraine was the publics in Finland and Sweden moving closer toward NATO membership. The Russian invasion of Ukraine inched the Nordic states closer to membership despite the uncertainty of the political elite. In an interesting development, the public called for membership. Finnish public opinion was 60% in favor of NATO membership while it had hovered at 25% for decades.[9] The support in the political class is also mirroring the popular support with the president, the prime minister and 95% of the parliament voting in favor of Finland joining the Atlantic alliance, in May 2022.[10] Finland's long-standing policy of collaborating with the West, while not provoking Russia, shifted. With some interlocutors discussing the Finlandization of Ukraine, it is notable Finland is underplaying a drastic, and public, move away from a policy developed over 70 years due to its geostrategic location and a powerful neighbor. Finlandization is when a powerful country (Russia) makes a smaller neighboring country (Finland) refrain from opposing the former's foreign policy rules, while allowing it to keep its nominal independence and its own political system. This worked for Finland because its political system was an established democracy when it struck the tacit bargain with Russia, uncomfortably as the cold war emerged.

Finland is a NATO European partner and can request membership without a Membership Action Plan within the Partnership for Peace because it is an established democracy with a professionalized military and a strong economy. It will benefit from a faster path to membership relative to the others joining post-cold war. There is a level of cooperation with NATO operationally in the Partnership for Peace 'policy planning and review process' and the Operational Capabilities Concept. It is a member of the EU and contributes to battlegroups. It is a member of the COE[11] on Cyber-Defense and Strategic Communications. It can collaborate on building the message around its membership. The Fins will contribute to the alliance's core missions of collective defense, cooperative security and crisis management/resilience. Finland offers defense capabilities, understands the complexities of cooperative security, and can contribute to crisis management. Its assets and experience reinforce the perception it will be a 'security provider' to the alliance. It participated in the International Security Assistance Force (ISAF) in Afghanistan and KFOR in Kosovo. It demonstrated resilience to Russian activities and incursions in the state's maritime and aerial zones. Finland brings impressive intelligence capacities for monitoring Russia as well as competent sea forces. Finland could accept a more active role in monitoring the Arctic for NATO partners. The Russians are accustomed to the Finns being present in Arctic waters—so this would not be a functional actor change. The Nordic duo increasing monitoring and surveillance in the Arctic would be supportive of ensuring Canada's territorial sovereignty and defense capabilities in the region as the trio share a strong mutual respect for the rules-based liberal international order. Finland's request to join NATO was formally deposited on May 12, 2022.[12]

Whether the Fins will accept NATO troops, bases and equipment is to determine but effectively the Danes entered the alliance, as an original member under the same bargain, as Copenhagen was closest to Moscow among initial NATO members. There are risks for Finland throughout the time period between requesting NATO membership and the ratification the accession protocols in national capitals—with 30 members, given parliamentary calendars, legislative recesses and the continuing violence in Ukraine. The Fins could request/invest in air defense/air denial assets to deter a Russian reaction. The accession protocols were delivered at the NATO Summit in Madrid in June 2022. There is risk with Finland moving formally closer to the alliance; Putin might reinvoke discourse of NATO advancement toward Russian border—while this is correct, Finland long grouped with the western block of states. A change in policy may draw Moscow's ire, but Finland will pursue the path the public requests because democracies react to public opinion, if not, leaders risk losing re-election.

Sweden watched its neighbor to the east attentively. Public opinion in Sweden steadily shifted toward membership but slower than in Finland, climbing weekly during the initial phase of the Russian invasion in Ukraine, from 51% in March supporting joining the alliance to 57% in April, and over 60% in May.[13] Between 1996 and 2019, polls showed a popular support ranging between 20 and 30%.[14] The political class followed suit, with the ruling party dropping in May its historical policy of 'non-alignment,' days before the prime minister signed the formal request for NATO membership, even though she declared in early March she would oppose. Her signature resulted in the ruling coalition effectively joining the opposition parties in supporting the alliance.[15] Sweden shares a water boundary zone with Russia, substantially less direct exposure than Finland. Sweden maintained a historical policy of military non-alignment. The 'Swedest deal' would have been letting Finland go first toward NATO accession to access information in facilitating its own process but before long, both states understood strategically moving their candidatures together was more effective and efficient regarding bargaining costs. The Swedes are cognizant security that risks to Finland are higher due to geography. That notwithstanding blocking two solid candidates from joining the alliance would be difficult for any single partner or subgroup of partners. Sweden collaborates in two NATO COE. It offers experience working with the alliance as a European partner to NATO. The Swedes bring increased cold weather capacities, recalling Cold Weather Operations is the smallest COE, and they could contribute securing the Arctic in the maritime and aerial domains. Sweden offers economic capacity and democratic resilience; it will be a net contributor/provider to collective defense, cooperative security, and conflict management/resilience for the alliance. Both Sweden and Finland are among the six members[16] of the Partnership Interoperability Initiative created in 2014 to contribute to NATO crisis management and, if needed, NATO Response Forces.

Turkey, as the NATO partner, who has relied on Russian arms imports in the past decade, signaled objections to their memberships. Notably due to internal political issues surrounding the Kurdish Worker's Party (PKK) considered a terrorist organization by Turkey and what Turkey considers to be Swedish tacit support for the PKK.[17] To prevent Turkey from blocking both candidacies, assurances were included in a trilateral memorandum containing 10 points.[18] Point 2 reaffirms alliance essentials such as collective defense, the indivisibility of security, and common principles and values in the NATO Treaty. Point 5 confirms both Finland and Sweden identify the PKK as a 'proscribed terrorist organization' and reject the PKK's goals and other affiliated terrorist organizations, individuals, inspired groups/networks and extensions. Finland and Sweden will tighten counterterrorism laws nationally and interdict financing/recruiting by the PKK. A Permanent Joint Mechanism was created enhancing cooperation on counterterrorism, organized crime and other mutually decided challenges. In exchange, Turkey agreed to support the Open-Door Policy and the duo's invitation to the alliance. Hungary indicated it will not block either candidate, but it will patiently wait to ratify the duo's accession protocols after Turkey.

Poland stated it will defend Sweden and Finland from Russian attack.[19] This speaks to Poland's acute knowledge of its geostrategic position and willingness to support their candidacies. Slovakia offered unequivocal support within days of the official request for membership.[20] Unlike the extensive internal debates from some enlargement rounds in some partner capitals. Finland and Sweden offer credible contributions to collective defense capacity, cooperative security building experience, and histories of participation in crisis management with NATO and the EU. About a third of NATO partners approved the Finnish and Swedish accession protocols within weeks at the national level, and Canada was the first to ratify accession protocols due to the structure of the parliamentary system permitting the PM to rapidly move policy.

Ukraine's Chances of "Rich Man's Clubs": Requests for EU (& NATO) Membership Offer Risks

Recent research on NATO and EU simultaneous enlargements to states in the post-Soviet geographic space after the cold war implies Ukraine is distant from getting membership offers. One notable tendency is all 14 states that entered those clubs after the end of the cold war entered NATO first. A criterion for entering NATO/EU is the absence of border disputes and reduced political risk. Ukraine represents a risky candidate because its economic environment is unstable, and it increases security risk to the alliance. NATO enlargement rounds started with those most distant from Russian direct borders. Poland's situation is complicated with the Russian–Belarus increasingly intertwined defense relationship exposing its border substantially to Russia. Poland hosts the US brigade and benefits from their logistical and transport support and the Forward Operating Post, that the US transitioned to a military base headquarters over the past year (but the US will not directly involve itself in Ukraine). Canada has extensive links in Ukraine from operation UNIFIER, the police and army training mission with tens of thousands of individuals already trained, and a large Ukrainian diaspora exceeding 1.3 million people including 77,000 persons born in Ukraine located in western Canada with some political power. The Trudeau government invested political and economic capital in supporting Ukraine and faces substantial internal pressures to do so from the media and public. It continued to donate and send economic aid, but it is no longer on the ground in Ukraine since UNIFIER was suspended in February 2022.

The resurgence of conflict due to Russian aggression reveals information about its projected aims in eastern Europe. Despite Putin's total war discourse, Russia may be content with stripping Ukraine of its eastern areas and southern access to the Black Sea to secure Russian naval access to warm water ports; this would happen at the disrespect of Ukrainian sovereignty by the rest of the international system. While the West signaled in 2014 Ukraine's territorial boundaries were permeable, the influx of military equipment, financial support and arms is limited by the 'human fighter' factor with more than 8 million Ukrainians displaced due to the conflict; those left will fight but many are untrained, defending civilians. Though defenders require less numbers (1/3), Russia has deeper access to manpower than Ukraine despite its welcoming and integrating foreign fighters. As the conflict moves toward a mutual hurting stalemate, the chances for resolution depend on a Russian decision it is costlier to continue to fight, than negotiate. The tipping point is not reached. Ukraine started bargaining EU membership, but this path for others was long. "Due to the broad scope and deep nature of EU integration covering financial, legal, and regulatory aspects across domains, the *acquis communautaire* demanding wide-ranging policy work requiring political will, political capital, and time" (Kimball, 2021b, 698).[21] There is no guarantee Ukraine will be granted a fast path to EU membership.

Conclusions: Beyond 2%: Why Another Book?

What is the value of another book on NATO burden sharing and why *Beyond 2%?* First, this book fills a gap in the literature and data offering pedagogical and policy tools. Few book-length studies of NATO defense economics study burdens with multiple methods. This work offers insight to policymakers negotiating a mandate on the part of government stakeholders.

Second, this research joins novel measures of partner-level risk, threats, informational improvement provided by US DSA along with contributions going beyond the budget share of 2% of GDP on military spending, a political goal from 2006. This is done by examining NATO Centres of Excellence, as side institutions, contributing to **collective defense, cooperative security and crisis management** based on 30 individual mandates. "COE establishment emerged as a result of the Prague Summit in 2002, when the Allied Command Atlantic became the Allied Command Transformation, responsible for transformation of the Alliance into a more efficient organization" (Simion, 2016, p. 72). Little extant NATO burden research examines aspects of COE despite a functional presence since 2005 (see Table 4.1). NATO COE are international military organizations established, run, and funded by subgroups of NATO partners. "NATO COE train and educate personnel from Allied and Partner nations on specialized topics of relevance to the Alliance."[22] COE cover a wide variety of topics, some are highly populated (28 participants), while others combine a handful of states. These institutions not only share the burdens but also signal issue areas partners want to focus collaboration on to increase cooperative security, collective defense and crisis management. NATO European partners, for example (Austria, Finland, Sweden), participate in COE.

Third, deconstructing burden sharing along multiple categories is worthwhile since the alliance enlarged to a variety of members, modified its strategic concept multiple times and is undergoing pressures from Russian activities. Both Finland and Sweden experienced increased public opinion in favor of joining NATO since the Russian invasion of Ukraine in February 2022 (notwithstanding the demands of Ukraine itself to enter EU and NATO in the last several weeks). One recent study of NATO and EU enlargement offered implications (Kimball, 2021b) and a risk management model. This book motivates analyses with delegation theory, collective action theory, realism, liberalism and its compliment, liberal intergovernmentalism, as well as constructivism.

Finally, the statistical modeling offers stand-alone contributions in terms of the: number of cases, temporal period under analysis, and testing claims of middle/second power states in the alliance without relying exclusively on discourse or critical analysis. Offering a new test of the middle power burden sharing within NATO mobilizes another subset of literature (Douch & Solomon, 2014; Zyla, 2016) with less statistical analyses compared to the larger set of burden sharing research. Burden sharing analysis of NATO must go beyond debates around a discrete number, more symbolic than significant at, operationalizing the concept. "An outcome measure, such as NATO members' compliance to the two per cent goal, is difficult to identify as NATO's contribution [to shared tasks, i.e., crisis management, cooperative security & collective defense]. In this example, non-compliance by several NATO members does not necessarily mean NATO has done a poor job" (Heinen-Bogers, 2022, p. 13).

The risk management model of burden sharing contends club partners present distinct capacities, face individual risks and can provoke threats (from Russia) such that information about partner defense commitment 'credibility' can be difficult to interpret. Increasing information about partner defense quality/credibility can be done through contracting agreements with the most powerful partner, the US, and importing arms from abroad. Club entrants after the cold war were variously capable militarily and offered risks; US defense and security agreements helped partners secure NATO membership offers while accounting for political risks consistent with rational institutionalist arguments (Kimball, 2021b). Research on collective burden sharing does not include risks, how partners can reduce uncertainties through bilateral contracting and the consequences of extra-institutional arrangements, i.e., hosting Centres of Excellence, on NATO operation participation. The risk management model of burden sharing uses two dependent variables and the same set of explanatory factors in statistical models and offers case studies to trace the links between design aspects of the agreement and constructivist claims concerning discourses, practices, and behavior. The result is a model offering flexibility and predictive capacity examining burden allocation behavior by partners with potential for future research advancement due to the availability of data and modeling details for interested readers. The policy implications of the results are discussed for policy makers and negotiators. The book proceeds next with a discussion on the complexity of burden sharing to make the case for extending beyond the GDP% target.

Notes

1. See pages 51–52, 1984 edition of Keohane's book.
2. https://www.rferl.org/a/slovakia-s300-air-defense-ukraine/31793133.html; https://www.thedrive.com/the-war-zone/45139/ukraine-situation-report-slovakias-donated-s-300-surface-to-air-missile-system-is-on-its-way; https://ecfr.eu/article/why-advanced-weapons-can-help-ukraine-defeat-russia/, last access 27 May 2022.
3. Research supported by Canadian Social Sciences & Humanities Research Council Partnership Grant, 95-2019-1000 for the Canadian Defence and Security Network. The author thanks C. Picard for compiling & disaggregating the literature, copyediting, and support throughout.
4. Formal models and research not employing methods comprise the remainder.
5. https://www.wsj.com/articles/germany-to-raise-defense-spending-above-2-of-gdp-11645959425, last access 21 April 2022.
6. https://www.defensenews.com/global/europe/2022/04/08/slovakia-confirms-patriot-s-300-air-defense-systems-are-heading-to-ukraine/, last access 21 April 2022.
7. https://www.rferl.org/a/us-troops-arrive-poland/31687938.html, last access 21 April 2022.
8. https://www.iss.europa.eu/content/becoming-military-district; https://www.opendemocracy.net/en/odr/why-is-belarus-hosting-russian-troops/, last access 27 May 2022.
9. https://www.eva.fi/en/blog/2022/03/22/russias-invasion-of-ukraine-shifted-the-opinion-of-a-majority-of-finns-in-favour-of-nato-membership/, last access 27 May 2022.

10. https://www.bloomberg.com/news/articles/2022-05-12/finland-s-leaders-support-joining-nato-as-formal-decision-nears, https://www.reuters.com/world/europe/finlands-parliament-likely-vote-nato-application-tuesday-2022-05-17/, last access 11 July 2022.
11. A multi-nationally, or nationally, established and sponsored entity offering recognized expertise and experience within a defined subject matter area to the benefit of the Alliance within the four pillars of NATO's COE program. 2020. *Catalogue of COEs*, page 4.
12. https://www.cnbc.com/2022/05/12/finland-announces-bid-to-join-nato-in-historic-move.html, last access 13 May 2022.
13. https://www.reuters.com/world/europe/growing-majority-swedes-back-joining-nato-opinion-poll-shows-2022-04-20/, last access 9 July 2022.
14. https://www.thechicagocouncil.org/commentary-and-analysis/blogs/major-shift-swedish-public-supports-nato-membership, last access 9 July 2022.
15. https://www.reuters.com/world/europe/swedens-ruling-party-poised-back-nato-bid-2022-05-15/; https://www.nytimes.com/2022/05/15/world/europe/sweden-nato.html, last access 9 July 2022.
16. Australia, Finland, Georgia, Jordan, Sweden, and Ukraine
17. See https://www.mfa.gov.tr/pkk.en.mfa, last access 13 December 2022.
18. https://www.nato.int/nato_static_fl2014/assets/pdf/2022/6/pdf/220628-trilat-memo.pdf, last access 13 July 2022.
19. https://www.politico.eu/article/mateusz-morawiecki-poland-defend-sweden-finland-attack-nato-accession/, last access 27 May 2022.
20. https://spectator.sme.sk/c/22912229/korcok-finland-and-sweden-joining-nato-is-in-our-interest.html, last access 27 May 2022.
21. If economic risks influence EU membership offers, then fast-track admitting a country in crisis due to invasion and conflict is inconsistent with the EU's previous actions post-cold war.
22. https://pm.gc.ca/en/news/backgrounders/2021/06/14/strengthening-transatlantic-defence-and-security, last access 15 May 2022.

References

Altfeld, M. (1984). The decision to ally: A theory and test. *Western Political Quarterly, 37*(4), 523–544. https://doi.org/10.1177/106591298403700402

Bogers, M., Beeres, R., & Bollen, M. (2020). NATO burden sharing research along three paradigms. *Defence and Peace Economics*, 1–14. https://doi.org/10.1080/10242694.2020.1819135

Bueno de Mesquita, B., Morrow, J., Siverson, R., & Smith, A. (1999). An institutional explanation of the democratic peace. *American Political Science Review,* 93(4), 791–807. https://doi.org/10.2307/2586113

Camerer, C. (2003). *Behavioral game theory: Experiments in strategic interaction*. Princeton University Press.

Douch, M., & Solomon, B. (2014). Middle powers and the demand for military expenditures. *Defence and Peace Economics, 25*(6), 605–618. https://doi.org/10.1080/10242694.2013.861652

Drake, P., & McCubbins, M. (Eds.). (1998). *The origins of liberty: Political and economic liberalization in the modern world*. Princeton University Press.

Hartley, K. (2020). NATO at 70: A political economy perspective. *Springer International Publishing*. https://doi.org/10.1007/978-3-030-54395-2

Heath, C., & Staudenmayer, N. (2000). Coordination neglect: How lay theories of organizing complicate coordination in organizations. *Research in Organizational Behavior, 22*, 153–191. https://doi.org/10.1016/S0191-3085(00)22005-4

Heinen-Bogers, M. (2022). *Burden sharing in security organizations: Broadening the burden sharing debate*. Tilburg University.

Katchanovski, I. (2011). Puzzles of EU and NATO accession of post-communist countries. *Perspectives on European Politics and Society, 12*(3), 304–319. https://doi.org/10.1080/15705854.2011.596308

Keohane, R. (2005). *After hegemony: Cooperation and discord in the world political economy* (1st Princeton classic edition). Princeton University Press.

Kim, W., & Sandler, T. (2020). NATO at 70: Pledges, free riding, and benefit-burden concordance. *Defence and Peace Economics, 31*(4), 400–413. https://doi.org/10.1080/10242694.2019.1640937

Kimball, A. (2006). Alliance formation and conflict initiation: The missing link. *Journal of Peace Research, 43*(4), 371–389. https://doi.org/10.1177/0022343306064816

Kimball, A. (2019). Knocking on NATO: Strategic and institutional challenges risk the future of Europe's seven-decade long cold peace. *The School of Public Policy Publications, 12*. https://doi.org/10.11575/SPPP.V12I0.68129

Kimball, A. (2019). Knocking on NATO: Strategic and institutional challenges risk the future of Europe's seven-decade long cold peace. *The School of Public Policy Publications, 12*. https://doi.org/10.11575/SPPP.V12I0.68129

Kimball, A. (2021a). L'OTAN peut-elle encore avoir un rôle multilatéral? In *L'après COVID-19: Quel multilatéralisme face aux enjeux globaux? Regards croisés: Union européenne – Amérique du nord – Chine* (pp. 343–356). Bruylant-Larcier.

Kimball, A. (2021b). Managing risks, side payments, and multi-institutional enlargement: The role of US defence, big four investment agreements and candidate risks on NATO and EU enlargement. *European Politics and Society, 22*(5), 696–715. https://doi.org/10.1080/23745118.2020.1820152

Koremenos, B. (2005). Contracting around international uncertainty. *The American Political Science Review, 99*(4), 549–565.

Koremenos, B., & Nau, A. (2010). Exit, no exit. *Duke Journal of Comparative & International Law, 21*(1), 81–120.
Lipson, C. (1991). Why are some international agreements informal? *International Organization, 45*(4), 495–538.
Martin, L. (2000). *Democratic commitments: Legislatures and international cooperation*. Princeton University Press.
Milner, H. (1997). *Interests, institutions, and information: Domestic politics and international relations*. Princeton University Press.
Morrow, J. (1991). Alliances and asymmetry: An alternative to the capability aggregation model of alliances. *American Journal of Political Science, 35*(4), 904. https://doi.org/10.2307/2111499
North, D. C. (1990). *Institutions, institutional change, and economic performance*. Cambridge University Press.
Palmer, G., & Morgan, T. C. (2006). *A theory of foreign policy*. Princeton University Press.
Powell, R. (1991). Absolute and relative gains in international relations theory. *American Political Science Review, 85*(4), 1303–1320. https://doi.org/10.2307/1963947
Powell, R. (1999). *In the shadow of power: States and strategies in international politics*. Princeton University Press.
Root, H. (1989). Tying the King's hands: Credible commitments and royal fiscal policy during the old regime. *Rationality and Society, 1*(2), 240–258. https://doi.org/10.1177/104346318900100200 5
Sandler, T. (2004). *Global collective action* (1st ed.). Cambridge University Press. https://doi.org/10.1017/CBO9780511617119
Sandler, T., & Hartley, K. (2001). Economics of alliances: The lessons for collective action. *Journal of Economic Literature, 39*(3), 869–896. https://doi.org/10.1257/jel.39.3.869
Simion, E. (2016). *NATO centres of excellence and the transformation of the North-Atlantic alliance*. University of Oradea. https://nbn-resolving.org/urn:nbn:de:0168-ssoar-73403-8
Smith, M., & Timmins, G. (2000). The EU, NATO, and the extension of institutional order in Europe. *World Affairs, 163*(2), 80–89.
Snider, L. (2005). Political risk: The institutional dimension. *International Interactions, 31*(3), 203–222. https://doi.org/10.1080/03050620500294176
Wiarda, H. (2001). Where does Europe end? The politics of NATO and EU enlargement. *World Affairs, 164*(4), 178–197.
Zyla, B. (2016). Who is keeping the peace and who is free-riding? NATO middle powers and burden sharing, 1995–2001. *International Politics, 53*(3), 303–323. https://doi.org/10.1057/ip.2016.2
Zyla, B. (2018). Transatlantic burden sharing: Suggesting a new research agenda. *European Security, 27*(4), 515–535. https://doi.org/10.1080/09662839.2018.1552142

CHAPTER 3

Complexity and Burden Sharing: Member Risks and Threats

Introduction

The agency of international institutions (II) depends on the powers delegated by state partners (Hawkins, 2006) and the structural design of the institution described in its founding documents (Koremenos et al., 2001). "Delegation is defined as a conditional grant of authority from a principal to an agent that imports the latter to act on behalf of the former. This grant of authority is limited in time or scope and must be revocable by the principal" (Hawkins, 2006, p. 7). One survey of over 145 agreements drawn randomly from those deposited with the United Nations Treaty Section presented the following categorizations: security/disarmament, economics, environment and human rights (Koremenos, 2013). Security agreements relative to others included the fewest non-state actors. Less than one in three discuss a pre-existing II. Distribution issues appeared more in those agreements (at 36%) than any category though uncertainty about the state of the future state of the world appeared in almost two of three agreements (Koremenos, 2013, p. 662).

Delegation, Agency, and NATO

Since NATO is an institution associated with 'high politics,' i.e., defense and security, states should be reticent to delegate decision authority in

A. L. Kimball, *Beyond 2%—NATO Partners, Institutions & Burden Management*, Canada and International Affairs,
https://doi.org/10.1007/978-3-031-22158-3_3

a domain closely related to national sovereignty. Those domestic agency costs represent a reminder that the opportunity costs of joining NATO may be higher than expected for some partners. While delegating the principal must be able to infer whether the agent's proposal is better, or worse, than the status quo AND the agent must have an incentive to make a proposal for the principal better than the status quo.

> Stated intuitively, when the agent faces a principal who can distinguish better proposals from worse proposals, then he knows that proposing any point that is worse for the principal than the status quo, including his own ideal point, leads to the status quo as the outcome of delegation. In these conditions, the agent should only make a proposal that makes both himself and the principal better off relative to the status quo. (Hawkins, 2006, p. 356)

Delegation is not without challenges, for example, the principal delegates some authority to the agent with specialized skills and precise mandates (e.g., Centres of Excellence). Employing a specialized actor for a task is a delegation advantage because it allows the principal to gain in efficiency while saving energy and resources. The possibility an agent undertakes autonomous actions, undesired by the principal, is a limitation (agency slack). Two forms of agent negligence are identified: when the agent does not make all efforts to achieve objectives set by the principal (shirking) and when the agent deviates from the principal's objectives in favor of their own preferences, known as slippage (Hawkins, 2006, p. 8). Slippage arises from information asymmetry between the agent and principal during mandate execution. Actors in the field acquire firsthand information about the crisis situation, they may adjust mandates to match newly informed preferences. However, such behavior may cause agents to deviate from the organization's (i.e., the principal's) preferences simultaneously. Moreover, once operations begin resources available may differ in quantity and quality from those mandated. As a result, it is not uncommon to revise mandates during a mission.

Another distinction is 'rule-based delegation' that tends toward a strict interpretation of mandate limits compared to more flexible 'discretion-based delegation' where the agent is granted an increased policy-making role (Hawkins, 2006, p. 27). When preferences vary about a mandate's interpretation then agent opportunistic behavior is likely but granting sanctioning power to II, as principals, can deter opportunism.

From a principal-agent perspective when weaker states join NATO, they should be reluctant to delegate if the club is dominated by a single actor, e.g., the US. Stone argued principal-agent models lack an explanation for why 'weak states consent to participate' (2011, p. 16). Stone distinguished formal and informal rules arguing, "formal rules specify voting rights and legitimate procedures that embody a broad consensus of the membership, while the informal rules allow exceptional access for powerful states to set the agenda and control particular outcomes" (2011, p. 13). Consistent with incomplete contracts, strong states relinquish formal powers to the benefit all partners under normal circumstances, this in exchange for informal power under extraordinary circumstances. According to the informal governance model, a powerful agent bypasses normal procedures through manipulation, information concealment and/or complex delegation schemes. Therefore, the relationship between the number of principals (and their preference heterogeneity) and policy implementation is not linear, as contended by some studies. Delegation from sovereign states to II presents the challenge of simultaneously examining complex principals (state governments) delegating to a complex agent (international institution), then granting said institution principal-type mandates in the name of state-partners. The institution is conferred agency, but said continuation depends on allocations and burden sharing when required.

Moreover, for an II to sustain, an inter-temporal quid pro quo exists between domestic principals, the institution and how agents in weak states interpret said quid pro quo under crisis conditions to understand burden management. And, the defense and security status quo, in the absence of NATO, for many partners leaves them at risk from a geostrategic view even within a community of 'like-minded' states in a constrained geographic space sharing norms of peaceful dispute resolution.

International organizations/institutions (IO/II) are granted a variety of tasks (Abbott & Snidal, 1998) and also take on informal governance functions (Abbott & Snidal, 2000; Stone, 2013; Vabulas & Snidal, 2013). IO can be forums for raising awareness about appropriate behaviors and socializing states to respect the norms structuring the international system according to constructivists. They provide a legitimizing function in permitting preference aggregation, thus presenting a common voice in the international community (Panke, 2020). IO, as agents (Dai et al., 2010; Hawkins, 2006), consider risks to the institution and individual members, though mandates provide no obvious tools to do so (King & Narlikar, 2003). IO are likened to policy advisors by sending persuasive credible signals to the national environments, but only if the IO is viewed as more moderate than national experts and diverges from their position (Fang & Stone, 2012). As independent actors, IO carry out a multitude of activities in a variety of environments from pre-crisis to post-conflict to crisis and conflict situations-prevention, mediation, management, monitoring, disarmament, demobilization and reintegration as well as peacekeeping, peace enforcement, peacebuilding and peace observation (Kimball & Lewis, 2011). In this way, NATO is like other II, yet collective defense, cooperative security and crisis management obligate continual risk analysis to ensure credible defense provision and NATO maintains troop forces to react rapidly to crises.

A nuanced view of burden sharing explains why Canada dislikes criticisms of its military spending under the 2% threshold does not include activities for which it overcontributes (i.e., missions) compared to members including those with larger militaries (Kimball, 2019; Massie, 2014; Massie & Zyla, 2018; Saideman, 2016). Disagreements over shirking, asymmetric allocations, and internal versus external trade-offs underlie negotiations across a number of strategic issues the institution faces with pressures from Russia alongside migration and transnational issues (i.e., cyber-defense, climate change, public health). A nuanced analysis demonstrates states collaborate to manage the strategic problems of credibility and uncertainty about the future state of the world differently within NATO due to its adaptive capacities. Domestic political considerations of threats and political constraints determine if partners increased allocations to the club. An improved understanding of how partners interpret threats facilitates future rounds of annual burden negotiations by reducing acrimony, increasing cohesion, and influences crisis burden management. Powerful members are defense underwriters for newer members, but one state dominates, the US (Kavanagh, 2014). Others discussed how US spending and collaboration affects partner and EU spending and how regionalized threats influenced spending by Black Sea states (Becker, 2017, 2021). Kimball (2010) and Becker (2021) using distinct cases and time periods examine differently the trade-off between 'guns and butter' a decade apart to conclude similarly. In NATO, the US served the role endorser reducing uncertainty surrounding defense capacities of newer partners; it may leverage its position (using informal governance mechanisms) with those states despite consensus rules.

Beyond Collective Action Models of Defense

As burden sharing research evolved and theoretical conceptualizations moved away from public goods models, theories were challenged to explain the internal dynamics of alliances, i.e., trends in burden sharing and disagreements about the credibility of defense given what NATO and its partners considered 'most at risk' invested in to collectively defend themselves. Post-cold war enlargement was pursued to reduce partner and club insecurities. Weak link arguments on public goods provision contend admitting members lacking criteria reduced the collective good level to a lowest common denominator, i.e., weakest link (Alley, 2021; Sandler, 2004). "Weak links may not affect average total goods levels provided by a club offering multiple diversified goods. However, clubs providing rare, costly goods (i.e., security) risk greater externalities admitting weaker partners. Exclusion is the recommendation for economic markets where the costs of externalities are diffused, but on the European geostrategic 'collective security' market it was costly to exclude certain states" (Kimball, 2021, p. 697). The US contracting bilateral defense and security agreements with partners and post-cold war entrants is one measure to capture if the US influences partner-level military spending and participation decisions concerning a new operation.

Considering the US as an Underwriter—Defense-Security Agreements and Arms

Public data on US defense and security agreements (Kavanagh, 2014) supports rationalist arguments stronger partners invest in weaker entrants based on agreements with post-cold war NATO entrants from 1993–2016. However, not all entrants benefited at the same rate or depth from US defense and security contracts despite the two clusters of states starting simultaneously in 1994. Figure 3.1 shows the cumulative evolution of US agreements with post-cold war entrants illustrating the differential rates of initial start and growth after the creation of the Partnership For Peace (henceforth, PFP). Despite contentions of

US dominance in NATO, some post-cold war entrants obtained more US attention, while others received less—one way to understand this phenomenon is to consider arms imports from the US, NATO partners, global partners, and rivals. If US arms importations dominate the same set of states with the most US bilateral defense and security agreements, it offers evidence of possible hegemonic influence. The arms importations of the trio of states representing the first round invited to join NATO after the end of the cold war is offered with Romania, Bulgaria, and the three Baltic states.

As an alternative to bilateral (defense and security agreement) contracting, the US supported post-cold war partners through arms transfers, Poland (panel a), while others supported Hungary and Czechia, see arms transfer data visualizations in millions of dollars. Hungary was not among those with the most US DSA, nor the most US arms imports that entered NATO in 1999. Upon entry Hungary accepted to contribute a share one-quarter the size of Poland and 60% the size of Czechia's (Kimball, 2019, p. 21) though its arms importations were not substantial smaller than Czechia's. That notwithstanding Poland purchased twice the number of US arms (plotted in orange), while Czechia (Fig. 3.2b) imported more arms from global partners (Austria, Finland, Israel, South Korea, Ukraine) followed by Russia, though still

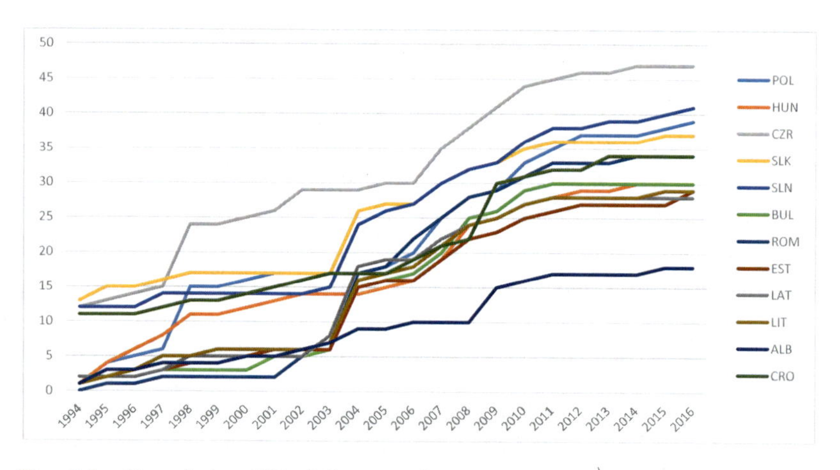

Fig. 3.1 Cumulative US defense and security agreements (DSA), NATO entrants before 2010

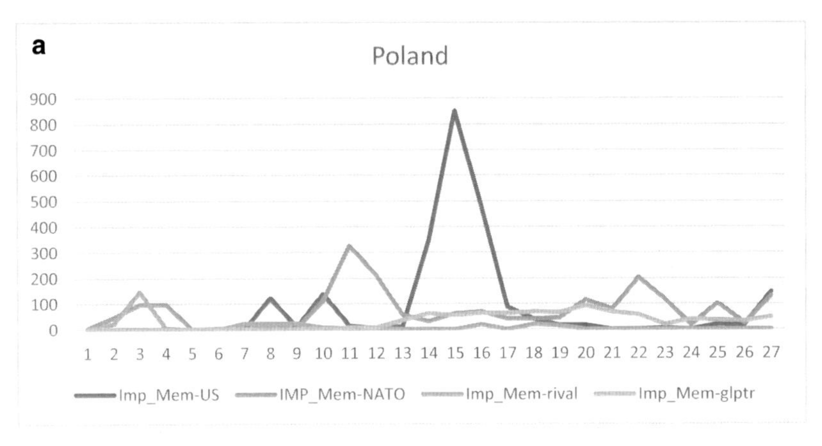

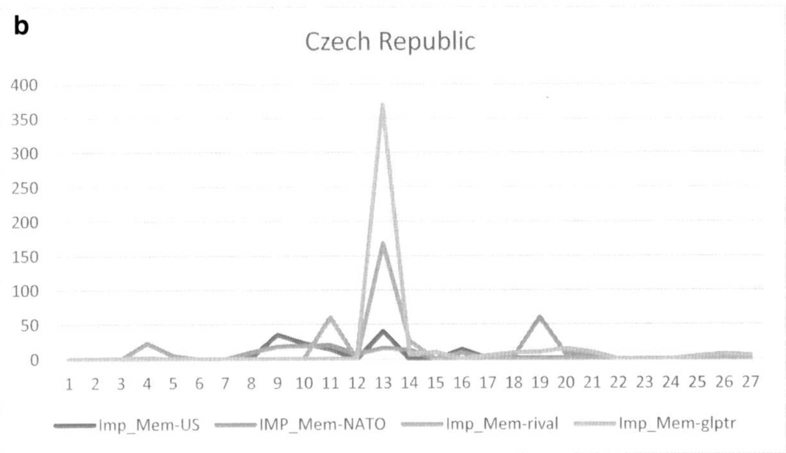

Fig. 3.2 **a** Arms transfers—Poland from US, NATO partners, Russia, global, 1993–2019. **b** Arms transfers—Czechia from US, NATO partners, Russia, global, 1993–2019. **c** Arms transfers- Hungary from US, NATO partners, Russia, global, 1993–2019

less than half of Poland. Figure 3.2c illustrates arms imports to Hungary indicating those from global partners dominated those from the US with some from Russia. Variation around Hungary's political risk was larger, than others, but its average risk similar to both Poland and Czechia in the late 1990s.[1] Based on risk versus investments trade-offs, it was the

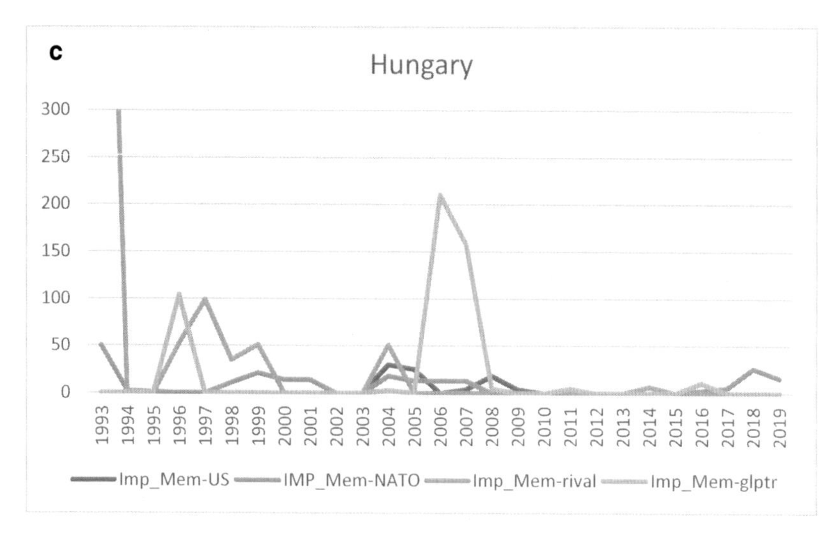

Fig. 3.2 (continued)

entrant closest to the reservation point of non-admissibility in a two-level win-set (Putnam, 1988); Hungary represented the least prepared entrant concerning defense credibility and most at risk politically. And subsequent democratic backsliding by Orban's government (Bernhard, 2021; Krekó & Enyedi, 2018; McFaul, 2002) upheld this position in the years after the 1999 enlargement. Hungary's process toward democracy supports the argument it is an unconsolidated regime with a partial transition (McFaul, 2002). And with Turkey, it is among the final states to ratify Finland and Sweden's 2022 request to join NATO. Others argued NATO expansion did not spread democracy (Reiter, 2001).

The two panels above offer Fig. 3.3a, b illustrate arms imports to Bulgaria and Romania. Romania was closer to importations at a credible level to join NATO in 1999 but the next chapter contends its political and investment environments were risky, as were Bulgaria's. Bulgaria had not invested in arms imports to offer a contribution to collective defense until after 2000 and again NATO partners transferred arms, not the US. Comparing the data visually illustrate—Bulgaria and Romania were invested in by other partners within the NATO club then the US. One study of burden sharing offered evidence the majority of NATO

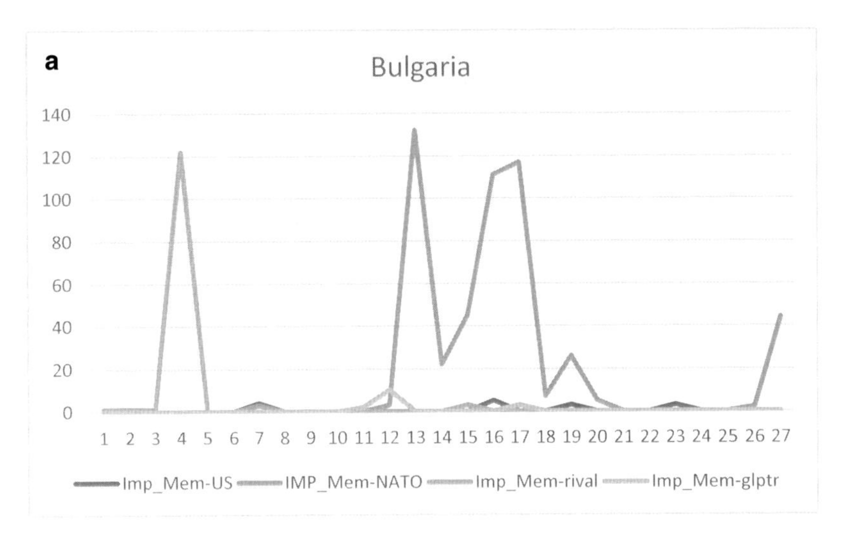

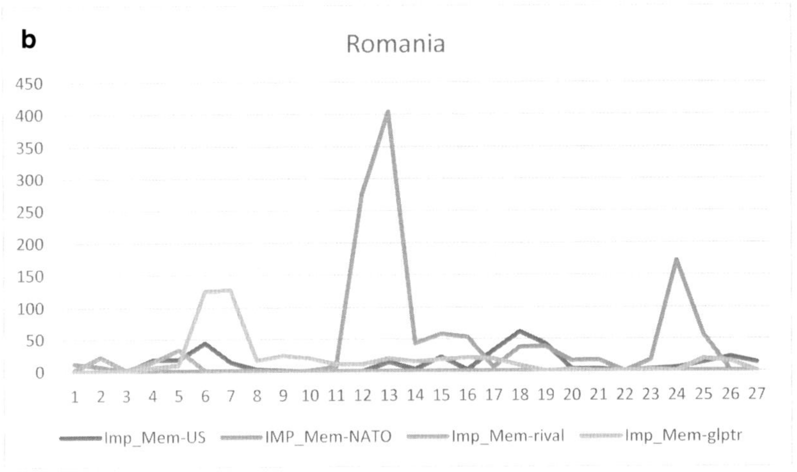

Fig. 3.3 **a** Arms transfers—Bulgaria from US, NATO partners, Russia, global, 1993–2019. **b** Arms transfers—Romania from US, NATO partners, Russia, global, 1993–2019

partner's military spending tracks with the UK and not the US, France and Romania being the sole exceptions (Liu et al., 2019).

The above series of figures shows arms importations to three Baltic states from 1993 to 2019. Each state joined NATO in 2004 with

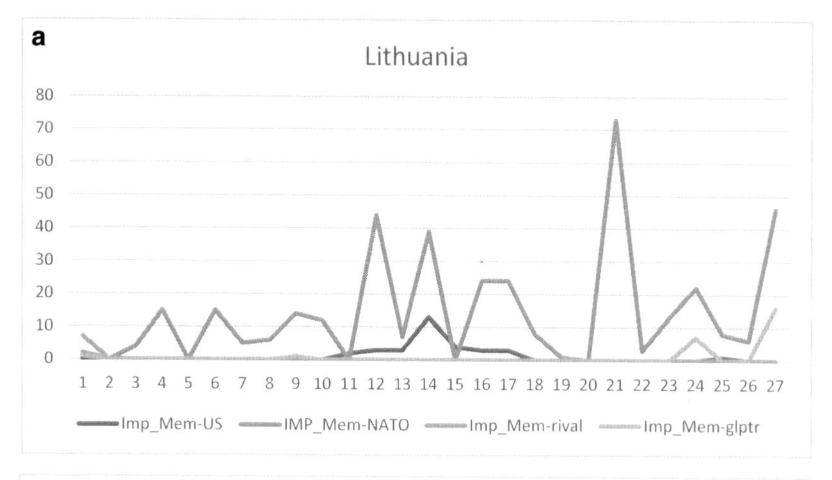

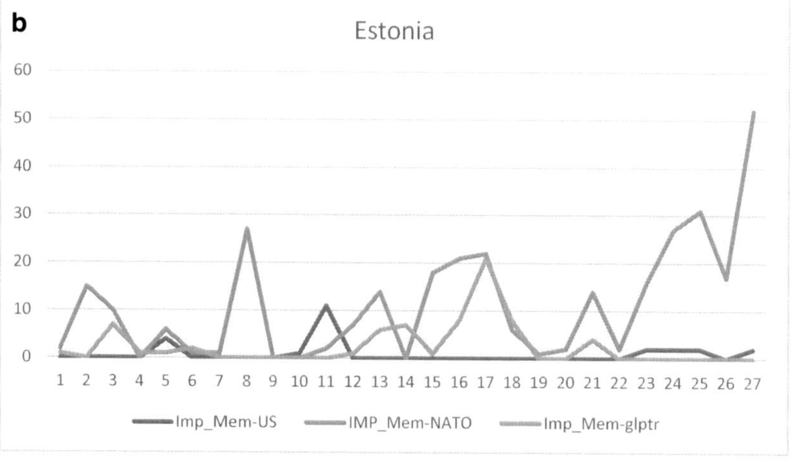

Fig. 3.4 **a** Arms transfers—Lithuania from US, NATO partners, Russia, global, 1993–2019. **b** Arms transfers—Estonia from US, NATO partners, Russia, global, 1993–2019. **c** Arms transfers—Latvia from US, NATO partners, Russia, global, 1993–2019

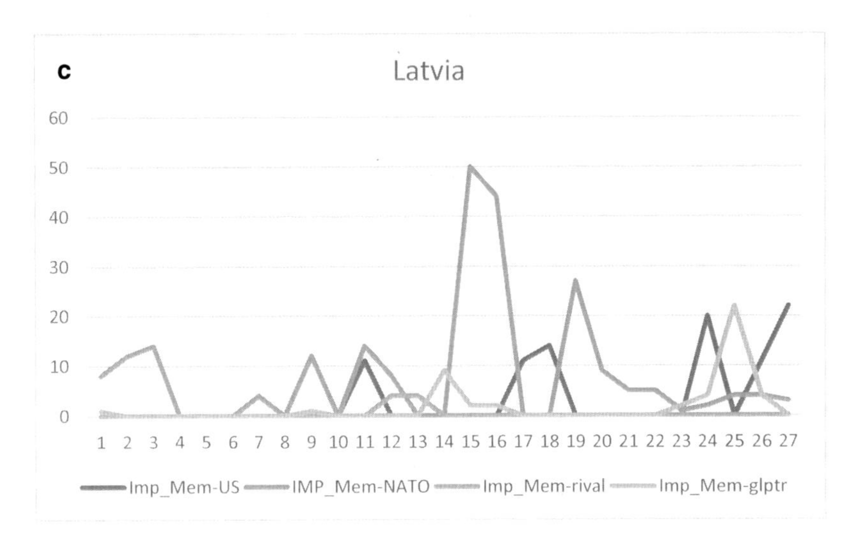

Fig. 3.4 (continued)

Romania, Bulgaria, Slovakia and Slovenia. The Baltic states illustrate a different pattern of arms importations sent by NATO partners with Estonia acquiring a small amount of Russian arms over a decade ago. The figures indicate the US played a strong role in enhancing defense by supplying arms to some newer partners after the cold war, but others joining after the cold war benefited from imports by global partners to NATO or non-US NATO partners, the UK and France.

Looking broadly,[2] few NATO partners imported arms from Russia (or China) since 1993 by pre-1999 members; it is limited to Greece and Turkey. While some entrants benefited from Russian arms; Bulgaria, Hungary and Poland had substantial trade for less than a decade, even then it was magnitudes smaller than importations from NATO or global partners. Estonia had low level arms transfers with Russia for a few years. Turkey distinguished itself as the only partner with arms transfers in the last decade with Russia and China, worthy of further analysis. An over-reliance on the US for arms imports is not supported by data for those joining after the end of the cold war; those advancing such claims rely on anecdotes over objective evidence presented here.

External Threats—As Motivation for Partner Behavior Within a Club

States differ from the club about their perceptions of external club threats versus those on a national level. Such differences affect military spending and allocations to club goods and operations. There can be political risks within states. When NATO enlarged, "geography relative to Russia shaped defence externalities for individual partners—some [possible entrants] increased defence (e.g., Poland, Hungary) while others provoked (e.g., Georgia, Ukraine)" (Kimball, 2021, pp. 700–701). Geography is an important vector for threats given not all partners equally perceived the salience of the threat from the Soviet Union, despite being the focus of strategic attention in 1949. Moreover, avoiding a faultline with Russia remained a concern as NATO enlarged after the cold war (Schimmelfennig, 2001; Wiarda, 2001). Geostrategic aspects enlargement of measured by the distance from a candidate's capital to Moscow relative to the NATO partner average offers a partial explanation for when candidates were invited to join (Kimball, 2021).

Some explanations fall short operationalizing and theorizing along external threat perceptions versus internal bargaining constraints producing theoretical and empirical limits in burden sharing studies. Few studies include aspects of geographic distance as threat and internal risks/constraints in quantitative analysis. NATO enlargement after the cold war created a buffer zone for original European partners from Moscow. Figure 3.5a offers a visualization of the distance from partner national capitals to Moscow. Data indicate the average inter-capital distance is 2303 km across the 14 (European) NATO partner after 1980, while the 13 NATO entrants after 1990 offered an average inter-capital distance of 1571 km indicating an average increase of 732 km. Of original partners Copenhagen is closest to Moscow, the entry of Poland added 400 km of buffer. In 2004, Lithuania's capital brought the institution within 800 km of Russia's capital but creates an equivalent distance buffer zone to Berlin, the second closest cold war partner capital (but not secured in 1949) representing the institution's defense perimeter, i.e., similar to Schelling's focal point. However, Eastern partners reduced average territorial exposure to threats when Poland joined in 1999 (Fig. 3.5b), 14 current partners increased geographic buffer space from Russia. Poland's threat exposure was highest of those that joined in 1999, yet Prague is closer to Moscow than 11 partner capitals. The

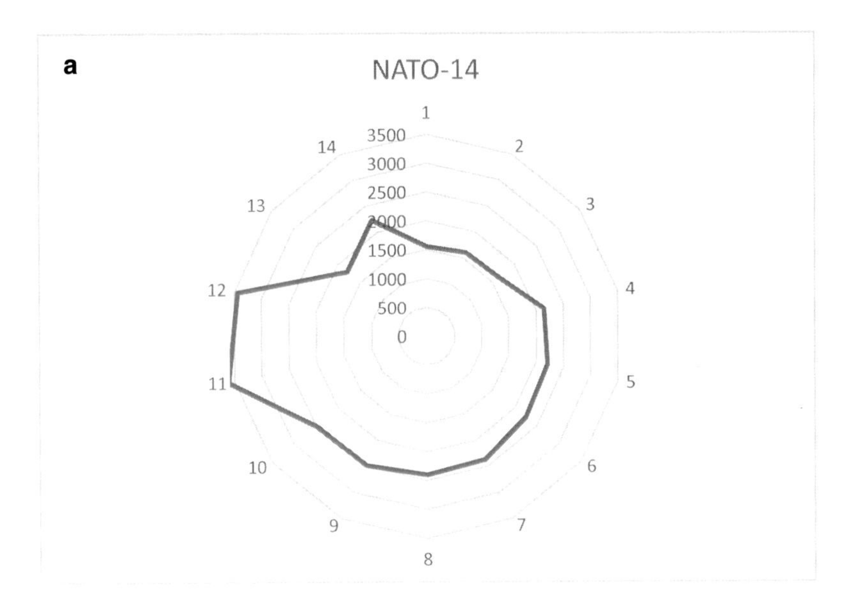

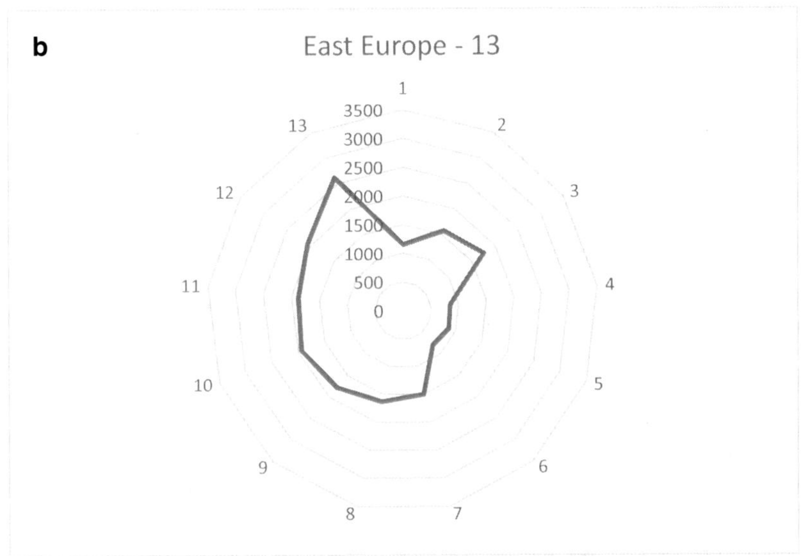

Fig. 3.5 **a** NATO-14 partner inter-capital distances; center is Moscow, ordered by entry date, distance; *original data*. **b** Eastern European-13 partner inter-capital distances; center is Moscow, ordered by entry date, distance; *original data*

2004 round added the three partners, highly exposed to Russia geographically, but simultaneously secured another layer of buffer as Poland's capital gained another 360 km of security with Vilnius, now most proximate, added at less than 800 km from Moscow providing all 17 regional partners reduced territorial risks.

Some allies with persistent insecurities demand others signal reassurance and defense commitment credibility (Blankenship, 2020).[3] Differing interpretations of Article V strain the foundations of the alliance. The joint allocation of troops in Poland, Romania, and the Baltic allies, for instance, shows a willingness to accept costs, while committing partners to a forced tripwire response. Russia maintains the ability to exert pressure through a wide array of methods, including (but not limited to) the dissemination of fake news, media manipulation and misinformation; financial destabilization; cyberattacks and other forms of cyberthreats; and the destabilization of global markets (especially through the manipulation of energy prices) and trade warfare. Military tactics are present, e.g., intrusions in foreign airspaces and waters, as well as the multi-pronged invasion of Ukraine in February 2022.

Multiple partners face individual risks combined with strategic uncertainties. This creates a situation where states differ in capacity and willingness to share burdens. A partner's willingness is affected by the possible differing levels of benefits obtained through collective action. When individual benefits increase, partners are more willing to partake in joint efforts (Sandler, 2004). Smaller states facing threats are willing to invest in prevention. Geography is also a crucial factor: it determines the salience of the individual threat relative to the geography of defense. An example of this is Russia. States in the European north and east are concerned with threats from the former, while southern European states are concerned with issues related to terrorism, cybersecurity and migration—these issues intersect geographically in the Mediterranean Sea. The observation multiple partners face risks combined with strategic uncertainties explains the behavior of those willing to deploy troops to Enhanced Forward Presence despite creating individual sunk costs with the risk of entrapment should the crisis escalate. This behavior enhances the credibility of the alliance's defense commitment. Finally, "when a collective action yields multiple results varying in publicness, those joint goods consequently vary. Willingness varies because partners differ in how much they benefit from individual initiatives and when individual benefits increase, then the cooperation game transforms into an assurance game" (Kimball, 2019, p. 8).

NATO: Regional and Out-Of-Area Crisis Actor

NATO's turn to out-of-area was less a strategic plan than a necessity in the post-cold war as tensions arose in the Balkans with divergent opinions regarding crisis management. NATO activities in the Balkans in the 1990s represented its first out-of-area mission due to the inability of the EU to effectively manage the crisis and re-establish stability. NATO was called upon second; Kosovo Force-KFOR remains the longest active mission of the Alliance as it enters its 23rd year of operation. The intervention in Libya—Operation Unified Protector— in 2011 was the first military operation of the Atlantic Alliance, led by Canada, a partner outside the top five alliance contributors. NATO maintains an operation near Syria since 2012 with ACTIVE FENCE. Canada ended up doing reconstruction in the NATO's Mission in Iraq after a 2003 public refusal to join the US coalition. The alliance's strategic concept caught up with mandates and missions underway by formalizing out-of-area operations in 1999. NATO undertook maritime operations to deter piracy in OCEAN SHIELD off the coast of Somalia and SEA GUARDIAN which succeeded ACTIVE ENDEAVOR in the Mediterranean Sea. ISAF and RESOLUTE SUPPORT represented the largest troop missions by the alliance. The next chapters present data on recent operations in the context of examining partner allocations.

Comparing Burden Shifts Across Decades, 1999 and 2019; NATO Civilian Budgets

Deploying a descriptive analysis of allocations to NATO's civilian budget, 1999 versus 2019, indicated a transfer of burdens across the top three contributors (US, UK, and Germany) benefiting from enlargement, followed by those in the last slots of the top 10. Those in the middle took on burdens, i.e., Turkey, Spain, France and Canada. As expected by RIT, the top contributors, with the most bargaining power, benefited from positive effects from enlargement, followed by those ranking in the last slots of the top 10 (Kimball, 2019, p. 13).

NATO partners outside top contributors remain sensitive to discourses and arguments about under-contributing (free-riding) and developing other criteria for contributions. Canada provides the same level of defense from threat with the most partners to manage in the mission it leads in Lithuania as part of Enhanced Forward Presence, (EFP) (Kimball, 2019). Subjectively, partners might not appreciate as they start with a different reference point/viewpoint of Canadian participation. Prospect theory argues a difference of perception is fundamental because actors have a higher sensibility to losses than gains (Levy, 1997, 89; Brunnermeier, 2004, 99). For partners perceiving Canada as under-contributing (i.e., short of the 2% target), increases of burden sharing by Canada will not have the same impact on its partners' perception as its own increase regarding effort. A comparative descriptive analysis of two points permitted a snapshot (Kimball, 2019).

As one opens defense burdens, the necessity for different theoretical, qualitative and quantitative approaches is evident. Frictions across partners over burden bargaining remain as NATO adapts and provides collective defense from threat, cooperative security and crisis management. Theoretical approaches and models homogenize states and threat perceptions across time.

Conclusions—Risks, Threats, and Information

Bargaining over sharing the burden of NATO creates a reiterated cooperative game structure between a seven-decade-old group of partners plus an expanded number of functionally equivalent, but not equally capable, peers in terms of allocation capacity, risk and threat exposure. Post-cold war entrants offered a level of protection from exposure to Russia but not without provoking reaction due to proximity. That notwithstanding—the measure of 2% is a political target representing an objective allocation level based a partner's economy. In the absence of direct threats, most cold war partners (outside the top contributors and Greece/Turkey) have not maintained this minimum threshold. Post-cold war entrants, for the most part, had smaller economies and benefited from strong socialized signals about the importance of defense spending to credibly commit to the alliance. Those states passed nearly a decade on average in the PFP before entering NATO learning norms and practices in training, exercises, building experience participating in operations, and reducing integration costs into the club's collective defense; again this is an under-studied aspect of burden sharing. The US endorsed defense capacity by signing bilateral DSA (Egel et al., 2016; Kavanagh, 2014). That information reduced noise concerning defense credibility and significantly increased the chances of a NATO offer (Kimball, 2021). The geostrategic effects of enlargement are omitted from most quantitative analytical work employing military spending as the outcome of interest, while qualitative work fails to go beyond a handful of states or missions. Moreover, the effects of political and economic risks remain absent from most burden sharing research despite the inclusion of economic capacity. The risk management model of enlargement indicated economic risk had a relationship to EU offers but GDP/capita did not (Kimball, 2021); economic transformation is an EU entry condition (Asmus, 2008; Schwarz, 2016). Finally, this book examines exploitation claims, i.e., small partners benefit from club goods without 'fairly' contributing. There is evidence of substitution concerning troop allocations for European NATO partners after 2012. From 2004, hosting/sponsoring NATO COE negatively effects the chances a partner participates in an operation. However, COE costs are calculated by partners in national budgets and excluded from NATO burden negotiations. COE are tasked with future alliance transformation concerning cooperative security threats and crises ranging from a variety of concerns—28 established and two in development. They are also locations of exchanging information, socializing (Johnston, 2001), education, and long-term collaboration on doctrine development and standardization. Partners sink considerable social, economic, political, defense, and security capital into said institutions and they offer new directions for burden sharing research.

Policy Pop Out 1

Complexity and burden sharing: member risks and threats

For the policymaker	*Complexity and burden sharing: member risks and threats*
What aspects of the background information does the reader/recipient need to know? What does the reader 'know' compared to what they 'do not know'?	NATO's political target of 2% of GDP on def/sec spending does nothing to functionally ensure 'credible defense capacity'. NATO's mandates cover collective defense, cooperative security, and crisis management by a club consensus. With the complexification of def/sec threats to states and the addition of stakeholders at the internal and external levels, a holistic view of alliance-level contributions to system crisis/conflict management relative to partner-level efforts inside NATO and with other IIs is germane. Partners must maintain national defense while contributing to the club's regular budget/personnel demands and crisis missions. Burden studies omit how differences across members in terms of risk and threat shape the decisions. With 30 diverse members, states differ about the salience of Russia, migration, terrorism, etc., indicating states may not all converge on the exact club goods to produce. Additionally, few studies examine the effects of enlargement on burden sharing though there is over two decades of data to do so. The political goal is insufficient to measure justice/fairness in burden sharing and this contributes to bargaining frictions. Finally, the emergence of NATO COE offer an institutional extension absent from studies. They are the functional social communities doing alliance transformation work among subsets of partners and exist outside the normal repeated burden bargaining game.

(continued)

(continued)

For the policymaker	*Complexity and burden sharing: member risks and threats*
What is their position on the matter? Who else is affected by the issue?	It is essential to work with partners towards broadening understandings of how burden is shared within the institution functionally as well as in the field operationally. Some partners are constrained in the field by mandates given from national governments. Those constrains influence club effectiveness to deliver on mandates and forces other partners to compensate by doing more. Post-cold war partners make essential contributions geostrategically by virtue of their location securing the majority of other partners. Recognizing different and distinct burdens that shift relative to risks and threats implies a monolithic measure is insufficient. This affects not only the NATO club but also national governments, their foreign and defense ministries, national militaries, civilian security sector, international defense communities and related actors.

(continued)

(continued)

For the policymaker	*Complexity and burden sharing: member risks and threats*
What are the costs and/or risks associated with this decision?	The agreement on 2% dates to 2006 at the Riga NATO Defense ministerial. It was struck after the second round of enlargement due to risks of adding partners with under developed militaries and having large political risks. It served as a signaling mechanism to partners also entering the EU at the same time that defense spending must remain a priority. While there was a period of US discourse about maintaining 2% under Trump, the invasion of Ukraine by Russia brought about commitments to 2% by Germany and others. That notwithstanding, the political environment within some countries, such as Canada, is unlikely to support that much spending, resting comfortably around 1.6%. New NATO partners commitment to 2% signals a socially legitimate target for them to be included but some countries remain central through other contributions, such as Netherlands and Italy hosting COE. NATO also draws from foreign affairs budgets though this is much less politicized nor accounted for in the larger burden discussions and scholarly research on burden sharing. A revised discussion must look more broadly and comprehensively to where all of the sources of support for NATO arise.

(continued)

(continued)

For the policymaker	*Complexity and burden sharing: member risks and threats*
What advantages and disadvantages should the reader know about who is to make the decision?	Burden sharing decisions involve a complex set of principals and agents simultaneously and two-level negotiation games with sequential endorsement and enforcement. As a result, state-partners make (com)promises at the international level with some uncertainty as to whether the domestic political environment can deliver upon those promises. This results in occasional friction and even a failure of NATO to act, and may require delegating some tasks onto smaller subsets of interested actors. The target represents something measurable comparatively but is not sufficient nor meaningful in crisis or conflict when it comes to tangible contributions of arms, equipment, troops, personnel etc. Risk exposure by partners and perceptions of threat shape willingness to over contribute as can along with other internal political forces. Such factors are not considered in the burden sharing discourse at the negotiation table nor in the scholarly research.

(continued)

(continued)

For the policymaker	*Complexity and burden sharing: member risks and threats*
What other evaluation criteria must the recipient use?	The evaluation criteria should be revised so the contributions of smaller partners reflect the relative cost paid by the partner 'at home' and internationally; i.e. the trade-offs. For example, partners with smaller militaries cannot participate in every NATO Operation without reducing national security even in the most secure environment. As the US has increasingly abandoned UN peacekeeping participation, other European states and increasingly post-cold war NATO partners accept those burdens. This speaks to a holistic view of burdens sliced across the different categories of need for the Atlantic alliance where contributions are disaggregated, as well as an examination of resources allocated to other IO by partners outside the top contributing half dozen states. For partners seeking to invest more in European defense autonomy, it will also mean greater collaboration with the EU, potentially to the detriment of NATO.

Notes

1. See Fig. 4.1.
2. See appendix figures A.1.a to A.1.g.
3. See also https://www.washingtonpost.com/politics/2021/03/04/biden-wants-reassure-allies-that-us-is-still-interested-their-security/, last access 26 July 2022.

References

Abbott, K., & Snidal, D. (1998). Why states act through formal international organizations. *Journal of Conflict Resolution, 42*(1), 3–32. https://doi.org/10.1177/0022002798042001001

Abbott, K., & Snidal, D. (2000). Hard and soft law in international governance. *International Organization, 54*(3), 421–456. https://doi.org/10.1162/002081800551280

Alley, J. (2021). Reassessing the public goods theory of alliances. *Research & Politics, 8*(1), 205316802110052. https://doi.org/10.1177/20531680211005225

Asmus, R. (2008). Europe's Eastern promise: Rethinking NATO and EU enlargement. *Foreign Affairs, 87*(1), 95–106.

Becker, J. (2017). The correlates of transatlantic burden sharing: Revising the agenda for theoretical and policy analysis. *Defense & Security Analysis, 33*(2), 131–157. https://doi.org/10.1080/14751798.2017.1311039

Becker, J. (2021). Rusty guns and buttery soldiers: Unemployment and the domestic origins of defense spending. *European Political Science Review, 13*(3), 307–330. https://doi.org/10.1017/S1755773921000102

Bernhard, M. (2021). Democratic backsliding in Poland and Hungary. *Slavic Review, 80*(3), 585–607. https://doi.org/10.1017/slr.2021.145

Blankenship, B. (2020). Promises under pressure: Statements of reassurance in US alliances. *International Studies Quarterly, 64*(4), 1017–1030. https://doi.org/10.1093/isq/sqaa071

Brunnermeier, M. (2004). Learning to reoptimize consumption at new income levels: A rationale for prospect theory. *Journal of the European Economic Association, 2*(1), 98–114. https://doi.org/10.1162/154247604323015490

Dai, X., Snidal, D., & Sampson, M. (Eds.). (2010). International cooperation theory and international institutions. *Oxford Research Encyclopedia of International Studies*. Oxford University Press. https://doi.org/10.1093/acrefore/9780190846626.013.93

Egel, D., Grissom, A., Godges, J., Kavanagh, J., & Shatz, H. (2016). *Economic benefits of U.S. overseas security commitments could far outweigh costs*. RAND Corporation. https://doi.org/10.7249/RB9912

Fang, S., & Stone, R. (2012). International organizations as policy advisors. *International Organization, 66*(4), 537–569. https://doi.org/10.1017/S0020818312000276

Hawkins, D. (2006). *Delegation and agency in international organizations*. Cambridge University Press. http://site.ebrary.com/id/10150378

Johnston, A. I. (2001). Treating international institutions as social environments. *International Studies Quarterly, 45*(4), 487–515. https://doi.org/10.1111/0020-8833.00212

Kavanagh, J. (2014). *U.S. security-related agreements in force since 1955: Introducing a new database*. RAND Corporation.

Kimball, A. (2010). Political survival, policy distribution, and alliance formation. *Journal of Peace Research, 47*(4), 407–419. https://doi.org/10.1177/0022343310368346

Kimball, A. (2019). Knocking on NATO: Strategic and institutional challenges risk the future of Europe's seven-decade long cold peace. *The School of Public Policy Publications, 12.* https://doi.org/10.11575/SPPP.V12I0.68129

Kimball, A. (2021). Managing risks, side payments, and multi-institutional enlargement: The role of US defence, big four investment agreements and candidate risks on NATO and EU enlargement. *European Politics and Society, 22*(5), 696–715. https://doi.org/10.1080/23745118.2020.1820152

Kimball, A. & Lewis. (2011). La délégation à l'épreuve du terrain: Les difficiles interventions militaires et civiles des organisations internationales dans les conflits et les crises. In *Conflits dans le monde, 2011.* Presses Université Laval.

King, D., & Narlikar, A. (2003). The new risk regulators? International organisations and globalisation. *The Political Quarterly, 74*(3), 337–348. https://doi.org/10.1111/1467-923X.00543

Koremenos, B. (2013). The continent of international law. *Journal of Conflict Resolution, 57*(4), 653–681. https://doi.org/10.1177/0022002712448904

Koremenos, B., Lipson, C., & Snidal, D. (2001). The rational design of international institutions. *International Organization, 55*(4), 761–799. https://doi.org/10.1162/002081801317193592

Krekó, P., & Enyedi, Z. (2018). Orbán's laboratory of illiberalism. *Journal of Democracy, 29*(3), 39–51. https://doi.org/10.1353/jod.2018.0043

Levy, J. (1997). Prospect theory, rational choice, and international relations. *International Studies Quarterly, 41*(1), 87–112.

Liu, T.-Y., Su, C.-W., Tao, R., & Cong, H. (2019). Better is the neighbor? *Defence and Peace Economics, 30*(6), 706–718. https://doi.org/10.1080/10242694.2017.1422321

Massie, J. (2014). Public contestation and policy resistance: Canada's oversized military commitment to Afghanistan. *Foreign Policy Analysis, 12*(1), 47–65. https://doi.org/10.1111/fpa.12047

Massie, J., & Zyla, B. (2018). Alliance value and status enhancement: Canada's disproportionate military burden sharing in Afghanistan: Canada's military burden. *Politics & Policy, 46*(2), 320–344. https://doi.org/10.1111/polp.12247

McFaul, M. (2002). The fourth wave of democracy and dictatorship: Noncooperative transitions in the postcommunist world. *World Politics, 54*(2), 212–244. https://doi.org/10.1353/wp.2002.0004

Panke, D. (2020). States in international organizations: Promoting regional positions in international politics? *International Journal: Canada's Journal of Global Policy Analysis, 75*(4), 629–651. https://doi.org/10.1177/0020702020965267

Putnam, R. (1988). Diplomacy and domestic politics: The logic of two-level games. *International Organization, 42*(3), 427–460.

Reiter, D. (2001). Why NATO enlargement does not spread democracy. *International Security, 25*(4), 41–67. https://doi.org/10.1162/01622880151091899

Saideman, S. (2016). *Nato in Afghanistan—Fighting together, fighting alone*. Princeton University Press.

Sandler, T. (2004). *Global collective action* (1st ed.). Cambridge University Press. https://doi.org/10.1017/CBO9780511617119

Schimmelfennig, F. (2001). The community trap: Liberal norms, rhetorical action, and the Eastern enlargement of the European Union. *International Organization, 55*(1), 47–80. https://doi.org/10.1162/002081801551414

Schwarz, O. (2016). Two steps forward one step back: What shapes the process of EU enlargement in South-Eastern Europe? *Journal of European Integration, 38*(7), 757–773. https://doi.org/10.1080/07036337.2016.1203309

Stone, R. (2011). *Controlling institutions: International organizations and the global economy*. Cambridge University Press.

Stone, R. (2013). Informal governance in international organizations: Introduction to the special issue. *The Review of International Organizations, 8*(2), 121–136. https://doi.org/10.1007/s11558-013-9168-y

Vabulas, F., & Snidal, D. (2013). Organization without delegation: Informal Intergovernmental Organizations (IIGOs) and the spectrum of intergovernmental arrangements. *The Review of International Organizations, 8*(2), 193–220. https://doi.org/10.1007/s11558-012-9161-x

Wiarda, H. (2001). Where does Europe end? The politics of NATO and EU enlargement. *World Affairs, 164*(4), 178–197.

CHAPTER 4

'Measuring' NATO Member Defense Burdens—Beyond 2%

Introduction

The previous chapters laid the foundation for revisiting and reconceptualizing state contributions to managing the burdens underlying institutions, their capacity to react to crises and fulfill precise mandates under changing external and internal conditions. NATO burden sharing is more than civilian and military budget allocations; this book offers alternative data and models.

Discord, Disagreement, and 'NATO Defense Spending' Targets

NATO burden sharing is the focus of a sizable literature because of fundamental disagreements over criteria, contributions, benefits distribution and the credibility of collective defense assets based on national budget spending shaped by distinct national defense policies and preference configurations. The repeated exercise of negotiating an institution's burdens creates cleavages due to partner differences concerning risks and capacities influenced by domestic constraints (political, economic, social). European partners face budget trade-offs about European autonomous defense versus NATO. The US favors partners increasing allocation to defense and accepting burdens as a European bloc but upon the tacit

A. L. Kimball, *Beyond 2%—NATO Partners, Institutions & Burden Management*, Canada and International Affairs,
https://doi.org/10.1007/978-3-031-22158-3_4

understanding NATO support is unaffected (financially, operationally, personnel, assets, etc.).

Despite an uneasy consensus on the target of 2%, partners formally contribute to military and civilian budgets plus the Security Investment Program. The civilian budget covers the HQ in Brussels and associated activities, whereas the military budget includes the Command Structure HQ and missions. "In 2021, €254.9 million of the military budget will go toward funding NATO's missions and operations".[1] This effort conceptualizes burdens along distinct axes of contributions. This categorization broadens the discussion beyond the bifurcating discourse, i.e., military spending ('defense commitment credibility') as a political target. Each category offers a number of indicators to measure, debate, and build upon. This project connects and centralizes as much of the quantifiable data possible to advance knowledge about burden sharing and open discussion with stakeholders.

Physical Capital (Partner Contributions to Fixed Assets)

These are the burdens partners take on hosting NATO's ground and mortar aspects of a physical presence (as an independent actor). The agency of IOs has received scholarly attention (Graham, 2014; Hawkins, 2006) though NATO escaped study. That notwithstanding, NATO has civilian secretariat, a military headquarters and subcommands throughout Europe. Partners host Centre's of Excellence, training centers and educational institutions in different defense and security domains. Some partners host US military bases (Germany, UK, now Poland). NATO also obtained agreements to extend its range e.g., ships can dock in Australia, New Zealand and Japan.

Table 4.1 offers an overview of US bases, NATO Centres of Excellence (COE), PFP—NATO Training Centres and NATO Colleges by partner with newer entrants followed by the 14 European partners, then European partners to NATO. The data compiled represent one of data contributions and are available disaggregated by state-COE in the digital appendix. Created in 2003, COE are a structural solution producing a minimal level of collective goods for partners with greater interests on a specific issue through an assurance structure provided by framework partner states. They offer experience and expertise on a defined subject to the benefit of the club within the four pillars of the COE program around

Alliance Transformation representing how the Alliance tries to reduce uncertainties associates with future actor behavior and the future state of the world with regularized communities developing functional forward-looking collaboration. COE permit burden sharing beyond the civilian and military budgets. Their precise specialized mandates are articulated around the four transformation pillars of *Education and training; Analysis and lessons learned; Concept development and experimentation;* and *Doctrine development and standards*. As institutional concepts, developed after enlargement to amplify and transmit expertise, they remain outside of the NATO chain of command and operate independently in an informal framework between partner states and the COE, as an actor/agent. Structurally, they are not part of the NATO Commands (per MCM-236-06) but report to Allied Command Transformation (ACT) and are guided by the Military Committee (MC) or other NATO entities. Global partners may join. They are institutions that are 'asked not tasked' speaking to their informal relationship with NATO.

Each COE has a Steering Committee (SC) guiding activities based on a Program of Work (POW) developed with ACT. To functionally sponsor a COE a state must: be a NATO Country; send at least one person to the COE (full time); pay its share of the yearly COE Budget; send national representation to SC meetings (NOT the staff member); and be a participant to both Memoranda of Understanding (MOU)—"a Functional Memorandum of Understanding, which governs the relationship between Centres of Excellence and the Alliance [with ACT] and an Operational Memorandum of Understanding, which governs the relationship between participating countries and the COE".[2] Once participants consent and sign, then ACT accreditation is sought.

> Framework and Sponsoring nations must also coordinate, draft, negotiate, and agree to a Functional MOU with ACT. The COE then enters into the accreditation phase. ACT develops accreditation criteria, after which the Framework Nation(s) request accreditation for the COE. A team from ACT then visits the COE and assesses it against the tailored list of points based on the Military Committee's accreditation criteria for COE.[3]

Sponsoring nations pay all costs resulting from COE operation; thus continued sponsor political will and financial support are essential.

Table 4.1 US bases, education centers, NATO assets hosted by (European) partners, original data

	US base	*PFP Train/Univ*	*NATO Commands*	*COE (host)*	*Total*	*Year COE established*	*COE framework (partners)*
Czechia	0	0	0	1	1	2007	1 (13)
Hungary	1	1	0	1	3	2009	1 (12)
Poland	0	0	1*	2	3	2014	2 (18)
Bulgaria	0	1	0	1	2	2015	1 (5)
Estonia	0	0	0	1	1	2008	1 (5)
Latvia	0	0	0	1	1	2014	1 (4)
Lithuania	0	0	0	1	1	2012	1 (5)
Romania	0	2	0	1	3	2010	1 (16)
Slovakia	0	2	0	2	4	2011	2 (9)
Slovenia	0	1	0	1	2	2015	1 (7)
Albania	0	0	0	0	0	–	0 (3)
Croatia	0	0	0	0	0	–	0 (4)
Montenegro	0	0	0	0	0	–	0 (1)
Belgium	3	0	2	2	7	2006	1 (5)
Canada	0	1	0	0	1	/2023/	/1/ (5)
Denmark	0	0	0	0	0	–	0 (7)
France	0	0	0	1	1	2008	1 (9)
Iceland	2	0	0	0	2	–	0 (0)
Italy	7	3	1	3	14	2012	3 (16)
Luxembourg	0	0	0	0	0	–	0 (0)
The Netherlands	2	0	1	3	6	2007	3 (13)
Norway	2	0	1	1	4	2007	1 (5)
Portugal	1	1	1	1	4	–	1 (4)
UK	5	0	1	0	6	2021	1 (10)
Germany	14	2	1	4	21	2005	4 (17)
Greece	2	1	0	1	4	2006	1 (15)
Turkey	2	1	1	2	6	2020	2 (11)
Spain	2	0	0	1	3	2010	1 (8)
US	–	0	2	1	3	2006	1 (14)
Finland	0	1	–	0	1	–	0 (3)
Austria	0	1	–	0	1	–	0 (3)

(continued)

Table 4.1 (continued)

	US base	*PFP Train/Univ*	*NATO Commands*	*COE (host)*	*Total*	*Year COE established*	*COE framework (partners)*
Sweden	0	1	–	0	1	–	0 (3)
Switzerland	0	1	–	0	1	–	0 (1)
Georgia	0	0	–	0	0	–	0 (1)
Total	43	17	10	28	107		32 (220)

*Transitioning from Forward Operation Post to military HQ
Source Author's creation, Jan. 2022.

There are 28 COE across NATO partners with all but Luxembourg and Iceland as partners. Because they remain outside the NATO framework structurally, partners negotiate MOU with each COE to join, resulting in possibility 220 bilateral-COE agreements.[4] NATO legal Deskbook defines the MOU as:

> used to record informal arrangements between States on matters which are inappropriate for inclusion in treaties or where the form is more convenient than a treaty (e.g., for confidentiality). They may be drawn up as a single document using non-treaty terms, signed on behalf of two or more governments, or consist of an exchange of notes or letters recording an understanding reached between two governments, or a government and an international organization. MOU *usually do not require ratification*. However, depending on the content and the agreement between the Parties on the nature of the document, MOU can be subject of a certain level of domestic ratification...NATO, in general, concludes MOU in numerous occasions. *MOU are a very flexible and adaptable instrument to record the will of entities with legal personality to achieve practical results* that do not amount to treaty obligations.[5] (emphasis added)

Two blocks of European states remain active in COE; Romania (17), Poland, Czechia, and Estonia are post-cold war partners in a dozen or more Centres, while Italy (17), Germany (17), Turkey, The Netherlands and Greece are partners to over a dozen COE.[6] Germany and The Netherlands are framework nations to the most COE (4, 3). Poland hosts the most COE and the US Forward Operation Post was upgraded to a base. Italy places itself with those hosting a significant diversity of physical assets without being a top financial contributor. In total, an impressive

107 installations are hosted by European states and NATO partners with a little under half (43 or 40%) being US military bases. Though Germany hosts the most total assets, reflecting its geographic risk for decades, the UK welcomes more US troops at few installations. Finland, Austria and Sweden are partners to three COE and each host one PFP training center, a level of support equal to 6 partners and exceeding Denmark hosting no physical assets due to Copenhagen's proximity to Moscow.

Continuing NATO Operations (i.e., Current Club Demands)

Table 4.2 presents continuing operations. The KFOR mission is led by the Italian Air Force for the last 5 rotations, whereas the Danes took over the Iraq mission from the Canadians. The UK leads SEA GUARDIAN because it hosts NATO's Maritime Command. Norway serves as a facilitator, and leads on the collaboration with the African Union through a special delegation in Addis Ababa. Finally, Germany and Spain settled on the splitting the leadership for air policing in eastern Europe but from home bases. EFP is a reassurance operation to Poland and the Baltic states. Those partners face threats to territorial sovereignty so extreme they requested the club place troops to ensure a 'trip-wire' of collective defense through entrapment. Kimball (2019) noted the importance of US defense of Poland's Suwalki Gap, a focal point for land access denial.

Demands arising from exogenous crises with short life-spans are included, in the category of punctual demands and partner troop allocations outside of NATO since 2013 presented in the next section. Partners contribute resources and capacities to missions with uncertainty about the state of the world on the ground and future partner behavior. Some may contribute to missions but with constraints on in the capacities and skills brought to theater. A continuing concern is limits on national military deployments since within NATO missions mandates are influenced by each partner's perception's of the particular operational conflict/crisis conditions resulting in possible caveats on national troop contingent participation in common missions. States with the greatest margin of action, such as Canada, accepted larger burdens in the operations in Afghanistan compared to Germany (Saideman & Auerswald, 2012). Mandate limits on militaries by partner national governments shifted burdens resulting in negative externalities for those less constrained. Canada offers an overcontributed EFP contingent with the

Table 4.2 Current NATO operations requiring partner contributions, public sources

Name	*Location(s)*	*Years active*	*Force size*	*Lead partner*	*Hub*
KFOR	Kosovo	22	3500	Italy	Naples
SEA GUARDIAN	MED sea	6	Varies	UK	MARCOM
NMI	Iraq	4 (17 total)	850	Denmark	Naples
AMISOM	Somalia	14	AU airlift aid	Norway	Addis Ababa
Air policing	East Europe	8	420	GER/SP	Uedem/Torrejon
EFP	EST, LAT, LITH, POL, ROM	8	5 battlegroups; 6105 (1146, 1650*, 1103*, 1058, 1148*)	UK, CAN, GER, US	Tapa, EST; Adazi, LAT; Rukla, LIT; Orzysz, POL; Cincu, ROM

*Up to, from February 2022, https://www.nato.int/nato_static_fl2014/assets/pdf/2022/2/pdf/2202-factsheet_efp_en.pdf, last access 15 June 2022
Source Appendix D

challenge of leading collaboration among the most multinational and multilinguistic battalion among the five while not being a top club contributor (Kimball, 2019, p. 17).

Punctual Demands (Crisis/Conflict Mission Contributions)

European partners to NATO and the EU face demands to shoulder operational burdens for both institutions (Dahl Thruelsen, 2009). At least one categorization of the types of crisis and conflict missions undertaken by NATO, EU, UN in an examination of how the extra-European missions are managed by states exists (Kimball & Lewis, 2010, 2011). Collective defense outputs vary by crisis determining what functional structure facilitates the successful provision of a good. For example, air policing and sea interdiction missions represent assurance games where once states with crucial capacities provide a level others contribute in complementarity, whereas counterterrorism resembles a collective action structure of weakest link, as the partner with the least sophisticated counterterror defense offers the entry point for any potential attack (Sandler, 2004, pp. 75–98). Peacekeeping operations resemble a threshold aggregation function which increases the chances of successful collective provision depending on the number and nature of the parties contributing (Sandler, 2004, p. 93); cost-sharing schemes and refunds induce cooperation along with coordination possibly through a leader-follower structure. Power asymmetry across actors requires a larger coordination to elaborate a collaborative crisis reaction to ensure collective security arises under incentives to defect by the stronger party. Finally, air refusal and air denial require sunk costs in fixed equipment to reduce exposure geospatially along with complementary mobile assets with strong information transmission and coordination across stakeholders.

That notwithstanding, the distribution of IO activities in conflict and crisis areas presents a different view of contributions by state partners. Activities vary across mandates and contribution size varies in terms of personnel and assets required.[7] Tables 4.3 and 4.4 examine troops contributed to various IO, state-led and national operations for all NATO partners and disaggregated across US, NATO cold war partners and NATO post-cold war partners. Table 4.3 indicates between 2013 and 2020 for all partners national commitments accounting for about 75% of national troop allocations. This included the draw down of Afghanistan and French-led missions in Mali. This is distributed with non-US cold war partners allocating between 58 and 69% and post-cold war partners from 66 to 87%, the rest of the troops for those nations distributed across EU and UN missions. The US reduced troop allocations to NATO activities to 3% in 2020 from 17% in 2013. Partners entering NATO after the Cold War demonstrate an increased willingness to take upon EU and UN troop burdens across the period alongside decreasing US troop commitments to NATO missions simultaneously, taken together evidence of substitution and a successful effort to increase burdens taken on by other NATO partners but escapes acknowledgement due to the political target's dominance as criteria. Table 4.4 is a snapshot of troop commitments by partner across the three areas of action in 2020. Cold war NATO partners, excluding the US, shouldered the most burden for operations to the South whereas the US offered about 81% of troops to Europe and Eastern areas. Troops in the Middle East were 46% other cold war NATO partners and 54% from the US supporting the claims of the risk management burden sharing model that partner contributions to collective operations differ regionally and are shaped by national risk perceptions and national political/economic constraints. For example, Turkish contributions are predominately in the Middle East, where it offers 32% of all troops, while France contributes around 30% of those guarding the Southern flank-an effort equal to the US in the region.

Disaggregated data in the appendix show NATO's ISAF/RESOLUTE SUPPORT represented a comparatively large force in 2013 with over 83,000 of troops and US troops dominated the collective force ranging from 61 to 82% from 2013 to 2016 when it reduced to less than 12,000. From 2017 to 2022, the US reduced this force from 57 to 40%. This alongside KFOR retaining a force of 3,600 to 3,825 and the US forces remained between 17 and 19% of combined troop allocations, while it took on a larger slice of KFOR, it never contributed over 24%. Offering evidence of the short-term qui pro quo intra temporal alliance entry costs, those states entering NATO after the cold war accepted the KFOR burden increasingly from 2013 to 2020, collectively taking on 22–38% of troops. Intra-alliance bargaining is essential to the continued provision of club goods under shifts in partner preferences over what missions were vital to club interests over time. From a risk management perspective, partners under threat bargain to ensure they are protected and the willingness of unthreatened allies depends on the individual salience of the crisis/threat for internal political audiences. Risks/salience cannot be equal for all members for bargaining to happen, Putnam's classic two-good, two-level bargaining win-set implicitly relies on said assumption (Putnam, 1988). This explains the delay and ramp up to EFP despite consistent pleas and increasing threats to eastern partners. Those behaviors are consistent with the risk management model of institutional burden sharing.

Ongoing missions of IO are ordered by intervention length since 1949 in Table 4.5, another data contribution. The UN is not only most engaged, with 28 activities, but manages six of the longest interventions. Three decades of OSCE activities resulted in 13 missions. UN activities in the Central African Republic, South Sudan, Somalia, Mali and Lebanon account for the deployment of around 58,000 troops from UN members. Troops contributed by NATO partners account for less than 4,800 troops or 8%. Those troops are located in Israel-Lebanon (about 3,600) and Mali (871). EU missions are more compact, as its seven operations deploy around 1,840 troops. NATO undertakes activities in about 11% of all crises and conflict but deployed 19 times. The UN acts in 52% of conflicts and crises followed by the OSCE in 24%. In most cases, NATO enters after another IO intervened (Kosovo, Afghanistan, Horn of Africa, Iraq). Its maritime deployment to the Mediterranean Sea and

Table 4.3 NATO partner troop allocations to operations by II and states alongside national commitments disaggregated, 2013–2020

All NATO partners	*NATO operations*	*EU operations*	*UN operations*	*US-led operations*	*French-led operations*	*National troop commitments*	*% NATO of total*	*% national troop commit of total*
2013	90,373	2034	3785	2764	2800	382,503	18.66	78.99
2014	42,671	2888	4796	5191	3000	341,458	10.67	85.36
2015	19,186	4240	3785	9750	3502	369,178	4.68	90.12
2016	18,467	3645	4839	18,112	3500	367,791	4.44	88.34
2017	23,364	2536	5552	20,885	4000	372,857	5.44	86.87
2018	26,098	2479	5911	16,774	4332	376,879	6.04	87.15
2019	27,123	1857	5337	16,226	4335	372,988	6.34	87.17
2020	20,293	2258	5692	12,063	2489	375,179	4.86	89.76
US	*NATO operations*	*EU operations*	*UN operations*	*US-led operations*	*French-led operations*	*National troop commitments*	*% NATO of total*	*% national troop commit of total*
2013	61,145	0	38	1720	0	298,691	16.91	82.60
2014	30,331	0	37	3370	0	260,234	10.32	88.52
2015	7822	0	30	5654	0	292,175	2.56	95.58
2016	7641	0	36	8834	0	291,358	2.48	94.64
2017	8645	0	49	14,506	0	300,550	2.67	92.83
2018	9934	0	45	10,791	0	307,256	3.03	93.67
2019	10,315	0	30	11,060	0	312,795	3.09	93.60
2020	5480	0	31	7563	0	307,689	1.71	95.92
Non-US NATO cold war partners	*NATO operations*	*EU operations*	*UN operations*	*US-led operations*	*French-led operations*	*National troop commitments*	*% NATO of total*	*% national troop commit of total*
2013	24,003	1641	3412	999	2800	83,812	20.57	71.84
2014	9287	2576	4428	1788	3000	81,224	9.08	79.40
2015	8308	3846	3412	3745	3502	77,003	8.32	77.15
2016	8082	3353	4364	8597	3500	76,433	7.75	73.26
2017	11,254	2139	4707	6003	4000	72,307	11.21	72.01
2018	11,822	2063	4966	5539	4232	69,623	12.03	70.87

(continued)

Table 4.3 (continued)

Non-US NATO cold war partners	*NATO operations*	*EU operations*	*UN operations*	*US-led operations*	*French-led operations*	*National troop commitments*	*% NATO of total*	*% national troop commit of total*
2019	12,380	1391	4503	4700	4235	60,193	14.16	68.87
2020	11,015	1842	4253	4034	2299	67,490	12.11	74.22

NATO post-cold war partners	*NATO operations*	*EU operations*	*UN operations*	*US-led operations*	*French-led operations*	*National troop commitments*	*% NATO of total*	*% (EU + UN) of total*
2013	5225	393	341	45	0	0	87.03	12.23
2014	3053	312	331	33	0	0	81.87	17.24
2015	3056	394	403	351	0	0	72.69	18.96
2016	2744	292	436	681	0	0	66.07	17.53
2017	3465	397	402	376	0	0	74.68	17.22
2018	4342	416	450	444	50	0	76.15	15.19
2019	4428	466	402	466	50	0	76.19	14.94
2020	3798	416	704	466	95	0	69.32	20.44

Source The Military Balance, 2014–2021 (London: International Institute for Strategic Studies)

air denial (ACTIVE FENCE) over Syria are examples where NATO was the first IO involved. Some overweight NATO operations though its intervening force size is similar sized to other II with the exception of ISAF.

Socialization (Considering Human Capital, Community)

NATO created effective institutions to socialize and train potential partners and extra regional collaborators alongside the club in an operational context. Since 1993, the PFP serves as an institutional forum to socialize possible alliance (and global) partners by collaborating in a variety of trainings, operations, etc. Its goal is to prepare potential members to join the institution, if they request, and ensure a level of operational capacity with the institution. Potential partners select from 1600 collaborative activities. NATO's mandate covers operating in crisis and conflict

Table 4.4 NATO partner troop allocations to Eastern flank assurance activities in 2020

	Calculations of effort by region, 2020			
	Europe and Eastern flank	*Southern flank*	*Middle East*	*Total (%)*
Cold War partners	127,696	**78,044**	**495,300**	**701,040 (37%)**
Belgium	1517	1255	1828	
Canada	6362	794	4851	
Denmark	1583	1192	3032	
France	17,546	36,457	21,601	
Germany	12,853	6833	18,633	
Greece	2025	271	8940	
Italy	6563	6579	28,086	
Luxembourg	146	97	21	
The Netherlands	2084	12,110	2509	
Norway	1361	1574	2581	
Portugal	1983	1474	999	
Spain	3486	2042	10,302	
Turkey	9282	1112	342,796	
United Kingdom	60,905	6254	49,121	
Post Cold War	**18,114**	**3467**	**21,820**	**43,401 (2%)**
Albania	307	21	667	
Bulgaria	638	35	1533	
Croatia	781	50	1012	
Czech Republic	644	867	2187	
Estonia	216	249	546	
Hungary	5191	219	2444	
Latvia	385	108	341	
Lithuania	382	146	595	
Poland	4195	315	4224	
Romania	1735	1342	5704	
Slovak Republic	1133	21	2310	
Slovenia	2507	94	257	
United States	**557,777**	**35,528**	**558,122**	**1,151,427**(61%)
Totals	685,473	117,039	1,075,242	1,877,754 (100%)

Source The Military Balance, 2014–2021 (London: International Institute for Strategic Studies)

Table 4.5 Crisis/conflict intervention by II ongoing since 1949

Current IO interventions in ongoing crises and conflicts since 1948 (N = 55) (31 in 26 crises) and (24 in 13 conflicts)

	Conflict/crisis	*IO*	*Name*	*Start date*	*Troop size (any formed police)*	*Years active (2022)*
Israël	Conflict	UN	UNTSO	1948–	59^	74
India	Conflict	UN	UNMOGIP	1949–	*2^	73
Pakistan	Conflict	UN	UNMOGIP	1949–	*2^	73
Cyprus	Crisis	UN	UNFICYP	1964–	729	58
Israël	Conflict	UN	UNDOF	1974–	6^	48
Lebanon	Conflict	UN	UNIFIL	1978–	*9669/3631^	44
Egypt	Crisis	UN	MFO	1981–	1154/609#	41
Morocco	Crisis	UN	MINURSO	1991–	0	31
North Macedonia	Crisis	OSCE	Mission to Skopje	1992–	–	30
Moldova	Crisis	OSCE	Mission to Moldova	1993–	–	29
Tadjikistan	Crisis	OSCE	Programme Office in Dushanbe	1994–	–	28
Ukraine	Crisis	OSCE	Project Co-ordinator in Ukraine	1994–	–	28
Bosnia-Herzegovina	Crisis	OSCE	OSCE Mission in B-H	1995–	–	25
Kyrgyzstan	Crisis	OSCE	Programme office in Bishkek	1998–	–	24
Turkménistan	Crisis	OSCE	Centre in Ashgabat	1998–	–	24
Kosovo	Crisis	NATO	KFOR	1999–	2885^	23
Kosovo	Crisis	UN	UNMIK	1999–	0/7^	23
Kosovo	Crisis	OSCE	Mission to Kosovo	1999–	–	23
Afghanistan	Conflict	UN	UNAMA	2002–2023	0	21
Serbia	Crisis	OSCE	Mission to Serbia	2001–	–	21

(continued)

Table 4.5 (continued)

Current IO interventions in ongoing crises and conflicts since 1948 (N = 55) (31 in 26 crises) and (24 in 13 conflicts)						
	Conflict/crisis	*IO*	*Name*	*Start date*	*Troop size (any formed police)*	*Years active (2022)*
Senegal	Crisis	UN	UNOWAS	2002–	0	20
Iraq	Crisis	UN	UNAMI	2003–		19
Bosnia-Herzegovina	Crisis	EU	EUFOR-ALTHEA	2004–	431^	18
Central Africa Rep	Conflict	EU	EUTM	2004–	116^	18
Montenegro	Crisis	OSCE	Mission to Montenegro	2005–	–	17
Uzbekistan	Crisis	OSCE	Project Co-ordinator in Uzbekistan	2006–	–	17
Israël	Conflict	UN	UNIFIL mandat +	2006–	*9669/3631^	16
Burundi	Crisis	UN	BINUB (political)	2007–	0	15
Croatia	Crisis	OSCE	Office in Zagreb	2008–	–	14
Georgia	Conflict	EU	EUMM	2008–	200	14
Kosovo	Crisis	EU	EULEX-Kosovo (rule of law)	2008–	0	14
Papua New Guinea	Crisis	UN	UN Bougainville Programme & Nation building through crisis prevention and recovery (development mandate)	2008–	0	14
Somalia-Horn of Africa	Conflict	EU	OP-ATALANTA (EUNAVFOR)	2008–	441^	14

Current IO interventions in ongoing crises and conflicts since 1948 (N = 55) (31 in 26 crises) and (24 in 13 conflicts)

	Conflict/crisis	*IO*	*Name*	*Start date*	*Troop size (any formed police)*	*Years active (2022)*
Niger	Crisis	UN/AU/ ECOWAS	Mission conjointe ONU/UA/CEDEAO à Niamey (development mandate)	2009–	0	13
Somalia-Horn of Africa	Conflict	NATO	OCEAN SHIELD	2009–	1173	13
Somalia	Conflict	EU	EUTM (Somalia)	2010–	176^	12
DR Congo	Conflict	UN	MONUSCO	2010–	12,713 (1224)/36^	12
Libya	Conflict	UN	UNSMIL	2011–	233/4^	11
Sudan	Conflict	UN	UNMISS	2011–	13,260 (849)/52^	11
Sudan	Conflict	UN	UNISFA	2011–	3042	11
Syria	Crisis	NATO	ACTIVE FENCE	2012–	150^	10
Mali	Conflict	UN	MINUSMA	2013–	11,788 (1443)/871^	9
Mali	Conflict	EU	EUTM	2013–	0/540^	9
Somalia	Conflict	UN	UNSOM	2013–	2^	9
Central Africa Republic	Conflict	UN	MINUSCA	2014–2022	11,189 (1894)/208^	8
Ukraine	Crisis	OSCE	Special Monitoring Mission to Ukraine	2014–	–	8
Somalia	Conflict	UN	UNSOS	2015–	623/10^	7
Med Sea	Crisis	NATO	SEA GUARDIAN	2016–		6

(continued)

Table 4.5 (continued)

Current IO interventions in ongoing crises and conflicts since 1948 (N = 55) (31 in 26 crises) and (24 in 13 conflicts)

	Conflict/crisis	*IO*	*Name*	*Start date*	*Troop size (any formed police)*	*Years active (2022)*
Columbia	Crisis	UN	UNVMC	2017–	0	5
Iraq	Crisis	NATO	NMI	2018–	379	4
Haiti	Crisis	UN	BINUH	2019–	0	3
Yemen	Crisis	UN	UNMHA	2019–		3
Med Sea	Crisis	EU	EUNAVFOR MED	2020–	554^	2
Sudan	Conflict	UN	UNITAMS	2020–	0	2
Somalia	Conflict	AU	ATMIS	2022–	0	

*Both hosts coded with same N
^data from 2020 NATO partners
#https://mfo.org/contingents
13 current NATO and EU operations & italicized actors/areas represent collective naval operations
Source Author's creation

regions where the transaction costs of miscommunication, misperception and lack of coordination are consequential. Potential entrants and extra regional partners opt into operational training and other activities with the PFP for the past three decades. NATO Defense College in Rome and cross-partner military training opportunities are additional aspects of socialization (Becker & Malesky, 2017; Johnston, 2001). These activities create the environment of trust contributing to social cohesion and the credibility the Article V collective defense relies upon. "We are NATO" is a shared identity and a unifying concept for those posted to NATO rotations under national flags. #WeAreNATO is a social media tag used by the institution as identifying with the club. This construction is reinforced and reproduced with a set of under two-minute videos: *PartnerName is NATO. #WeAreNATO.* Social media campaigns are for domestic audiences; English subtitles appear.[8] It is a communication campaign in various media addressing military members, politicians and populations to reinforce NATO's positive, cohesive club image. It also serves as an external signal to potential aggressors the organization, with its global partners, is prepared to react to a multitude of defense and security threats across the domains of defense and security efficiently and effectively. COE continue socialization into the future with analysis, training, and doctrine development concerning future risks and collaborative challenges on specific defense and security issues among subgroups of participating partners. COE remain understudied in both the NATO burden and international institution cooperation research.

US Defense Agreements—As Informational Improvement by Endorsement

Partners differ in capacity to produce to defense goods at home creating bargaining to produce the essential defense goods. Some with larger defense sector capacities may act as underwriters for the defense capacity of others. Kimball (2021) offered evidence of the role of the US defense agreements reducing uncertainty and signaling the credible defense capacity of post-cold war new partners while other analyses support the pivotal role of the UK in shaping the allocations of European partners (Liu et al., 2019). Kavanagh (2014) and Fig. 3.1 offer data indicating the US serves as a defense underwriter for some post-cold war partners.

Post-cold war partners offered strategic benefits but extending the institution's collective defense frontier was prioritized over political risks from new entrants.

Considering intra-alliance arms transfers and bilateral defense and security agreements with the US by partners is among the contributions. Defense influence varies and an asymmetric system developed with US as an essential partner due to its oligopolistic role on the market (Kimball, 2015). Some partners rely strongly on US arms transfers and agreements to maintain NATO commitments, while others diversify using more intra-NATO arms trade (The Netherlands, Belgium, and Norway). Close partners to the US face transaction costs and trade-offs cooperating or purchasing outside the US market. Substantial reliance on the US may deter individual dissension over burdens or missions supported by the US.

Partner Level Risks Brought to NATO

Adding post-cold war partners required identifying risks incurred from each. All candidates had the capacity to enact legislation and enact reforms when candidates entered were determined by politics (Wiarda, 2001). "Political risks remained important. Institutions managed costs including the risk of conflict with Russia, uncertainties about security/economic externalities from suboptimal partners, and the effects of new partners on distributional aspects, e.g., decision-making and budgeting" (Kimball, 2021, p. 699).

Side bargains, such as US DSA, offered information to existing partners improving perceptions of potential entrant credibility. Another way to examine if dominant states influence II behavior is through bilateral arms transfers.[9] Cross-national studies of burden sharing must account for how post-cold war entrants created threats from Russia, reduced geographic exposure for existing partners and differently offered relative political or economic risks.

Box Whisker plots of the distribution of political and economic risk for 13 post-cold war entrants appear in Figs. 4.1 and 4.2 ordered by entry group during a period of 25 years. Box Whisker plots offer a graphical method of displaying the variation in a set of data through identifying the upper and lower quartiles of the data and displaying the variability of the annual observations. The lines extending parallel from the boxes are known as the "whiskers," indicate variability outside the upper and lower quartile. For each country an X marks the average while the median is identified with a straight line. The International Crisis Risk Guide measures of political and investment risks are used provided by the Political Risk Group. For the former, the dataset employs 12 factors and a 100-point scale, where higher values indicate lower risk. Those factors include government stability, conflict, bureaucratic quality, investment profile, and socioeconomic conditions. The qualitative cut-offs are 50, where risk is considered very high; 50–59.9, high risk; 60–69.9, moderate risk; and 70–79.9, low risk (Kimball, 2021). The X for each country identifies its average and the blocked rectangle shows limits of the upper and lower quartile, while the median is marked with a straight line. The 1999 trio of entrants distinguished themselves with averages at or above the median for political risk. Only Slovakia, of the states in the second round, had a median similar to their averages and equally high. The accompanying economic risk Box Whisker plot uses a scale of 50 points and supports the 1999 trio that had means and medians nearly the same. The larger variance in economic risk in Slovakia meant it was a less good candidate compared to others at the time despite similar political risks. Examining these descriptive figures and including both risks in quantitative models offers a distinct contribution to NATO burden sharing research and the international cooperation and bargaining literature, writ large.

Conclusions: Multiple Measures for Multiple Models

A nuanced, comprehensive understanding of risks and threats affirmed enlargement to the 1999 trio reduced partner risks and was unlikely to provoke Russia. Poland's military imports were several times larger than its first-round peers. The second-round included the Baltic states, likely to trigger Russian response due to proximity, with larger (in terms of arms transfers) but less stable states, politically, and economically, i.e., Romania and Bulgaria. A risk management model of institutional burden sharing for NATO presented herein covers a sizable period and number of states, while considering state attributes and risks versus public policy trade-offs concerning allocations. A novel measure of informational improvement provided by US bilateral DSA is examined with the 'status quo measure' of defense effort (military spending as a % of GDP, i.e., the 2% target) along with measures of political and economic risk and geostrategic threat

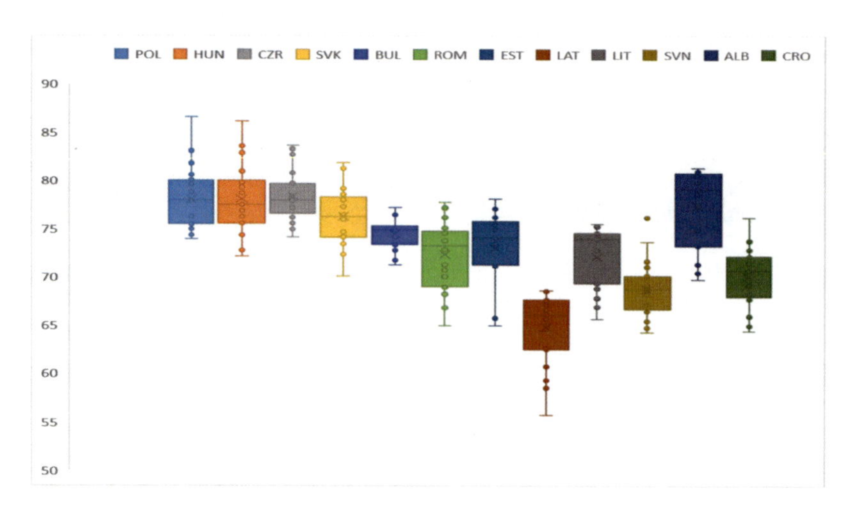

Fig. 4.1 Box Whisker plots of political risk, 1994–2018, post-cold war entrants (pre-2010)

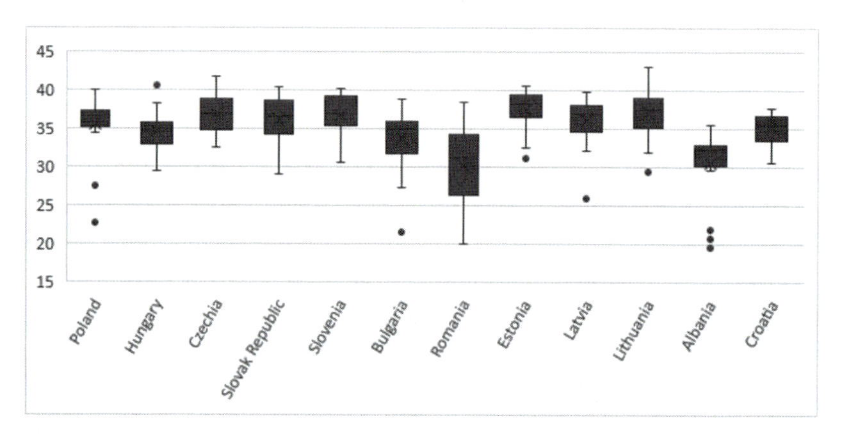

Fig. 4.2 Box Whisker plots of economic risk, 1994–2018, post-cold NATO entrants (pre-2010)

constructing risk management models of burden sharing, using NATO as a case for analysis.

Those measures are examined across partner decisions concerning military spending and participation in new alliance operations, more original data. Quantitative analytical models covering two temporal periods examine military spending (from 1949 onwards and after 1993). A second set of analytical models predicts the chances a NATO partner contributes troops to missions after 1990. This research also discusses how NATO Centres of Excellence redistribute burdens while supporting alliance transformation in the areas of collective defense, cooperative security and crisis management. Two COE are selected for an intensive study of their primary founding documents, the MOU, using constructivist and rational institutionalist approaches. This research contributes new data, uses multiple methods to propose and examine risk management models of burden sharing.

Policy Pop Out 2

Measuring NATO partner burdens: Beyond 2%

For the policymaker	*Measuring NATO partner burdens: beyond 2%*
What aspects of the background information does the reader/recipient need to know? What does the reader 'know' compared to what they 'do not know'?	Going beyond the 2% target requires a comprehensive view of what contributions support NATO functioning on a day-to-day level, at its various physical locations and in a theatre of operations. There must be a consideration of the requirements to achieve the mandates of collective defense, cooperative security and crisis management as a club within the NATO area and beyond. Partners face different internal constraints and political environments, enlargement remains untreated in studies as are reflections of how an enlarged and transformed alliance shares the costs of the club while distributing access to the benefits. Bargaining over the costs of club burdens and the distribution of club benefits in the presence multiple semi-private structures, i.e., COE, requires an understanding of how those structures redistribute burdens consistent with collective action and rational approaches. COE serve as communities in a co-constructed environment to advance common and partner-level goals consistent with sociological explanations. The implications are two-fold; first, an improved longitudinal picture of burden sharing accounting for risks, threats, the effects of US support with special attention to the effects of enlargement after the post-cold war and the shifting nature of def/sec threats to NATO, as a club, and partners individually is required. Second, aspects of contributions outside the budget percentage line and a political target require transparency and reporting deserve further study. Research can also be advanced through a better understanding of how NATO's institutional structures are self-enforcing and why practices, behaviors and information exchanges at COE institutions support identity building and socialization while also providing functional semi-exclusive club goods.
What is their position on the matter? Who else is affected by the issue?	Reflecting on new ways to account for and conceptualize burden sharing requires shifting thinking among some defense and foreign affairs stakeholders. The 2% target measure is instrumentalized and politicized by partners, leaders and governments in discussions on defense sharing, defense policy planning and defense investment. That notwithstanding increasing the information available to everyone at the bargaining table about how to categorize and rethink contributions may increase burden sharing effectiveness and redistributive justice in the long term, even, if there are increased bargaining costs caused by transparency. Those costs reduce overtime with efficiencies and institutionalization of cost-sharing agreements, as is the case with COE. It also incurs upon states to consider what contributions make the institution function and how to account for them more transparently and consistently in burden sharing negotiations.

(continued)

(continued)

For the policymaker	*Measuring NATO partner burdens: beyond 2%*
What are the costs and/or risks associated with this decision?	Requests for transparency and budgeting detail concerning def/sec triggers state inclinations to protect autonomy and secrecy of information. Transparency is a virtue of democracy, liberalism and freedom which are shared values of the Atlantic Alliance and its members. As much as NATO entrants passed thresholds publicly to enter based on multiple criteria guided by the PFP (Kimball, 2021), NATO burdens should be treated similarly with criteria and monitoring. This requires the normalization of stakeholders sharing information and data about contributions, such data will reveal over contribution or under contribution across aspects of club outputs producing a more nuanced image of the complex concept. The US is not likely to be in favor of such a change of criteria (away from the 2% target). States are strategic actors cognizant of such concerns, researchers and analysts could have access to 'reliable' data from governments, and some willingly offer data for empirical study, otherwise publicly available data are used or original data complied by researchers to understand burden sharing. NATO could adopt new norms and/or adapt norm practice about transparency by consensus. This is possible around COE financing through ACT mandate because they are external to the NATO financing structure and cannot duplicate existing NATO capacities. However, COE represent how the alliance looks forward and transforms to the future; COE partners are subsets of member states accepting extra costs of a particular burden today to enable the club have a better level of future collective response capacity to the shifting environment of threats, evidenced by the variety of COE thematic areas.
What advantages and disadvantages should the reader know about who is to make the decision?	This decision should be taken at the defense ministerial level or above as the output of a meeting, summit, in a written communique, strategic concept, MOU or any other informal negotiated, formalized document through signature by National Representatives. The decision should taken by consensus per the status quo. The entry of new members with substantive capacities to contribute, i.e., Finland and Sweden, presents the opportunity to take on this task systematically and transparently. Partners must understand participation is key to a process that is flexible, fair, and forward-looking the club given expected risks and threats. The largest disadvantage of this change will be reshaping culture and norms about transparency so that information is made public for study. As always, the secrecy of def/sec politics may be invoked as one of several countervailing pressures.

(continued)

(continued)

For the policymaker	*Measuring NATO partner burdens: beyond 2%*
What other evaluation criteria must the recipient use?	The criteria should include aspects of contributions offered across various categories accounting for the cost/risk exposure for each partner. Burdens in missions compared to the running of the institution require inclusion in research. The role of partners in information accumulation and transmission across the alliance through PFP and COE represent club burdens undertaken bilaterally excluded from studies as well. For example, Poland's important participation role in COE's along with being the strongest of the trio entering in 1999 permitted it to serve as a transfer point of knowledge—its role and leadership is worthy of recognition along with its position as a top-tier contributor. The research program outlined in the book offers a starting point for mobilizing efforts to adapt and advance this agenda in the short to medium term with the appropriate alignment of stakeholders, political will, norms/behavior change, and openness to systematically examine and adopt a more rigorous burden contribution evaluation and analysis structure for the institution and its partners.

Notes

1. See https://www.nato.int/cps/en/natohq/news_180185.htm, last access 13 July 2022.
2. https://c2coe.org/about-coes/, last access 28 June 2022.
3. https://c2coe.org/about-coes/, last access 28 June 2022.
4. On NATO and MOU, NATO Legal Gazette, issues 34, 37 (Munoz Mosquera, 2014, 2016). http://www.act.nato.int/publications, last access 25 May 2022.
5. NATO Legal Deskbook (2010, p. 127). http://publicintelligence.net/nato-legal-deskbook/, last access 10 May 2022.
6. See Table 4.2.
7. Sources in Appendix A.3.1 (Béraud-Sudreau & Giegerich, 2018; Oma, 2012; Richter, 2021).
8. https://www.youtube.com/watch?v=MDQYSbl0g4Q for Canada; https://www.youtube.com/watch?v=Wwz7hr8gOMQ for Slovakia, last access 25 May 2022.
9. Refer to Figs. 3.1–3.4.

References

Becker, J., & Malesky, E. (2017). The continent or the "Grand large"? Strategic culture and operational burden-sharing in NATO. *International Studies Quarterly, 61*(1), 163–180. https://doi.org/10.1093/isq/sqw039

Béraud-Sudreau, L., & Giegerich, B. (2018). NATO defence spending and European threat perceptions. *Survival, 60*(4), 53–74. https://doi.org/10.1080/00396338.2018.1495429

Dahl Thruelsen, P. (2009). *International organisations: Their role in conflict management*. Royal Danish Defence College.

Graham, E. (2014). International organizations as collective agents: Fragmentation and the limits of principal control at the World Health Organization. *European Journal of International Relations, 20*(2), 366–390. https://doi.org/10.1177/1354066113476116

Hawkins, D. (2006). *Delegation and agency in international organizations*. Cambridge University Press. http://site.ebrary.com/id/10150378

Johnston, A. I. (2001). Treating international institutions as social environments. *International Studies Quarterly, 45*(4), 487–515. https://doi.org/10.1111/0020-8833.00212

Kavanagh, J. (2014). *U.S. security-related agreements in force since 1955: Introducing a new database*. RAND Corporation.

Kimball, A. (2015). What Canada could learn from U.S. defence procurement: Issues, best practices and recommendations. *The School of Public Policy Publications, 8*. https://doi.org/10.11575/SPPP.V8I0.42517

Kimball, A. (2019). Knocking on NATO: Strategic and institutional challenges risk the future of Europe's seven-decade long cold peace. *The School of Public Policy Publications, 12*. https://doi.org/10.11575/SPPP.V12I0.68129

Kimball, A. (2021). Managing risks, side payments, and multi-institutional enlargement: The role of US defence, big four investment agreements and candidate risks on NATO and EU enlargement. *European Politics and Society, 22*(5), 696–715. https://doi.org/10.1080/23745118.2020.1820152

Kimball, A., & Lewis. (2010). Le rôle accru des organisations internationales dans les conflits contemporains. In *Conflits dans le monde 2010*. Presses Université Laval.

Kimball, A., & Lewis. (2011). La délégation à l'épreuve du terrain: Les difficiles interventions militaires et civiles des organisations internationales dans les conflits et les crises. In *Conflits dans le monde, 2011*. Presses Université Laval.

Liu, T.-Y., Su, C.-W., Tao, R., & Cong, H. (2019). Better is the neighbor? *Defence and Peace Economics, 30*(6), 706–718. https://doi.org/10.1080/10242694.2017.1422321

Munoz Mosquera, A. (2014). NATO legal cornerstones: "Memorandum of understanding (MOU)": A philosophical and empirical approach (Part I).

NATO Legal Gazette, 34, 55–69. http://www.act.nato.int/images/stories/media/doclibrary/legal_gazette_34a.pdf
Munoz Mosquera, A. (2016). MOU: A philosophical and empirical approach (Part II), *NATO Legal Gazette, 37,* 48–61.
Oma, I. M. (2012). Explaining states' burden-sharing behaviour within NATO. *Cooperation and Conflict, 47*(4), 562–573.
Putnam, R. (1988). Diplomacy and domestic politics: The logic of two-level games. *International Organization, 42*(3), 427–460.
Richter, A. (2021). NATO in the age of Trump: Alliance defense spending during the Trump presidency. *Comparative Strategy, 40*(3), 285–304. https://doi.org/10.1080/01495933.2021.1912511
Saideman, S., & Auerswald, D. (2012). Comparing caveats: Understanding the sources of national restrictions upon NATO's mission in Afghanistan: Comparing caveats. *International Studies Quarterly, 56*(1), 67–84. https://doi.org/10.1111/j.1468-2478.2011.00700.x
Sandler, T. (2004). *Global collective action* (1st edition). Cambridge University Press. https://doi.org/10.1017/CBO9780511617119
Wiarda, H. (2001). Where does Europe end? The politics of NATO and EU enlargement. *World Affairs, 164*(4), 178–197.

CHAPTER 5

Theoretical Perspectives on Collective (Defense and Security) Burden Sharing

Introduction

Scholars employ theories to simplify and examine actor behavior. Those frameworks offer sets of assumptions about the state of the world, actor motivations, and the types of behavior one might expect under certain conditions. Theories are ideas about how the world functions. They serve the purposes of those employing them and are not apolitical (Cox, 1981).

Theories are sets of statements proposing causal explanations about social behavior for those seeking explanatory definitions. They are internally consistent, logically complete, i.e., the arguments flow from the assumptions. They offer falsifiable implications to be examined using different types of empirical evidence. Constitutive theories offer a different approach to international interactions seeking to understand the underlying discursive and practice-related processes contributing to outcomes through socialization and interactions. The process is as important as the outcome. Predictive theories are evaluated upon the basis of post-diction, generality, simplicity and the number and types of arguments. In comparison, constitutive theories focus on action interpretation by understanding language. Such theories focus on the language internal to the practices of actors-structures, understanding the rule-boundness and meaning of the terms of that language and the ethics embedded in the practice-structure-actor co-creation. Constitutive theories are not

A. L. Kimball, *Beyond 2%—NATO Partners, Institutions & Burden Management*, Canada and International Affairs,
https://doi.org/10.1007/978-3-031-22158-3_5

seeking to offer causal explanations as their focus is on an understanding ideational/representational intersection of actor behavior at a particular moment. Theories inform scholars about fundamental concepts (e.g., power, safety, well-being) and identify causal relationships between the concepts and the theoretical assumptions. A scholar identifies measures of the concepts in order to translate theoretical factors into operationalizable and falsifiable information to 'test'. Theories differ in terms of epistemological[1] foundations but contribute toward a common goal of seeking to advance knowledge and understanding from how scholars examine, perceive and study research objects. An empiricist epistemology claims knowledge is based on experience and observation as the source, and this is countered by critical approaches focusing on the production of knowledge as influenced and co-constructed power relations across social groups and within a social environment. There is no single theory claiming to explain all international interactions; therefore, researchers use theories as a discursive backdrop to advance arguments. This research explores military spending, troop contributions, and the development of alliance transformation institutions while mobilizing several theoretical approaches. This book is intended for the student, the informed reader as well as the scholar seeking to advance knowledge. For students, this chapter situating the major IR theories relative to the research objects brings basic elements of IR to the study of burden sharing. Classic theories are treated to prepare the reader for the discussion of rational institutionalist theory which serves as the base for the risk management model used in this research project.

Threat-Based Theories

Theories explain complex interactions between independent actors based on sets of simplifying assumptions shared about the state of the world. For example, the absence of a central authority in the international system for realists is a permissive force for states to proactively manage power relations with others. Realism is a theory where states react to external threats by seeking to increase power. The absence of an external regulatory force encourages power maximization through conflict, conquest or internal investments in arms (Walt, 1987). "The literature treats alliances as a potential cause of conflict as if alliances arise from a process largely divorced from the process that leads to conflict. In fact, it is almost certainly the case that the decision to ally and the decision to fight arise from many of the same causal factors" (Kimball, 2006, p. 372). The problem is the incentive structure for states derived from realism creates crosscutting incentives. This is because many early formal and economic studies of defense alliances assume increasing capabilities are the tacit raison d'être, i.e., the capability aggregation model of alliances (Morrow, 1991). As a result, states cannot trust each other in the joint pursuit of ensuring stability in the distribution of power in the system because each state has incentives to individually defect by working to increase individual power. Thus, interstate cooperation rests fragile for realists.

The emergence of collective security in a realist system is possible, as states seek to balance power globally. Those clubs are fragile and managed, possibly dominated, by the strongest partners. Asymmetric partnerships are cast as contracts trading security gains for policy autonomy losses (Altfeld, 1984) confirming the internal trade-offs between security, autonomy and wealth when allying. Alliances impose opportunity costs as actors balance across competing demands (Kimball, 2010, p. 408). Some argued capacity aggregation models (and pure public goods models) are inappropriate to study products resembling semi-private goods, i.e., NATO is better conceptualized as a club (Kimball, 2019; Sandler, 2004). Realist theory fails to explore NATO design and the delegation of powers because its endurance and increasing partner collaboration remain at odds with the theory due to pessimist views on the chances egoist actors credibly commit to defend each other under the duress of conflict or crisis.

Realism explains why states, defending from common threats, contract among themselves to defend, but cannot explain aspects of collaboration around burden sharing leaving a gap. The US has not hesitated to invoke the argument NATO partners contribute more to the alliance in the past. Trump's transactional approach (Wolf, 2017) placed the credibility of the Article V collective defense commitment to newer partners as conditional upon their defense spending meeting the political target of 2% (Kimball, 2019, p. 12; Sperling & Webber, 2019; Ubriaco, 2017). However, his discourse with cold war NATO partners was less strong.

Realists focus on dominant powers under-contributing relative to the remainder of the club due to concerns about relative gains and short-term exploitation. Alliances designed consistent with realist considerations should demand high entry costs, as strong partners offer security in exchange for policy influence in weaker partners (Altfeld, 1984: Morrow, 1991). Small partners understand the trade is conceding policy autonomy to acquire security those states cannot acquire otherwise (i.e., though internal arming, war and/or conquest). **Membership costs** are high under such conditions to induce commitment credibility (i.e., enforcement). And within the club should the allocation and distribution of goods become asymmetric, then intra-club bargaining reshapes burdens rather than forcing exit by those not contributing fairly. Aspects of treaty design implicitly increase **costs of exiting**; for example, to renounce the treaty is to renounce the fundamental concepts of the alliance, i.e., democracy, liberty and economic freedom. This approach favors a **centralization of powers** into an individual, a delegation of special powers to smaller group of individuals (e.g., UN Security Council) or based on financing the institution, for example, the allocation of voting power relative to funding as in the World Health Organisation. *Consensus decision procedures rank as least favorable by realists*. As club size increases so do bargaining costs and complexity, encouraging the use of other tactics, such as logrolling,[2] to advance negotiations. Club decisional outcomes should fall as close as possible to the position supported by the strongest.

If the entire club cannot agree on a position—a motivated subgroup may act. The 2003 mission in Iraq was carried out by a coalition of NATO partners including the UK and the Netherlands with global NATO partner, Australia, but without the explicit support of the alliance. The US provided 3 in 4 troops for the force. Denmark, Italy, the Netherlands, Spain and the UK were partners joining the coalition with notable contributions along with a Turkish contingent, while minimal contributions came from Czechia, Hungary, Iceland and Portugal (11 of 19 partners or 58%). Future NATO partners made small contributions in 2003 including Albania, Bulgaria, Estonia, Latvia, Lithuania, (North) Macedonia, Romania and Slovakia for a total of 19 current partners. The withdrawal of US combat forces was necessary for NATO's Training Mission in Iraq (NTM-I) in 2011. There were 23 partners participating including Germany and Canada offering financial support as well as hosting trainings outside of Iraq along with combinations of the French, Poles, Bulgarians, Spaniards and Norwegians. When it became NATO's Mission in Iraq, a non-combat mission, in 2018 Canada accepted command of the mission despite its 2003 public refusal to join the coalition because of the lack of alliance consensus. The evolution of missions in Iraq points to the flexibility of activities IO undertake (Abbott & Snidal, 1998; Kimball & Lewis, 2010, 2011) and the existence of trade-offs for state members facing demands to contribute to multiple IO activities. Those activities are identified along with a presentation of which II intervened in crises and/or conflicts from 1990–2020 in next chapters.

Realists would limit the **scope of issues** to facilitate enforcement and reduce distribution issues. However, as the sources of threat and security expanded since the 1990s, the club faced challenges responding to new threats due to the state-centric nature of threats for realists influencing allocation choices. This uncertainty about the future state of the world points to **asymmetry in internal control of an institution** increasing with differences in contributions and partners. NATO enlargement created countervailing pressures for realist predictions. For example, increasing membership and member differences should lead to an external delegation of dispute resolution mandates, a behavior common in economic than security agreements (Koremenos, 2013) and the systematic study of economic agreements is comparatively more advanced than DSA.[3] **Research employing realist approaches omits how contributions shifted with the nature of threats and how perceptions of club partners changed across time. Much is limited to an object (a mission), time period and/or set of countries.**

Concerning NATO's specific mandates, realists consider collective defense and cooperative security aspects essential tasks over crisis management (Kaplan, 2004; Sirici & Coletta, 2009). Data collected on NATO involvement in crises and conflicts show both the UN and OSCE were hosted and undertook mandates ranging from peace-making/building/keeping along with rule of law and DDR missions more frequently. Given NATO's crisis management mandate, another way of measuring contribution is participation in a new club operation by partners. Regarding crisis management, NATO, as a club, remains reticent to act until called upon by the international community. When the club failed to locate a common position concerning an intervention, then smaller subgroups of partners led missions after which NATO and others followed. Post-cold war states shifted allocations within the club to goods offering the best individual threat protection as illustrated by examining troops across the defensive flanks. This is possible because punctual operation decisions take place within national constraints. If the club was controlled by top contributors then, those outside 'the top' would carry burden from the strongest partners when forces are retained over a number of years. NATO Air Policing operation burdens shifted across partners but retained of effectiveness because of a consistent efforts to renegotiate the pre-determined collective level of capacity as the contributions annually shifted. The focus of realism on great powers constrains its capacity to explain NATO enlargement and the behavior of non-major contributors.

The US is not a sizable troop contributor to UN missions. Italy is the NATO partner contributing most troops to UN missions and it ranks 18th with 1,025 troops across multiple operations.[4] The UN has missions in 28 conflict regions and crises with troops contributed to 11 missions though only nine states host over 500 troops; they include the Central African Republic, Mali, Somalia and Sudan/S. Sudan, as well as Israel/Lebanon, Cyprus and Iraq. Four UN missions with trained police units are in Africa and the percentage of trained units relative to troops varies from 6% (South Sudan) to 14% (Central African Republic). Untrained police individuals are attracted to those missions ranging from 290 individuals in Mali to over 550 participating in South Sudan, a rate lower than trained police units. Crisis management is undertaken by IO other than NATO, but if NATO is called upon then, its force is sizable, ex. KFOR, Libya. Again, NATO attracted attention due to the troop numbers and the efforts it deployed in Kosovo at under 4,000 troops in 1999 (KFOR). NATO's KFOR peacekeeping presence launched days after UNMIK and included support by most post-cold war partners (similar to ISAF/RESOLUTE SUPPORT).

The US-led coalition in Afghanistan began at less than 5,000 troops in 2003, ballooning to above 132,000 in 2011 after the Obama surge with 90,000 US troops providing 68% of the force.[5] The US reduced troops to under 29,000 by 2014—a two-thirds reduction shifting to RESOLUTE SUPPORT. NATO cold war partners benefited from a 75% reduction from 2013 to 2014 (19,319 to 4,520 troops) though post-cold war partners reduced troops at a smaller rate (43%).

In 2015, Hungary was the only post-cold war NATO partner participating in INHERENT RESOLVE (against ISIL, an Islamic state in Iraq, Syria after Libya). Five years later six post-cold war partners were contributing including a sizable Polish contingent (>100 troops). Nine cold war NATO partners contributed to that mission with six offering over 100 troops, and this is despite a 53% troop reduction from 2017 to 2020 (18,711 to 9,939).

NATO's ACTIVE FENCE offers border stability to Turkey in the ongoing Syrian civil conflict since 2012 with contributions by Turkey, US, Germany and the Netherlands until replaced by Italy and Spain, respectively, in 2015. Germany participated in 2016 in INHERENT RESOLVE and joined Air policing in 2017. SEA GUARDIAN is a flexible maritime security operation in the Mediterranean Sea, and OCEAN SHIELD is a maritime security operation engaging in anti-piracy around Somalian coastal areas. No post-cold war partners contribute to ACTIVE FENCE, SEA GUARDIAN or OCEAN SHIELD; again their contributions to collective efforts are focused on those offering the most individual protection relative to total club protection consistent with the arguments presented in this book. NATO's force capacity attracts attention but operational burdens shift regularly within the club because of the shifting locality of threats to partners.

Realism would not favor the addition and complexification of institutions to manage club burdens. This decentralized approach reduces the capacity of the powerful state(s) to access influence. Five NATO partners participate in more COE than the US. With one exception (Germany), partners outside the top contributors sponsored and participated in the most COE. While the COE institutional structure indicates a diffusion of activities, COE report to Allied Command Transformation (ACT) in Norfolk, US—resulting in a centralization of COE information. A pooling of information reduces the effects of the strategic problem of uncertainty about the future state of the world (Koremenos, 2008; Koremenos & Nau, 2010). The MC endorses COE and ACT accredits them. ACT is led by an American commander giving the US de facto influence on collaborating in the programming, agenda, development, and survival of COE. The US is "a global leader in establishing/ influencing directions in global security and NATO politics. ... (It has) a central role in NATO, with a major contribution in concepts and doctrine development, operational procedures, capability development, technology advancement, and institutional resilience" (Simion, 2016, p. 92).

A plurality of burden sharing research focused on military spending so a set of realist propositions regarding military spending are presented. A second dependent variable captures participation in a new crisis and conflict operation NATO has undertaken. *Threats* represent a source of insecurity for realists inciting clubs/subgroups to react. They increase military spending and the chances of a partner participates in an operation. One threat measure offers geographic distance from Russia and the other, distance from the crisis/conflict region when considering operation participation.

At least one study suggested partner military spending tracks with the UK (Liu et al., 2019). To examine that claim a variable identifies *the top four club contributors*. And top contributors are likely to participate in a new operation and are positively associated with military spending. *Non-US cold war partners* have smaller increases, if not decreases, in spending relative to top contributors and post-cold war NATO partners. Finally, post-cold war partners are more likely to participate in a new operation relative to cold war partners after accounting for top contributors due to pressures to socialize with the club and contribute to collective efforts.

Group Preferences

Liberal theory offers normative and structural explanations for a convergence of group preferences on cooperation for collective defense. Arguments, from Kant to the democratic peace, explain liberal 'like-minded' states prefer aligning over fighting. The lack of central governance for liberals allows actors to collaborate and prevent violence among themselves through diplomacy. States should protect the gains of liberalism (economic, social and political) by creating institutions to stabilize relations and reduce uncertainties. In Europe, multiple overlapping institutional frameworks (i.e., EU, OSCE, NATO, UN, etc.) imply resource competition for punctual missions and regular demands from II commitments. That notwithstanding, NATO and the EU subscribe liberal behavior in their respective founding documents. Both reference UN principles (i.e., peaceful resolution of conflicts, refraining from threats of force) and within the North Atlantic Treaty Article II, as well as parts of Article I, identify partners shall strengthen free institutions, eliminate economic conflict and encourage economic collaboration.

Liberalism offers few predictions on cooperative agreement design but anticipates cooperation frequently due to welfare maximization. The welfare of states incorporates economic well-being, internal and external security. Cooperation is probable since states recognize gains from coordination and forsake competitive behavior (as uncertainty is inefficient). Coordination gains include reducing foreign policy risks, economic gains from coordinating in costly endeavors (e.g., collective goods, trade rules) and the possibility to produce security efficiently relative to the unilateral provision of security. Cooperation arises from convergent individual preferences on welfare efficiency to advance joint gains. Preferences are informed by internal factors (i.e., re-election concerns) but liberalism cannot predict what triggers convergence on cooperation differently across domains. The convergence of preference-driven behavior offers no explanation about which security policies to pursue given partner and alliance level calculations of costs and benefits across alternatives. Current institutional activities reducing defense collaboration costs through mechanisms, such NATO's PFP and COE contributing to the regularization of training, exercises, education, etc., require study.

For liberals, the strategic decisions of states derive from internal structures and processes. The state is no longer an autonomous actor but "a representative institution constantly subject to capture and recapture, construction and reconstruction by coalitions of social actors" (Moravcsik, 1997, p. 518). The "ideas, interests and institutions of society [that] influence the behavior of states by shaping their preferences, i.e., the fundamental social objectives that underlie the strategic calculations of governments" (Moravcsik, 1997, p. 518). For liberals, preferences remain essential to explain behavior; yet the variation in behavior, that is decisions to go to war or cooperate, is explained by the diversity of preferences and interests of national actors (Moravcsik, 1997). States represent a dominant subset of society whose preferences and interests they serve, and the configuration of preferences across the system determines behavior on the international stage. From a realist perspective national interests are fixed, idealized and determined by the international system's external constraints as shaped by the distribution of power and beliefs about rival behavior (state capabilities, threat perceptions). In comparison, liberals recognize the interaction between social groups seeking to maximize welfare within national political institutions acting on their behalf determine interest aggregation and coalition formation (Moravcsik, 1997, pp. 516–521). The nature of a political regime influences defense strategies by determining competition between the interests of social groups that are rational but divergent and repercussions on the strategic choices available. According to Moravscik, "[b]etween theoretical extremes of tyranny and democracy, many representative institutions and practices exist, each of which privileges particular demands; hence the nature of state institutions, alongside societal interests themselves, is a key determinant of what states do internationally," (1997, 518). This trend partly explains the 'democratic peace,' the absence of war between democracies (Moravcsik, 1997). Finally, Moravscik converges with Wendt asserting the ability of states to acquire preferences in the international arena is influenced by the preferences of others (Moravcsik, 1997, pp. 520–521; Wendt, 1992, p. 395).

Liberals identify collective institutional emergence but do not consider how actor difference over threat perceptions, capabilities and internal constraints affects burden bargaining to support the institution. Differences in democracies concerning executive powers, military-state links and civilian government combined with external pressures regarding allocations (annual and mission related) are omitted. Social theorists argue the focus on institutions and individual actors, as separate, is artificial, inexistent in practice.

Liberals offer normative and structural explanations for the emergence of cooperative institutions. Normative explanations favor the emergence of cooperation under many conditions and around strategic issues. Liberals view cooperation as an improvement to the status quo of unilateral defense and security policy management. Due to the essentialness of NATO's tasks, not only is partner contribution expected, but essential for continuity. Structural explanations contend leaders, cognizant of the need to provide national security and social goods to retain political power, work to ensure demands are met and security assured through defense pacts (Kimball, 2010). A liberal proposition would be increases in *demand for social goods* reduce military spending and the chances a state contributes to a new Operation.

Strategic Culture and Critical Approaches

Social interactions are constraining as much as constrained by how power, knowledge and legitimate behavior is proscribed and prescribed within a context. Social theories emerged as the cold war ended with reflexive and reflective turn in positivist thinking. Where positivist theories examined evidence (collected facts) and studied patterns (data), critical and reflexive scholars examined *discourses and structures of power, identities and interests*, understanding how relations are socially reproduced and naturalized within different contexts (i.e., strategic cultures, see (Becker & Malesky, 2017)), while drawing attention to the co-constitution of the agent and structure. Intersubjectivity is understood by actors as significations and shared understandings emerging from agent-structure interactions. The facts scholars observe and interpret are the production of relationships with each other, our social groups and the ideational structures in the social world. Facts are culturally and historically bound but also malleable over time and across contexts. Meanings are constructed from a mix of history, norms, ideas and beliefs scholars interpret to explain behavior. Together they create *representational practices* populating the world with subjects (that is agents) and objects, define the relations among and between these subjects, as well as between subjects and objects, and, in doing so, endow subjects with interests. Sovereignty is a construct relying upon a shared structural understanding by internal and external stakeholders ensuring its continuation as well as sets of reinforcing institutions (Johnston, 2001; Zarakol, 2018). The practices of states and stakeholders reinforce, reproduce or counter the shared understanding of a concept witnessed through the support of logics of appropriateness. Ideas, norms and rules influence the formation of the identities, interests and actions of agents (Wendt, 2006). There are no standard reactions to anarchy or the distribution of power as realists contend (e.g., self-interest is a product of egoism and anarchy). Perceptions of social place, fairness, justice and power relations become essential to examining actors enmeshed within a social structure seeking to understand the origin and meaning of IR studying social relations and power in communities (Barnett & Duvall, 2005; Barnett & Finnemore, 1999; Mattern & Zarakol, 2016).

Constructivists focus on three aspects of IR: first, the role of rules, norms, cultural values, ideologies and representational practices in shaping the form and substance of IR (i.e., *ideational structures*). Those structures are understood as intersubjective sets of meanings, dispositions, and perceptions shared by actors. Second, they focus on the analysis of the process of constructing the social identities of actors (agents) in IR for understanding interests and actions. Finally, they consider how ideational structures and social agents interact, form and influence each other; this is referred to as the co-constitution of agency and structure.

Conceptions of self and other, and consequently security interests, develop only in interaction within communities (Wendt, 1992, p. 401; Zehfuss, 2001). NATO's identity is as much a social construction it projects and sustains through repeated interactions, as well as a set of iterative processes (i.e., institutions) creating interactions and shared understandings. State actions in international politics are understood in terms of identity. Constructivist analyses of identity formation offer three perspectives: seen from the system, seen from the state (or unit) and seen from both simultaneously. Seen from the systemic point of view, state identity is formed by the normative structure of society and the practices dominating it, leaving aside internal factors (ideology, etc.) giving a state its identity. Individualist constructivists, on the other hand, are interested in how internal, social and legal norms influence identities and interests. The agent and structure are co-constituted and cannot be distinguished-delineated as realists posit. The agency of institution arises from the shared and reproduced powers conferred by partners, as well as by the rest of the system. NATO variously sought mandates from the UN (Balkans, Libya, the Iraq Training Mission) and called to act when others proved ineffective (e.g., EU in Kosovo). NATO fulfilled requests for logistical support for UN peacekeeping in Africa (Sudan & Somalia) and supported UN disaster relief in Pakistan. It secured the delivery of World Food Programme humanitarian aid to Somalia and a field hospital to Ghana in the C-19 pandemic; crisis management activities accepted due the absence of alternatives.

Ideas become a part of the structure when they have reached a level of a collectively held knowledge, rules, beliefs and norms such that they constrain actors. Ideational structures include the rules, norms, cultural values, ideologies and representational practices shaping the form and content of IR. The resulting structures include material capabilities and the values of actors. Focusing on the development of shared identity to create communities and adopt appropriate behaviors while identifying problematic challenges to expected behaviors is an aspect of interactions the theory seeks to understand using different logics of behavior. The 'logic of appropriateness' sees human action as driven by rules of appropriate or exemplary behavior, determined by institutions, practices, norms, etc. Rules are followed because they are seen/internalized as natural, rightful, expected and legitimate. Whereas a 'logic of consequences' contends states respect the rule of institutions because of the anticipated consequences of non-respect from the community. Both logics rely upon shared understandings of power relations by stakeholders, vertically and horizontally. Scholars emphasize the importance of discursive and identity construction around shared conceptual understandings, e.g., 'like-minded,' 'free institutions,' 'liberal,' 'democracy,' 'second-tier (middle) power,' 'credible,' etc.

The #WeAreNATO publicity campaign serves as a rallying concept for the identity of NATO as constructed in a shared (operational) context but using the language and images of personnel from partners narrating video segments. The socialization aspects of NATO include the importance of its power to teach liberal democratic norms to states entering post-cold war (Gheciu, 2005). NATO created a shared ideational framework through which it influenced definitions of national interests and club identity in central and eastern European states (Becker & Malesky, 2017; Gheciu, 2005). When the processes of socialization occurred is less clear for others (Zyla, 2015, p. 54) as is what triggers participation in individual operations for individual members.

Constructivists contend conflict is possible from differences over how anarchy structures interactions (i.e., Hobbesian-conflictual, Lockean-competitive, Kantian-amical) (Wendt, 1992). If states perceive a situation as conflictual, relations reflect said perception. This is why how NATO casts adversaries is important, i.e., strategic partner, competitor, threat and opportunity. Discourses produced and reproduced are 'othering,' identifying an in-group and out-group. Messages transmitted to sanction 'others' for behavior inconsistent with the group invokes a 'logic-of-appropriateness', as in what states should do to comply with the norm and refrain from provoking a 'logic of consequences' incurring actions from the sender(s).

The discourses states invoke communicating to each other, the IO and within an IO, are the evidence constructivists examine. Discourses reflect the practices of partners. The discourse tone (positive, negative, neutral) and language activeness are important. Language-proscribing behavior is important as is that invoking-group behavior. The study of language acts explores the use of declaratory, directive and engaging language. Declarative statements are about the nature of an aspect of social life, situation or condition. They become declarative rules informing about a state of affairs in the social world and consequences of ignoring said information. Directive statements are imperatives. Directive rules suggest ideal behavior agents could ignore knowing consequences. Finally, engaging statements are promises. Committing multiple speech acts can become a rule/norm when a number of speakers hold them valid and commit to consequence action for non-respect. The repetition of similar speech acts by particular agents changes the perception of others. And from this point on, speech acts become rules of expected behavior or conduct in a community.

Conflict arises because of differences in identity. NATO builds its identity; its positionality is a product of co-constructed perspectives' shared states, the system and other actors. Simpson questions NATO's actions in "Northern, Rich, and White Nations defending NATO," (Badcock & Marks, 2010, Chapter 2). Post-colonial scholars ask if socialization or stigmatization are the forces shaping identity (Zarakol, 2014) due to a Western-centric focus on norm creation and reproduction. This structuration implicitly limits non-Western states to agency in non-compliance by committing 'bad' deeds (Zarakol, 2014). There is an amount of stigmatization of partners not meeting the 2% political target discursively and politically. States are sensitive to remaining 'credible' partners and contributors to the alliance. They want to comply with the 2% collective target—the gap between a state's spending and the target is also known as a 'compliance gap' in the literature (Heinen-Bogers, 2022). The name, itself, invokes a perspective of shame/failure causing friction for those in the subgroup.

Constructivist theory offers insights about relations within a group/community through the analysis of text, discourse and social interactions. It does not seek to be causal, explanatory, or predictive as do realism, liberalism and rational approaches. As a critical theory, its focus is on understanding the environment where choices are made and tracing the process creating a narrative/discourse that agents share. Focusing on the production (and reproduction) of social knowledge from institutions though developing shared tasks, new interests and new forms of organization (Barnett & Finnemore, 1999), the theory eschews realist and liberal explanatory, predictive approaches. Critical studies of burden sharing share skepticism of empirical and quantitative analytical studies. Reflexive scholars criticize the 2% criteria (Zyla, 2009, 2015), as a metric for identifying the operational, structura, and punctual burdens by partners to support the institution. The political target is unrelated to how partners understand burden sharing, how states bargain over individual, shared, and club roles to produce common goods. The resurgence of states committing to the 2% spending target following the Russian invasion of Ukraine in spring 2022 returned the criteria to the political and public discourse. The German public commitment to the club target evidenced[6] a substantial shift from a partner historically bound to limited military commitments. Spending 2% of partner state's annual GDP may become the norm if most states, or a tipping point of key partners, converge upon the target in the next few years including norm entrepreneurs (Cortell & Davis, 1996; Finnemore & Sikkink, 1998). The norm could be effectively shifted by making the 2% political target the minimal threshold, i.e. floor, for partner defense spending.

The interests of states are malleable through a process of deep politics via norm diffusion. The emergence of COE, as shared learning, information transmission, and collaborative environments offers a novel structure to reshape state interests and capacities around 30 different issues engaging in alliance transformation. Original research on NATO Centres of Excellence offers insight on how subgroups of partners collaborate to develop supporting institutions serving as loci of socialization, learning and knowledge creation. Finally, individual-leader sociological arguments on the role of the Secretary General (Schuette, 2021) offer interlocutors a voice shaping military spending and partner participation in NATO operations.

As a critical theory, constructivism focuses on the shared symbolism of understanding if a 2% threshold is socially just, feasible and reliable to ensure a national contribution to collective defense and why NATO partners, as a divided group, consented to said target over 15 years ago. This puzzle was examined by others (Becker, 2017; Zyla, 2015, 2018). The observation, in 2019, that less than one-third of NATO partners attained said threshold offers supports to the claim not all are convinced of the target's validity; yet, after the Russian invasion of Ukraine in February 2022, multiple partners stepped up with public announcements, including a reticent Germany.

Securitization theory is a critical approach to examining the process through which one identifies and interprets security issues/threats. It can explain why members identify diverging and/or converging threats. Insofar as risks made it possible to identify future threats, the problem arises in the definition a risk in an 'objective' way. Actors react differently, depending on their level of risk aversion (O'Neill, 2001, p. 618) and their perception of the salience of the identified risk. From then, it is not only a question of naming a risk to identify it, but also determining what led concerned actors to see said issue as a risk. Securitization explores that process, when an issue becomes a security issue (and therefore a risk or a threat) and when actors consider it is, or may be, a threat (Balzacq, 2005, p. 172; Buzan et al., 1998, pp. 21–24). Club cohesion and the credibility of its commitment is built on the socialized practices and shared intersubjective understandings. Rational institutionalist theory presents an approach also based on studying founding written documents and jointly approved agreements, etc. but with a focus on how they resolve or reduce strategic problems partner face which challenge cooperative behavior.

Rational Institutionalist Theory

Rational institutionalists focus on the structural aspects of the agreement text and the strategic problems states seek to resolve through collaboration. Rational institutionalist theory (RIT) identifies the importance of agreement design characteristics such as flexibility, the obligations and level of discretion as important to the durability and effectiveness of international agreements (Koremenos et al., 2001). An analysis of the NATO treaty's features including obligations, precision, and delegation revealed,

> … it retains flexibility with provisions, such as Article IV (consultations in case of threat to territorial integrity, political independence or security), Article X (new members), Article XII regarding review, and Article XIII on duration and withdrawal. It offers opportunities for discretion in the interpretation of Article III (national and collective military capabilities) and Article V (collective defence). (Kimball, 2019, p. 4)

The resilience of NATO is evidenced through adapting to extra-regional operations and non-conventional missions, while providing credible defense for newer partners on the edges of threat tripwires. Kimball noted NATO and EU expansion after the cold war was simultaneous but unlinked structurally; however, the unmeasured factors related to NATO membership are positively correlated with EU membership (2021b).

According to RIT, states design contracts representing how the institution and partners view the essential strategic problems they must resolve to collaborate, which include:

1. enforcement—incentives to cheat; agreements aimed at solving these problems offer rewards-punishments, dispute resolution provisions, and notice periods to reshape short-term incentives to defect;
2. commitment—domestic commitment problems due to electoral constraints, time inconsistency (i.e., the need to tie one's hands in the long run due to an inability to medium-term commitment), and intergenerational time inconsistency;
3. allocation/distribution (concerning club resources, 'defending' territory, burdens, political power)—different preferences actors have over alternative possible agreements, when a series of possible arrangements producing possible bargains exist;
4. uncertainty about future actor behavior (measures/actions taken by others, detecting defection);

5. uncertainty concerning a partner's preferences (e.g., states are prone to misrepresent preferences, verbally, or through actions); and uncertainty about the future state of the world (knowledge about the consequences of actions, the actions of others AND/OR the actions of institutions, that is the consequences of cooperation—the security, and economic and political consequences of previous agreements concerning scientific and technical knowledge, and political and economic knowledge).

Other structures include export/codification of norms (e.g., human rights & environment); encouraging positive externalities; discouraging negative externalities; gridlock; and pure coordination games without uncertainty.

As per essential intervening factors—the number of partners and the heterogeneities across them (e.g., geographies, political risks, defense capacities, previous agreements) remain important and, "Institutional arrangements (including agreements) can magnify or diminish the distributional impact of exogenous shocks or unexpected changes" (Lipson, 1991).

Several aspects of institutional design include: membership rules (restrictive to inclusive); scope of issues included in mandate; and centralization of tasks required for collaboration and how they are delegated. Tasks include information collection, rulemaking, monitoring and surveillance, dispute settlement, etc. (see appendix A offering 20 tasks);

Centralization increases with uncertainty about behavior, the state of the world, the number of actors and/or their heterogeneity, and the severity of the enforcement problem. The club's autonomy using the term 'body' invoked by Bradley and Kelly argued the "autonomy of a body is determined by the level of state oversight, including the reporting requirements, the precision of the body's mandate, the decision-making procedures for the body (unanimity reduces the body's independence/autonomy), the permanence of the body, and the mechanism through which it gets funding" (Koremenos, 2008, p. 169).

Koremenos (2008 & Nau, 2010) argued: centralized monitoring reduces *uncertainty about behavior*, whereas *uncertainty about the state of the world* can be offset by pooling information, which is efficiently done through delegation. When there exists *enforcement problems* then delegating punishment helps. In the face of *internal commitment problems*, states may delegate authority. Thus, when problems are complex (italicized above) states are likely to delegate. When heterogeneity is high then, administration and decision-making are difficult and delegation facilitates policy collaboration.

Moreover, the rules controlling the institution (unanimity, simple majority, super majority, special majority, varies depending on issue, other/unspecified) are to be examined. As are the rules determining representation for internal delegation (fixed number of representatives per partner, number representatives proportional to population size or financial contribution, number of representatives determined by another characteristic (geography, dispersion, nuke status), other/unspecified). A final consideration is the allocation of votes for internal delegation (one per partner, number of votes proportional to partner's population, number of votes proportional to partner's financial contribution, number of votes determined by something else, other/unspecified).

Provisions Associated with Flexibility (I.E., Review, Amendment, Renegotiation and Renewal).

Lipson argues "the idea is to forge agreements that provide sufficient benefits to each side, when evaluated at each point during the life of the agreement, so that each will choose to comply out of self-interest in order to perpetuate the treaty" (Lipson, 1991, p. 522).

Withdrawal versus escape clauses: "Withdrawal clauses are responses to shocks that alter a state's basic interest in cooperation" (Helfer, Exiting treaties, 2005, cited in (Koremenos & Nau, 2010, p. 93)), that is "bedrock" preferences are fundamentally stable. "Withdrawal clauses are used in the event of "bedrock" changes, while escape clauses are used in the event of unchanged bedrock preferences but different domestic constraints" (Koremenos & Nau, 2010, p. 93). The same observation can be made of exit and re-entry of partners from COE or NATO mission rotations in order to alleviate domestic pressures and/budgeting concerns.

"The high costs of self-enforcement and the dangers of opportunism are important obstacles" to informal agreements (Lipson, 1991, p. 507). Indeed, costs may be so high that it is difficult to resolve basic problems, such as moral hazard and time inconsistency, the author continues, "resolving them depends on the parties' preference orderings, the transparency of their preferences and choices (asymmetrical information) and the private institutional mechanisms set up to secure their bargain" (Lipson, 1991, p. 507). Therefore, informal agreements are designed with endogenous enforcement (i.e., settle their own disputes, enforce commitments, sanction defectors, etc.) and offer room to maneuver through review, burden negotiations and joint collaboration in goods associated with the institutions' core missions (collective defense, cooperative security, crisis management). "Rationalists contend intra-institutional bargaining is facilitated if candidates signal commitment credibly by incurring costs (i.e., tying hands through accepting side-bargains)" (Kimball, 2021b, p. 699). Hand tying and sinking costs are mechanisms through which states increase defensive commitment credibility (Fuhrmann & Sechser, 2014).

Table 5.1 offers a summary of RIT recommendations for institutional and bargaining strategies to resolve six relevant strategic problems from the 11 identified above. These recommendations are examined in the context of NATO's institutional design and burden sharing aspects. NATO COE offer a novel set of comparative cases to study since they operate at no cost to NATO (NATO-Accredited Centres of Excellence, 2021, 2).

> COE totally or partially assume the extension of the work program (given by the MC of NATO) on all these directions supporting the transformation; while some focus almost exclusively on education and training, assuming a status similar to the one of a training Centre, others aim to define a "think-tank" profile or a comprehensive range that reaches all defining dimensions of transformation and development of the force capabilities. (Simion, 2016, p. 72)

A major concern for partners is how to enforce commitments once made; this is done by tying hands through agreements retaining some flexibility and sinking costs in the institution (Fuhrmann & Sechser, 2014). The host/sponsor and framework partner agreement structure of each COE permits the subset of partners to bargain among themselves the mandate, obligations and expected deliverables of the institution. The agreement obligates states to sink costs by identifying what partners must allocate to remain in 'good standing' (Zarakol, 2014) though there is flexibility evident there as well. Agreements centralizing authority and higher levels of restrictions/costs for entry ensures partners credibly commit, yet countervailing forces to manage enforcement by increasing issue scope affects the set of acceptable bargains available. Uncertainty about the future state of the world also encourages flexibility in agreements and centralization

Table 5.1 Strategic problems & rational institutionalist recommendations *Source* author's creation

The STRATEGIC problem.	*increase/decrease*	*then, institutional design recommendation*
severity of the ENFORCEMENT	increases	Membership costs/restrictions & rules
UNCERTAINTY—preferences	increases	Membership costs/restrictions & rules
severity of the DISTRIBUTION/ALLOCATION	decreases	Membership costs/restrictions & rules
ENFORCEMENT	increases	Flexibility provisions
severity of the DISTRIBUTION/ALLOCATION	increases	Flexibility provisions
UNCERTAINTY re: state of the world	increases	Flexibility provisions
severity of the DISTRIBUTION/ALLOCATION	increases	Scope of issues
severity of the ENFORCEMENT	increases	Scope of issues
UNCERTAINTY re: actor behavior	increases	Centralisation
severity of the ENFORCEMENT	increases	Centralisation
UNCERTAINTY re: state of the world	increases	Centralisation
UNCERTAINTY re: state of the world	increases	ASYMMETRY in internal control
If XXX		**intervening factor**
ASYMMETRY in internal control	increases asymmetry in	contributions
ASYMMETRY in internal control	increases asymmetry in	member heterogeneity
ASYMMETRY in internal control	increases	with UNCERTAINTY about the state of the world
INDIVIDUAL control	increases	with UNCERTAINTY about the state of the world
Centralisation	increases	with membership
EXTERNAL delegation of dispute resolution	increases	with membership
EXTERNAL delegation of dispute resolution	increases	with member heterogeneity
Centralisation	increases	with member heterogeneity
Flexibility	decreases	with member heterogeneity

(continued)

Table 5.1 (continued)

The STRATEGIC problem.	*increase/decrease*	*then, institutional design recommendation*
The scope of issues	increases	with membership*heterogeneity

but at the cost of leaning toward an asymmetry in internal control of the institution, running countercurrent to consensus norms within the institution. RIT propositions concerning the design of agreements' flexibility and review are associated with longevity, while focusing on the underlying strategic problems facing actors to collaborate in the provision defense goods with a minimal threshold and increased access for those willing to invest in surplus for individual, and collective, reasons.

Describing the Partner Participation in NATO COE

That being said aggregated data identify the most active COE stakeholders in 2021 as Poland (a member of 18 COE) from Table 4.1 is offered in Table 5.2, Germany, Italy and Romania, Greece followed by the US (in 14), Czechia, the Netherlands, Hungary, and Turkey (11). Germany hosts the most COE (3) followed by Italy and the Netherlands, then Turkey, Slovakia and Poland. Poland, Germany, Italy and the Netherlands form a group key entrepreneurs and investors in COE. All are members of the civil-military-CCOE, Jt. Air power-JAPPC, and STRATCOM; three are in ENSEC and MILMED. COE contribute to socialization, learning and functional collaboration across partners as they relate to NATO's core mandates of collective defense, cooperative security and crisis management. COE offer expertise in three of four pillars: education and training; analysis and lessons learned; concept development and experimentation; and doctrine development and standards (i.e., supply of products and services specific to the standardization process (doctrines, standards, procedures, evaluation instruments, etc.)) supporting the requirements of interoperability (Simeon, 2016, p. 71). COE permit partners to "contribute to NATO whilst at the same benefiting one or more nations" (NATO-Accredited Centres of Excellence, 2021, 2). This converges with collective action arguments analogous to a threshold scheme which transforms the interaction context into an assurance game (Sandler, 2004). In those games, individual actors contribute private benefits that are sufficiently large. "As the share of a good's excludable benefits increases, markets and clubs tend to allocate resources more efficiently to its provision and the appropriate institutional design is increasingly important" (Kimball, 2019, 8–9).

Table 5.3 offers the list of COE with host country and number of participants. COE organizing themes represent challenges facing alliance transformation e.g., air operations, command and control, and joint air power competence; cooperative security concerns requiring more investment, e.g., security force assist, stability policing, and maritime security; and aspects of crisis management the alliance foresees as increasing in importance, e.g., crisis management and disaster response, maritime geospatial, meteorological and oceanographic challenges and strategic communications. Finally, COE touch on traditional defense and security challenges such as JCBRN defense, military engineering and cyber-defense. The variety of COE demonstrates the club's commitment to transformation and the substantial investments some partners allocate to support the future.

Comparative case studies on the institutional design of four NATO COE by the author serve as a foundation for the discussion herein appear in bold. This book includes insights from complementary research on burden sharing and the institutional design of COE JCBRN and

Table 5.2 Top stakeholders in NATO COE by participation, N of COE = 28, *original data*

	Top 10 COE stakeholders	*Hosts*	*Framework partner*
1	Poland	2	18
2	Germany	4	17
3	Italy	3	16
3	Romania	1	16
4	Greece	1	15
	US	1	14
5	Czechia	1	13
5	Netherlands	3	13
6	Hungary	1	12
7	Turkey	2	11
	Canada	0	5

Source author's creation, last update 1 Jan 2022

Table 5.3 NATO COE, alphabetical order, original data *Source* author's creation

	COE name	*yr of estab*	*N of sponsors*	*N of partners (2022)*	*Host*
AO	Air Ops	2008	1	0	France
CIMIC	Civil-Military Cooperation	2007	2	6	The Netherlands
CWO	Cold Weather Ops	2007	1	0	Norway
CJOS	Combined Joint Ops from Sea	2006	1	12	USA
C2	Command & Control	2008	1	7	Germany/The Netherlands
CSW	Command Confined & Shallow Waters	2009	1	8	Germany
CCD	Cooperation Cyber-Defense	2008	1	28	Estonia
C-IED	Command - IED	2010	1	11	Spain
CI	Counter-Intel	2017	2	9	Poland
CMDR	Crisis Management & Disaster Response	2015	2	1	Bulgaria
DAT	Defense Against Terrorism	2006	1	9	Turkey
ENSEC	Energy Security	2012	1	11	Lithuania
EOD	Explosive Ordinance Disposal	2011	1	4	Slovakia
HUMINT	Human Intel	2010	1	8	Romania
IAMD	Integrated Air & Missile Defense	2020	1	4	Greece
JAPCC	Joint Air Power Competence Centre	2005	1	15	Germany
JCBRN Defense	Joint Chem, Bio, Radiological & Nuclear Defence	2007	1	13	Czechia
MARSEC	Maritime Security	2020	1	2	Greece

(continued)

Table 5.3 (continued)

	COE name	*yr of estab*	*N of sponsors*	*N of partners (2022)*	*Host*
MGEOMETOC	Maritime Geospatial, Meteorlogical & Oceanographic Centre	2020	1	3	Portugal
MILENG	Military Engineering	2009	1	15	Germany
MILMED	Military Medicine	2014	1	10	Hungary
MP	Military Police	2014	1	10	Poland
M&S	Modeling & Simulation	2012	1	3	Italy
MW	Mountain Warfare	2015	1	6	Slovenia
NMW	Naval Mine Warfare	2006	2	2	Belgium
SFA	Security Force Assistance	2015	1	2	Italy
SP	Stability Policing	2015	1	8	Italy
STRATCOM	Strategic Communications	2014	1	13	Latvia
Totals			32	220	
	FUTURE COE				
CCAS	Climate change & security	*(2023)*			Canada
SPACE	SPACE-Toulouse	*(2022–3)*			France

MILMED. Research on burden sharing has not considered how COE contribute to NATO mandates relative to which partners invest as key stakeholders and entrepreneurs since their 2005 emergence.

This research draws from multiple approaches to develop a set of propositions concerning what factors influence military spending for partners over two temporal periods with the aim of maximizing the number of cases and presenting a parsimonious model. The next portion of the book offers a descriptive empirical analysis of arms imports, inter-capital distance and US defense and security agreements with NATO partners. That presentation informs sets of models contributing a multi-method analysis. This research presents alternative burden measures, as well as different independent variables (contributions to non-NATO missions, COE participation, national elections) and case studies offering methodological and theoretical advancements.

Conclusions—Burden Sharing from Multiple Views

Theories are not apolitical (Cox, 1981). They are selected by researchers to serve the purpose of understanding social phenomena. Despite aspects of realism being traced as far back as Thucydides (Allison, 2018), several years into the cold war, 1949, the approach was detailed by Morgenthau in explaining the search for power influences opportunities for peace among nations (Morgenthau, 1973) and refined by Waltz in 1959 (Waltz, 2018) in an examination of which level of analysis explains the emergence of conflict between sovereign states. Realist theory converged nicely with US conceptions of its place in the world at the end of the second world war, as one of the few allies better positioned to face threats from the Soviet Union in the short to medium term. Realism relies upon motivating national interest with the quest for power to balance the system and in doing so it creates an international system wrought with conflict unless states credibly commitment to not take advantage of each other in future interactions; cooperation is considered fragile. However, decades later Waltz continued arguing structural conditions give rise to balancing by states, as similar-units, to produce international stability (Waltz, 2010). That narrative converges nicely with the emergence of the NATO and Warsaw Pacts balancing power within the same geographic space but one of the first empirical studies of realism (Walt, 1987) revealed (Middle Eastern) states bandwagon more frequently than they balance. That notwithstanding, the theory offers little about how cooperation should be designed aside from portending more powerful states are crucial and attempt to retain control over cooperative endeavors, usually through suggesting power within the group be linked to partner allocations.

Bandwagoning is consistent with liberal arguments about cooperation maximizing security and well-being relative to the status quo of providing security unilaterally. Liberal arguments also explain the depth and width of cooperation (Bernauer et al., 2013; Friedrichs et al., 2005) by European states within the EU, despite its lean collective defense offerings. The prospects for cooperation are higher for liberals though the design of cooperation should be focused on consensus and partner equality because all are equally sovereign. Because partners share similar beliefs about the long-run benefits from cooperation, the incentives for short-term defection are low, even given a high benefit from abandoning a partner, because norms and practices encourage states to respect commitments; reputations are important. Moreover, states should seek cooperation across domains of interest and the high negotiation costs to cooperation should not deter its chances of arising. While cooperation is likely, liberal explanations of cooperative arrangements focus on fair-divisions of club goods and exclusions will be unlikely. Cooperation design schemes, such as NATO Centres of Excellence, where those not contributing do not access the goods equally, are unlikely to arise within communities influenced by liberalism norms and practices of fairness, justice and transparency.

Social theories of state behavior emerged as a critique to the explicatory and predictive foci of realism and liberalism. Critical theories are less focused on predicting behavior than understanding the sense of how states interact to produce shared meanings in a co-constituted world. The focus for constructivists remains understanding how representational practices are naturalized and reproduced within the club. Understanding why partners accept to share more burden depends upon club socialization by those promoting the '2% target' (Sperling & Webber, 2019). For example, Trump's repeated calls for partners to meet the target to those joining post-cold war may explain why the Baltic states meet the target. Trump used a logic of consequences with warning new partners failure to meet that target might lead to a lack of the US defending in an Article V crisis (Ubriaco, 2017). The Russian invasion of Ukraine in the spring of 2022 also re-invigorated interest in the political target as partners sought to signal NATO's defense credibility by supporting a non-NATO Partnership For Peace member, Ukraine. NATO partners and the institution invoked democracy, respect for international law, human rights and sovereignty as shared reasons why partners should bilaterally contribute to supporting the defense of Ukraine. With four partners bordering Ukraine and others bordering a complicit Belarus, increasing the defense of the borders on NATO's eastern flank accomplished with actions and rhetoric was essential. Many partners contributing to Enhanced Forward Presence increased troop allocations bilaterally in bordering states. In addition, the Ukrainian President's invitation to the June 2022 NATO Madrid Summit represents a symbolic first, as does its invitation by the EU to start accession negotiation discussions the same month. Symbolic actions indicate a legitimation of Ukraine's membership requests despite

Russian attempts to discursively compare its leadership to fascists, link it to corruption and the failures of capitalism forced by democratic political liberalism.

IR theories offer insight about the emergence of cooperation, its durability and some design aspects. Moreover, concerning club burden sharing to produce a collective good or contribute to punctual operations most theories cannot explain differences across NATO partners. This is because research treats the club's threats as monolithic and does not account for structural constraints within states affecting decisions about defense spending and participation in activities. This project contributes theoretically and empirically with rich data and multi-method analyses.

Policy Pop Out 3

Theoretical perspectives on collective (defense & security) burden sharing

For the policymaker -	*Theoretical perspectives on collective (defense & security) burden sharing*
What aspects of the background information does the reader/recipient need to know? What does the reader 'know' compared to what they 'do not know'?	Theories offer different explanations for burden sharing and the causes of cooperation as frameworks for understanding international interactions. The realist prognosis for cooperation is fragile and clubs would be dominated by the largest contributors. There should be large entry costs to encourage self-enforcement of the promises made by partners. Dominant states prefer voting rules with veto powers rather than consensus according to realism. The emergence of cooperation under liberalism is common as would be cooperation designs aggregating capacity and seeking fairness/justice in allocations. Where realists seek relative gains for cooperation, liberals are satisfied with absolute gains to the status quo so the threshold for cooperation is lower as should be the entry costs. Constructivists focus on how identities merge on cooperation and the development of a socialized co-constructed community. The focus is understanding how actors interpret and conceptualize alliance burdens and commitments and how that discourse is reproduced and legitimized nationally. Social practices and activities produce and reproduce the sense of club and its capacity to survive is shaped by the unity of action/discourse among diverse members at different levels. Rational institutionalists focus on the strategic problems and what institutional design characteristics would mitigate them. They focus on design aspects of institutions facilitating self-enforcement and prevent defection.

(continued)

(continued)

For the policymaker -	*Theoretical perspectives on collective (defense & security) burden sharing*
What is their position on the matter? Who else is affected by the issue?	Despite credible commitment and compliance remaining issues, no IR theory points to military spending as a solid measure for club burden sharing - this explains the variety of measures, cases and methodological approaches in extant research. Defense budgets and actors may feel pressure, yet the fact civil security actors and foreign policy actors are excluded from models will prove favorable for many states in a future with improved burden sharing calculations. Recalling security threats are no longer limited to defense and other actors are called upon to react, i.e. national police, disaster management, etc. future burden sharing needs to adopt a holistic view of where partner allocated NATO personnel and financial resources originate outside defense budgets. A challenge will be convincing actors of the appropriateness of transparency and avoid stigmatizing consequences for partners falling short of 'club' expectations. The fact more than half of members do not meet the 2% target is reason for reconsideration of this target, not continuation. Logics of defense solidarity (integration) and defense pluralism (openness) should be promoted over defense sovereignty and exclusiveness. Sovereignty and exclusiveness tending to be associated with realist approaches. Plurality and inclusion is representative of liberal approaches.
What are the costs and/or risks associated with this decision?	To undertake a shift in rethinking burdens requires political capital, strong argumentation developed around fairness/justice, transparency, information sharing and collaboration to recast the entire process and system of bargaining burdens. The strong investment in legitimizing the criteria by the US and exceptional efforts by post-cold war partners with smaller economies that suffered under economic austerity and made difficult decisions to meet the spending criteria to enter NATO will argue against changing criteria. Again, the argumentation must be from democratic and collaborative ideals partners share by virtue of being inside the alliance. Partners should voluntarily contribute information to improve the consistency, efficiency and institutionalization of the burden process with the understanding a more coherent and comprehensive progress can contribute to community perceptions of justice, fairness and equity as the club plans to meet future def/sec needs.

(continued)

(continued)

For the policymaker -	*Theoretical perspectives on collective (defense & security) burden sharing*
What advantages and disadvantages should the reader know about who is to make the decision?	Partners would not deny the importance of foreign affairs nor diplomacy to NATO mandates, but recasting burden sharing beyond defense spending offers insight into the myriad of factors and contributions facilitating the institution's crisis/conflict operations and day-to-day existence. Again, norms and practices are ingrained concerning the 2% criteria despite continuous debates. Those arguing in favor of the social community and collaborative aspects of reconceptualizing burdens position themselves with constructivists and liberals. Actors supporting retaining the current target are concerned about relative 'credible' defense capacities without opening up to see which defense and security capacities are procured. Treating partners as 'like-units' downplays the importance of heterogeneity across partners concerning risks, threat exposure and capacities influencing operation participation and national budget allocations. Those with realist views are protectors of the status quo and also top contributors to the club. However, French and British cross-bidding for contributions will likely reduce due to Brexit and with capable entrants, Finland & Sweden, requesting membership; a critical moment to open such discussions is present.
What other evaluation criteria must the recipient use?	As theories differ about what to measure to confirm a 'partner shoulders club burden' so too do they differ on evaluation criteria. A military spending criteria speaks to realist conceptions of defense and security capacity. It also illustrates the observation most perceive NATO as a def/sec institution more than a political/diplomatic institution. Pluralism in criteria requires diversifying reflection about what constitutes contribution to the institutionS of NATO and the relative value of different components. It incurs considering distinctions between continuing and punctual operations. The process is revising evaluation criteria and rethinking negotiations with long term implications for club cohesion and future collective goods production potential.

Notes

1. Epistemology is interested in how knowledge is acquired, what constitutes valid versus invalid knowledge. It is interested in knowledge as such, i.e., in the reflection on what it means to know, to know and to believe in the truth, validity, or correctness of a proposition, a belief, a fact or a theory. Whereas, ontology is the philosophical branch concerned with the study of being as being, i.e., the study of entities that can be said to exist and what it means to say they exist.
2. Logrolling is vote trading, the exchange of favours (quid pro quo) concerning support on upcoming policy proposals in exchange.

3. Most volumes/issues focus international political economy (Hawkins et al., 2006; Stone, 2013).
4. https://peacekeeping.un.org/en/troop-and-police-contributors, last access 10 May 2022.
5. https://www.nato.int/isaf/placemats_archive/2011-07-26-ISAF-Pla cemat.pdf, last access 10 May 2022.
6. https://www.euronews.com/2022/03/25/germany-s-military-spending-spree-what-can-you-buy-for-100-billion, last access 27 May 2022.

References

Abbott, K., & Snidal, D. (1998). Why states act through formal international organizations. *Journal of Conflict Resolution, 42*(1), 3–32. https://doi.org/10.1177/0022002798042001001

Allison, G. (2018). *Destined for War: Can America and China escape Thucydides's Trap?* (First Mariner Books edition 2018). Mariner Books.

Altfeld, M. (1984). The decision to ally: A theory and test. *Western Political Quarterly, 37*(4), 523–544. https://doi.org/10.1177/106591298403700402

Balzacq, T. (2005). The three faces of securitization: Political agency, audience and context. *European Journal of International Relations, 11*(2), 171–201. https://doi.org/10.1177/1354066105052960

Barnett, M., & Duvall, R. (2005). Power in international politics. *International Organization, 59*(1), 39–75. https://doi.org/10.1017/S0020818305050010

Barnett, M., & Finnemore, M. (1999). The politics, power, and pathologies of international organizations. *International Organization, 53*(4), 699–732. https://doi.org/10.1162/002081899551048

Becker, J. (2017). The correlates of transatlantic burden sharing: Revising the agenda for theoretical and policy analysis. *Defense & Security Analysis, 33*(2), 131–157. https://doi.org/10.1080/14751798.2017.1311039

Bernauer, T., Kalbhenn, A., Koubi, V., & Spilker, G. (2013). Is there a "Depth versus participation" dilemma in international cooperation? *The Review of International Organizations, 8*(4), 477–497. https://doi.org/10.1007/s11558-013-9165-1

Badcock, G., & Marks, D. C. (Eds.). (2010). *War, human dignity and nation building: Theological perspectives on Canada's role in Afghanistan*. Cambridge Scholars.

Buzan, B., Wæver, O., & Wilde, J. de. (1998). *Security: A new framework for analysis*. Lynne Rienner Pub.

Cortell, A., & Davis, J. (1996). How do international institutions matter? The domestic impact of international rules and norms. *International Studies Quarterly, 40*(4), 451. https://doi.org/10.2307/2600887

Cox, R. (1981). Social forces, states and world orders: Beyond international relations theory. *Millennium: Journal of International Studies, 10*(2), 126–155. https://doi.org/10.1177/03058298810100020501

Finnemore, M., & Sikkink, K. (1998). International norm dynamics and political change. *International Organization, 52*(4), 887–917.

Friedrichs, J., Mihov, J., & Popova, M. (2005). Synergies and tradeoffs in international cooperation: Broadening, widening, and deepening. *EIoP, 9*(13). https://ssrn.com/abstract=827224

Fuhrmann, M., & Sechser, T. (2014). Signaling alliance commitments: Hand-tying and sunk costs in extended nuclear deterrence. *American Journal of Political Science, 58*(4), 919–935.

Gheciu, A. (2005). Security institutions as agents of socialization? NATO and the "New Europe." *International Organization, 59*(4), 973–1012.

Hawkins, D., Lake, D., Nielson, D., & Tierney, M. (2006). *Delegation and agency in international organizations.* Cambridge University Press.

Heinen-Bogers, M. (2022). *Burden sharing in security organizations: Broadening the burden sharing debate.* Tilburg University.

Johnston, A. I. (2001). Treating international institutions as social environments. *International Studies Quarterly, 45*(4), 487–515. https://doi.org/10.1111/0020-8833.00212

Kaplan, L. (2004). *NATO divided, NATO united: The evolution of an alliance.* Praeger.

Kimball, A. & Lewis. (2010b). Le rôle accru des organisations internationales dans les conflits contemporains. In *Conflits dans le monde 2010b.* Presses Université Laval.

Kimball, A. & Lewis. (2011). La délégation à l'épreuve du terrain: Les difficiles interventions militaires et civiles des organisations internationales dans les conflits et les crises. In *Conflits dans le monde, 2011.* Presses Université Laval.

Kimball, A. (2019). Knocking on NATO: Strategic and institutional challenges risk the future of Europe's seven-decade long cold peace. *The School of Public Policy Publications, 12.* https://doi.org/10.11575/SPPP.V12I0.68129

Kimball, A. (2006). Alliance formation and conflict initiation: The missing link. *Journal of Peace Research, 43*(4), 371–389. https://doi.org/10.1177/0022343306064816

Kimball, A. (2010a). Political survival, policy distribution, and alliance formation. *Journal of Peace Research, 47*(4), 407–419. https://doi.org/10.1177/0022343310368346

Kimball, A. (2021b). Managing risks, side payments, and multi-institutional enlargement: The role of US defence, big four investment agreements and candidate risks on NATO and EU enlargement. *European Politics and Society, 22*(5), 696–715. https://doi.org/10.1080/23745118.2020.1820152

Koremenos & Nau. (2010). Exit, no exit. *Duke Journal of Comparative & International Law, 21*(1), 81–120.

Koremenos, B. (2008). When, what, and why do states choose to delegate? *Law & Contemporary Problems, 71*(1), 151–192.

Koremenos, B. (2013). The continent of international law. *Journal of Conflict Resolution, 57*(4), 653–681. https://doi.org/10.1177/0022002712448904

Koremenos, B., Lipson, C., & Snidal, D. (2001). The rational design of international institutions. *International Organization, 55*(4), 761–799. https://doi.org/10.1162/002081801317193592

Lipson, C. (1991). Why are some international agreements informal? *International Organization, 45*(4), 495–538.

Liu, T.-Y., Su, C.-W., Tao, R., & Cong, H. (2019). Better is the neighbor? *Defence and Peace Economics, 30*(6), 706–718. https://doi.org/10.1080/10242694.2017.1422321

Mattern, J. B., & Zarakol, A. (2016). Hierarchies in world politics. *International Organization, 70*(3), 623–654. https://doi.org/10.1017/S0020818316000126

Moravcsik, A. (1997). Taking preferences seriously: A liberal theory of international politics. *International Organization, 51*(4), 513–553. https://doi.org/10.1162/002081897550447

Morgenthau, H. (1973). *Politics among nations: The struggle for power and peace* (5th edition). Knopf.

Morrow, J. (1991). Alliances and asymmetry: An alternative to the capability aggregation model of alliances. *American Journal of Political Science, 35*(4), 904. https://doi.org/10.2307/2111499

O'Neill, B. (2001). Risk aversion in international relations theory. *International Studies Quarterly, 45*(4), 617–640.

Sandler, T. (2004). *Global collective action* (1st edition). Cambridge University Press. https://doi.org/10.1017/CBO9780511617119

Schuette, L. (2021). Why NATO survived Trump: The neglected role of Secretary-General Stoltenberg. *International Affairs, 97*(6), 1863–1881. https://doi.org/10.1093/ia/iiab167

Simion, E. (2016). *NATO centres of excellence and the transformation of the North-Atlantic alliance.* University of Oradea. https://nbn-resolving.org/urn:nbn:de:0168-ssoar-73403-8

Sirici, J., & Coletta, D. (2009). Enduring without an enemy: NATO's realist foundation. *Perspectives, 17*(1), 57–81.

Sperling, J., & Webber, M. (2019). Trump's foreign policy and NATO: Exit and voice. *Review of International Studies, 45*(3), 511–526. https://doi.org/10.1017/S0260210519000123

Stone, R. (2013). Informal governance in international organizations: Introduction to the special issue. *Review of International Organizations, 8*(2), 121–136. https://doi.org/10.1007/s11558-013-9168-y

Ubriaco, J. (2017). NATO'S Baltic problem: How populism, Russia, and the Baltic can fracture NATO. *Harvard International Review, 38*(1), 13.

Walt, S. (1987). *The origins of alliances*. Cornell University Press.

Waltz, K. (2010). *Theory of international politics* (Reiss). Waveland Press.

Waltz, K. (2018). *Man, the state, and war: A theoretical analysis* (Anniversary Edition). Columbia University Press.

Wendt, A. (1992). Anarchy is what states make of it: The social construction of power politics. *International Organization, 46*(2), 391–425. https://doi.org/10.1017/S0020818300027764

Wendt, A. (2006). *Social Theory of International Politics*. https://doi.org/10.1017/CBO9780511612183

Wolf, R. (2017). Donald Trump's status-driven foreign policy. *Survival, 59*(5), 99–116. https://doi.org/10.1080/00396338.2017.1375260

Zarakol, A. (2018). *A non-Eurocentric approach to sovereignty*. https://doi.org/10.17863/CAM.26865

Zarakol, A. (2014). What made the modern world hang together: Socialisation or stigmatisation? *International Theory, 6*(2), 311–332. https://doi.org/10.1017/S1752971914000141

Zehfuss, M. (2001). Constructivism and identity: A dangerous liaison. *European Journal of International Relations, 7*(3), 315–348. https://doi.org/10.1177/1354066101007003002

Zyla, B. (2009). NATO and post-cold war burden-sharing: Canada "the laggard?" *International Journal: Canada's Journal of Global Policy Analysis, 64*(2), 337–359. https://doi.org/10.1177/002070200906400203

Zyla, B. (2015). Sharing the burden?: NATO and its second-tier powers. *University of Toronto Press*. https://doi.org/10.3138/9781442668386

Zyla, B. (2018). Transatlantic burden sharing: Suggesting a new research agenda. *European Security, 27*(4), 515–535. https://doi.org/10.1080/09662839.2018.1552142

CHAPTER 6

Risk Management Model of Institutional Burden Sharing

Introduction

There is a large literature on burden sharing in II. A review produced several conclusions: most studies do not cover the majority of members during the period examined and limit themselves to one method and object of analysis. Across quantitative studies, some variation of state military spending appears in most research though again, alternative measures include levels of burden sharing, attribution of defense assets, force levels in Europe, etc.[1] The variety of empirical measures is another indicator that the political 2% target can be improved. This project offers measures for conceptualizing burdens while restraining itself from arguing one measure should unify or dominate because of the complexity of sharing collective burdens across heterogenous partners. The risk management model of burden sharing argues partners balance threats to national security and club defense while managing institutional constraints at home. This simultaneous multi-level game (Evans et al., 1993; Hawkins, 2006; Putnam, 1988) explains partner variations in participation in punctual and ongoing missions as the geopolitical environment shifted throughout the institution's seven-decade history while enlarging. With geographic expansion and the increasing nature and complexity of defense/security threats shifting from the end of the cold war to post-9/11 to the

A. L. Kimball, *Beyond 2%—NATO Partners, Institutions & Burden Management*, Canada and International Affairs,
https://doi.org/10.1007/978-3-031-22158-3_6

current configuration, the institution adapted functionally, structurally, and socially to accomplish core mandates.

Studies of burden sharing should capture aspects of shifting geostrategic threats temporally, partner internal constraints and national perceptions of risks relative to the club perceptions as they affect how the club's burden is distributed functionally across partners. Proposing a model from previous research and the major IR theoretical approaches while ensuring it is functionally testable across measures and actors, offers a challenge from scholarly and policy perspectives and the potential to offer multiple contributions to the literature. II represent complex delegation systems (Hawkins, 2006) of state-partners that are also multi-level hierarchical agents in competitive internal budgeting environments embedded within national governments having different, perhaps even divergent, perceptions of risks and threats at the partner level relative to the alliance (Heinen-Bogers, 2022). This project advances research and offers avenues for study and greater discussion while providing data to test falsifiable propositions drawn from theoretical approaches.

Proposing a Risk Management Model of Institutional (Defense and Security) Burdens

The risk management model of institutional enlargement (Kimball, 2021) indicated the importance of information to reduce risks and uncertainties while accounting for threats. The *Beyond 2%* research offers a test of NATO burden sharing from theories deploying measures using the longest temporal domain and maximum number of cases available. Five theoretical claims propose a number of arguments, most examined in quantitative models, analyzing two dependent variables across full and limited time periods with shared and different independent variables. Each model is distinguished by several independent variables and is a contribution comparable to research using the same dependent variable. Trying to interact with the broadest portion of the extant quantitative literature, this research uses regression with clustering on country or year, then extends to probabilistic analysis with models predicting the chances a partner contributes to a new NATO operation accounting for cross-partner variations.[2] These samples include over 80% of possible cases since 1950 and 87% of cases since 1993, offering an extensive and original study.[3] Going beyond descriptive data employing statistical analyses permits a comparison test of competing claims though scholars can append the data to explore additional propositions with supplementary materials. A series of statistical models tests burden sharing and 'special' arguments concerning middle powers using a technique designed to identify irregularities around average crisis participation behavior. If there is a subset of states tending to overcontribute under identifiable conditions, such as perceived threats, then their behavior should be observably distinct compared to those consistently under-contributing, i.e., the smallest partners having little to contribute and those always contributing, e.g., top four plus Poland over the last several decades.

One way NATO reduced club risks, as an agent, was through enlargement to diminish threats to cold war partners; however, it remained sensitive to political risks. In contrast, the EU's concerns about market liberalization implied longer timelines for candidate completion. The availability of US DSA increased information about the credibility of candidates, as well as the extent of global NATO partner arms transfers to partners, taken together that information conveyed updated shared understandings of candidate quality. Revealed information about defense capacities changed risk perceptions for current partners increasing the likelihood of a membership offer (Kimball, 2021).

The lexicon of burden sharing refers to military spending and mission participation; both are used as measures in various contributions by others. Some examine troop allocations to missions (Dorussen et al., 2009; Heinen-Bogers, 2022; Zyla, 2015) while others the chances a state contributes to a collective mission/activity undertaken by a set of states (Ringsmose, 2010; Tago, 2014).

Across the following pages some factors explaining defense and security burden sharing behavior are discussed, this is not an exhaustive list but presents factors identified by existing research and IR theories. The explanatory factors discussed are threats, informational improvement, the exploitation of large partners by small peers, political risks and democracy. Each factor is discussed, operationalized and then connected via proposition to military spending and the chances a state participates in an operation. Descriptive figures are presented to support propositions along with references to added figures in appendix. The claims are constructed to measure empirically—a simplification of information for statistical purposes to identify patterns. The accompanying figures offer snapshots of implications before the analyses. The data matrix offers

NATO partner-year values of military spending and partner participation in a new NATO operation. Below several factors identified in the theoretical portions of this book are discussed in greater detail.

One state dominated NATO strategic thinking, club behavior and individual partner behavior, i.e., Russia. The club draws its defense and security limits with the 'weakest link', i.e., least secure front line to Russia while the club's political weaknesses remained more difficult to identify. In a system dominated by how states understand the distribution of power, boundaries remain focal points for defense and access denial. NATO burden research has examined the trade-off between geography and burden contribution to the club (Banka, 2022; De La Fe & Montolio, 2001; Dvorak & Pernica, 2021; Jakobsen, 2018; Tonelson, 2000). Sunk costs in defending areas with troop investments, physical assets are associated with partner/club threat assessments and military spending.

Threats

1: Partners with geographic exposure to Russia[4] (or the Mediterranean Sea) have lower military spending.

Figure 3.5a and b illustrated inter-capital distance to Moscow. States with greater exposure to Russia should prevent the security dilemma to avoid the perception military allocations are a threat. Partners closer to Russia host fewer physical assets by similar logic. Partners on the edge of risk exposure should seek reassurance while not provoking entrapment requiring collective response. This logic explains why Denmark hosts no NATO club assets on its territory of the 1949 signatories. The Fins and Swedes should contribute NATO outbound operations but are not likely to insist on, nor accept NATO physical assets, on national territories in negotiations toward full membership. Both should step into maritime awareness and warning in the Arctic and North Sea regions and air operations in Europe with ease.

Informational Improvement—Rational Institutionalism

The 2% military spending target is a signal of what the club considers 'enough' to ensure a contribution to the common club goods. That political target says very little about what partners should invest in though consultations between partners and NATO guide purchases. However, decisions are taken within partner states as funding is internal. That notwithstanding the US remains an important security partner and there is a playbook in terms how the US collaborated with post-cold war entrants (Kimball, 2022). US bilateral DSA conveyed information reducing uncertainty around a partner's 'true' military capacities. Such defense and security agreement contracting attracts less public attention due to limited agency involvement and is useful in domains requiring secrecy, e.g., defense (Kimball, 2017, 2018; Lipson, 1991). Informal agreement contracting with the dominant supplier endorse(s) and sends external signals of defense and security credibility. Contracted agreements served as costly signals shaping beliefs; they offer information important to partners (Kimball, 2021). Rationally designed agreements counter the strategic problems rationalists, such as Koremenos (2013) and Koremenos et al. (2001), identify (e.g., distribution of power, commitment, adjudication and enforcement, issue indivisibility, etc.). By addressing strategic issues, those contracts improved information available to partners and other states in the international system (Kimball, 2022) which converges nicely with RIT (Koremenos, 2005). US DSA in partners reduce uncertainty around defense credibility by providing information about how linked a partner is with the largest economy and defense good supplier. Egel and co-authors demonstrate the importance of US defense and security commitments increasing global trade, economic growth, and via the affects of US troops on local economies (Egel et al., 2016; Kavanagh, 2014).

2: As the number of partner bilateral DSAs with the US increases, then partner military spending increases [a partner is more likely to participate in a new operation].

Figure 3.1 visually presented the growth of US DSA with NATO partners that joined since the end of the cold war. Not all partners attracted similar attention from the club's central defense actor.

Risk Management—Rationalism, Trade-Offs

Though NATO set a policy target for club partners, those budgeting decisions remain functionally internal processes in states. Despite being a club of liberal democracies, NATO joins states reflecting 30 different democratic bargains within national contexts. IR scholars tend to treat them all equally despite literatures in comparative politics distinguishing presidential from parliamentary from hybrid political systems along with differences in civil-military relations, relations across bureaucratic stakeholders and the military branches. Policy choices involve trade-offs for leaders concerning defense and security. The political survival literature places choices in stark contrast for leaders choosing policies to enhance personal political survival, also known as the selectorate theory (Arena & Nicoletti, 2014; Bueno de Mesquita et al., 1999). The distributional dilemma (Arena, 2010; Becker, 2021; Kimball, 2010; Powell, 1999) forces leaders to choose between social policy goods (i.e., butter) or security policy goods (i.e., guns for defense). The policy trade-offs leaders make affect their capacity to response in crisis. Political risks are linked to NATO membership offers (Kimball, 2021) and include government stability, conflict, bureaucratic quality, investment profile and socioeconomic conditions, data from PRS Group (2019) visualized in figures offered in Chapter 4. Political risk was shown to be comparatively more important than economic risk in NATO and EU membership offers (Kimball, 2021). NATO partners facing competing economic and political risks may be forced to prioritize. This could mean allocating resources towards political concerns over military spending while simultaneously using military spending, investment and recruitment to affect the national economic situation. Sub-national or regional economic offsets present national-level collaboration schemes to post-contract agreement retrofit into internationally negotiated bargains.

- 3a: As ‘political risk’ increases, military spending decreases.
- 3b: As ‘economic’ risk increases, military spending increases.
- 3c: Increasing ‘economic risks’ are associated with smaller increases in military spending relative to ‘political risks’.[5]

Exploitation (Free-Riding)—Collective Action

Arguments about exploitation of large contributors by small partners are as old as the collective action literature itself extending over six decades (Banka, 2022; Dvorak & Pernica, 2021; Goldstein, 1995; Heinen-Bogers, 2022; Jakobsen, 2018; Kwon, 1998; Männik, 2004; Olson, 1971; Olson & Zeckhauser, 1966). Under or overcontributing is the purpose of a subset of the literature (Dorussen et al., 2009; Haesebrouck, 2017; Khanna & Sandler, 1997; Kim & Sandler, 2020; Marton & Hynek, 2012) as are fairness discussions (Kunertova, 2017, 2019). This literature was enriched with discussions on the role of domestic political concerns/constraints (Becker & Malesky, 2017; Saideman, 2016; Saideman & Auerswald, 2012). That research addressed issues associated with delegation slippage and inefficiency. Partners least affected by Russian threat should spend less on the military to benefit from collective benefits. This explains why partners such as Spain (De La Fe & Montolio, 2001) and Canada remain under the political target of 2%. There is a subset of research including comparative studies of Canada (Douch & Solomon, 2014; Massie, 2014; Massie & Zyla, 2018; Saideman, 2016; Zyla, 2009) recalling distributional concerns are a source of II emergence (Dai et al., 2010, p. 18; Koremenos, 2013).

4a: Partners increasing the security of members relative to Russia have lower military spending [are less likely to participate in a new operation].

Democracy—Liberalism (a, b) & Constructivism (c, d)

Social theorists insist NATO cohesion is due to convergent identities and interests across members (Gheciu, 2005; Johnston, 2001; Schimmelfennig, 1998). Institutions are as forums for socialization (and stigmatization [Zarakol, 2014], e.g., if partner does not meet 2%, the 'compliance gap' [Heinen-Bogers, 2022]) and states use language acts to advance preferred policies through negotiations (Barnett & Finnemore, 1999; Kratochwil & Ruggie, 1986). NATO's consensus decision-making ensures continued consultations. Shared understandings about identities and interests were identified as important to holding the EU together (Checkel, 2001; Schimmelfennig, 2001, 2005). The strategic culture of NATO partners defined as 'Atlanticist' versus 'Europeanist' shapes partner cohesion and unity (Becker & Malesky, 2017) based on evidence drawn from national security documents. Similarly, #WEARENATO is a public relations and diplomacy campaign offering its own instructions.[6] The North Atlantic treaty invokes economic freedom and liberalism as shared commitments by members. Liberal perspectives as far back as Kant discussed the virtuous circle of democracy, free trade creating economic interdependence and IO (Russett & Oneal, 2001) contributing to a peace between democracies. Such absence of conflict is partially attributed to norms of conflict resolution and respect for rule of law (Cortell & Davis, 1996).

5a: As a partner's level of democracy increases, then spending on the military increases [partners are more likely to participate in a new operation].
5b: As demands for social policies increase, then military spending increases.
5c: Hosting/sponsoring a COE reduces the likelihood a state participates in new operation.

Multiple measures of democracy exist and could be included in models of burden sharing, the goal is not to provide an exhaustive test of different operationalizations, nor study all claims in this book. Recognizing democratic diversity, several measures are explored including the extent of the majority political party control of the legislature and proxy measures, i.e., the infant mortality rate, to alternatively measure spending on social demands (Abouharb & Kimball, 2007). Infant mortality rates are associated with defense alliances having been previously examined in the study of guns versus butter trade-off claims (Kimball, 2010) of state behavior and are publicly available.

Constructivist arguments focus on loci of socialization, such as a COE, as an indicator. The portion of this book examining NATO, as an agent in the global system, compared to other IOs and the emergence of its COE as socialized environments where actors train, learn, engage, and collaborate in smaller subgroups offers material to explore constructivist claims. The effort here is on deconstructing and providing pathways for linking theoretical arguments to empirical techniques. The factors identified in propositions represent some claims examined with the use of multiple methods in the next pages.

Conclusions—Moving Toward Multi-method Analyses of the Risk Management Model

One benefit of a book-length project is the capacity to deploy several methods to examine the concept alongside different measures. That being said, to ensure the comparability of this research, one set of analyses examines the 'classic' measure, military spending. Another set of analyses examines if a partner participates in a new operation using the same explanatory factors when possible and the final portion considers NATO, as an actor, and a complex agent in a delegation game in the international system as other efforts exclude defense and security institutions (Hawkins, 2006; Vaubel, 2006). This triangulation of methods includes descriptive data analyses, quantitative analyses, and comparative studies of NATO's institutional delegates, i.e., COE, to explore the claims of theories on burden sharing using NATO as a case. Not only is there much research on NATO but the presence of a 'common' spending target offers a metric, though debated, for a contribution to the institution's efforts to provide the common goods. While the political target is a good faith signal within the club and externally, decisions to participate in crisis and conflict operations occur at the national level because forces are drawn from armies and funding from government budgets which involves trade-offs. There must be political willingness including an alignment of the major internal political stakeholders with international counterparts to create the collective goods offered by NATO in crisis/conflict activities. Internal stakeholders include political parties, ministries, militaries, banks, NGOs and others depending on issues at stake—creating a balance between competing internal demands is complicated (Evans et al., 1993; Moravcsik, 1997; Putnam, 1988). The use of multiple methods was offered studying international cooperation (Milner, 1997) linking formal modeling, descriptive analysis and quantitative analysis with the same unit of study, i.e., state decisions, this research extends to the alliance level. That effort examined different cases of cooperation and different sets of actors leaving room for a single-institutional focus contribution provided here.

This research deconstructs burden sharing within the Atlantic alliance offering measures. It also invokes extant literature by examining the importance of political and investment risks on state decisions and the informational improvement in the form of bilateral US DSA with partner states. It proposes analyzing burden sharing using military spending, participation in operations and comparative analyses tracing the emergence and development of COE. COE are a solution to complex burden sharing concerns in the future and NATO's response to the changing complexity of defense and security threats associated with alliance transformation. COE are forward-looking institutions, proactive in planning to prevent the need for reaction. They are NATO's institutional response to managing the club's strategic problems over allocations, commitment, enforcement and uncertainty about the future, while actively socializing states, creating a forum for collaboration, and a level of collective goods for the club with (some) exclusiveness. A COE begins with a set of partners sponsoring inviting others. A COE attracting increasing members over years experiences budget expansion and influence, e.g., STRATCOM and CYBERDEF. A host country's continued political and financial support remain crucial for mandate delivery. Data indicate several COE remain under-developed, stalled and under-populated by partners, e.g., Naval Mine Warfare and Cold Weather Operations. Finally, the use of multiple techniques and sources of data to examine burden sharing creates opportunities for others to advance with the information centralized herein while advancing a risk management model of burden sharing.

Risks are managed by states through the inclusion of direct measures and new measures of threats. The model accounts for the effects of enlargement shifting the focus of risks and how the institutional innovation of COE respond to future defense and security threats and contribute to alliance transformation while openly shifting burdens away from the club. The near exclusion of COE from burden sharing models in the last 15 years is notable in such context.

Notes

1. See literature compilation included in appendices.
2. If clustering over 'country' vs. 'year' is equivalent based on the IV specification, the clustered results should be similar across specifications of the Dependent Variable indicated an inclusion of state-level factors to ensure estimates are not affected by slicing data panels based on country vs. year.
3. Some form of military spending is used in over a dozen publications.
4. Measured as over or under the larger of the median OR average inter-capital distance. Seven newer partners reduced exposure relative to the mean. That notwithstanding NATO faces threats from multiple sources, this measure aims at capturing the geostrategic concerns as seen by partners in 1949 and the end of the cold war. See appendix for information on data sources. The

sensitivity of the measure is indicated by the fact across the NATO-14 states a predicted inter-capital distance over or under 2400 km or shifting between the mean or observed median affects minimum—maximum geographic exposure for UK and France, exposed at maximum distance, as well as Italy and Belgium, unexposed at minimum.

5. Supported by comparing coefficient estimates and model predictions.
6. https://www.act.nato.int/application/files/7415/6529/0612/nato-dsct.pdf, last access 26 June 2022.

References

Abouharb, M. R., & Kimball, A. L. (2007). A new dataset on infant mortality rates, 1816–2002. *Journal of Peace Research, 44*(6), 743–754. https://doi.org/10.1177/0022343307082071

Arena, P. (2010). Why not guns and butter: Responses to economic turmoil. *Foreign Policy Analysis, 6*(4), 339–348. https://doi.org/10.1111/j.1743-8594.2010.00116.x

Arena, P., & Nicoletti, N. P. (2014). Selectorate theory, the democratic peace, and public goods provision. *International Theory, 6*(3), 391–416. https://doi.org/10.1017/S1752971914000347

Banka, A. (2022). Neither reckless nor free-riders: Auditing the Baltics as US treaty allies. *Journal of Transatlantic Studies*. https://doi.org/10.1057/s42738-022-00096-3

Barnett, M., & Finnemore, M. (1999). The politics, power, and pathologies of international organizations. *International Organization, 53*(4), 699–732. https://doi.org/10.1162/002081899551048

Becker, J. (2021). Rusty guns and buttery soldiers: Unemployment and the domestic origins of defense spending. *European Political Science Review, 13*(3), 307–330. https://doi.org/10.1017/S1755773921000102

Becker, J., & Malesky, E. (2017). The continent or the "Grand large"? Strategic culture and operational burden-sharing in NATO. *International Studies Quarterly, 61*(1), 163–180. https://doi.org/10.1093/isq/sqw039

Bueno de Mesquita, B., Morrow, J., Siverson, R., & Smith, A. (1999). An institutional explanation of the democratic peace. *American Political Science Review, 93*(4), 791–807. https://doi.org/10.2307/2586113

Checkel, J. (2001). Why comply? Social learning and European identity change. *International Organization, 55*(3), 553–588. https://doi.org/10.1162/00208180152507551

Cortell, A., & Davis, J. (1996). How do international institutions matter? The domestic impact of international rules and norms. *International Studies Quarterly, 40*(4), 451. https://doi.org/10.2307/2600887

Dai, X., Snidal, D., & Sampson, M. (Eds.). (2010). International cooperation theory and international institutions. *Oxford Research Encyclopedia of International Studies*. Oxford University Press. https://doi.org/10.1093/acrefore/9780190846626.013.93

De La Fe, P., & Montolio, D. (2001). Has Spain been free-riding in nato? An econometric approach. *Defence and Peace Economics, 12*(5), 465–485. https://doi.org/10.1080/10430710108404999

Dorussen, H., Kirchner, E., & Sperling, J. (2009). Sharing the burden of collective security in the European Union. *International Organization, 63*(4), 789–810. https://doi.org/10.1017/S0020818309990105

Douch, M., & Solomon, B. (2014). Middle powers and the demand for military expenditures. *Defence and Peace Economics, 25*(6), 605–618. https://doi.org/10.1080/10242694.2013.861652

Dvorak, J., & Pernica, B. (2021). To free or not to free (ride): A comparative analysis of the NATO burden-sharing in the Czech Republic and Lithuania—Another insight into the issues of military performance in the Central and Eastern Europe. *Defense & Security Analysis, 37*(2), 164–176. https://doi.org/10.1080/14751798.2021.1919345

Egel, D., Grissom, A., Godges, J., Kavanagh, J., & Shatz, H. (2016). *Economic benefits of U.S. overseas security commitments could far outweigh costs*. RAND Corporation. https://doi.org/10.7249/RB9912

Evans, P., Jacobson, H. K., & Putnam, R. (Eds.). (1993). *Double-edged diplomacy: International bargaining and domestic politics*. University of California Press.

Gheciu, A. (2005). Security institutions as agents of socialization? NATO and the "New Europe." *International Organization, 59*(4), 973–1012.

Goldstein, A. (1995). Discounting the free ride: Alliances and security in the postwar world. *International Organization, 49*(1), 39–71. https://doi.org/10.1017/S0020818300001570

Haesebrouck, T. (2017). NATO burden sharing in Libya: A fuzzy set qualitative comparative analysis. *Journal of Conflict Resolution, 61*(10), 2235–2261. https://doi.org/10.1177/0022002715626248

Hawkins, D. (2006). *Delegation and agency in international organizations*. Cambridge University Press. http://site.ebrary.com/id/10150378

Heinen-Bogers, M. (2022). *Burden sharing in security organizations: Broadening the burden sharing debate*. Tilburg University.

Jakobsen, J. (2018). Is European NATO *really* free-riding? Patterns of material and non-material burden-sharing after the Cold War. *European Security, 27*(4), 490–514. https://doi.org/10.1080/09662839.2018.1515072

Johnston, A. I. (2001). Treating international institutions as social environments. *International Studies Quarterly, 45*(4), 487–515. https://doi.org/10.1111/0020-8833.00212

Kavanagh, J. (2014). *U.S. security-related agreements in force since 1955: Introducing a new database*. RAND Corporation.

Khanna, J., & Sandler, T. (1997). Conscription, peace-keeping, and foreign assistance: NATO burden sharing in the post-cold war era. *Defence and Peace Economics, 8*(1), 101–121. https://doi.org/10.1080/10430719708404871

Kimball, A. (2010). Political survival, policy distribution, and alliance formation. *Journal of Peace Research, 47*(4), 407–419. https://doi.org/10.1177/0022343310368346

Kimball, A. (2017). Examining informal defence and security arrangements' legalization: Canada–US agreements 1955–2005. *International Journal: Canada's Journal of Global Policy Analysis, 72*(3), 380–400. https://doi.org/10.1177/0020702017723931

Kimball, A. (2018). Future uncertainty, strategic defense and North American defense cooperation: Rational institutionalist arguments pragmatically suggest NORAD's adaptation over replacement. In C. Leuprecht, J. Sokolsky, & T. Hughes (Eds.), *North American strategic defense in the 21st century: Security and sovereignty in an uncertain world* (pp. 122–137). Springer-Verlag International (Collection: Advanced Sciences and Technologies for Security Applications).

Kimball, A. (2021). Managing risks, side payments, and multi-institutional enlargement: The role of US defence, big four investment agreements and candidate risks on NATO and EU enlargement. *European Politics and Society, 22*(5), 696–715. https://doi.org/10.1080/23745118.2020.1820152

Kimball, A. (2022). Deliberative institutional design & U.S. defense and security agreements: Comparing Canadian agreements to those with partners and competitors. *Journal of Transatlantic Studies, 20*(2), 230–250. https://doi.org/10.1057/s42738-022-00098-1

Kim, W., & Sandler, T. (2020). NATO at 70: Pledges, free riding, and benefit-burden concordance. *Defence and Peace Economics, 31*(4), 400–413. https://doi.org/10.1080/10242694.2019.1640937

Koremenos, B. (2005). Contracting around international uncertainty. *The American Political Science Review, 99*(4), 549–565.

Koremenos, B. (2013). The continent of international law. *Journal of Conflict Resolution, 57*(4), 653–681. https://doi.org/10.1177/0022002712448904

Koremenos, B., Lipson, C., & Snidal, D. (2001). The rational design of international institutions. *International Organization, 55*(4), 761–799. https://doi.org/10.1162/002081801317193592

Kratochwil, F., & Ruggie, J. (1986). International organization: A state of the art on an art of the state. *International Organization, 40*(4), 753–775. https://doi.org/10.1017/S0020818300027363

Kunertova, D. (2017). The Canadian politics of fair-share: The first burden-sharing debates about NATO. *Journal of Transatlantic Studies, 15*(2), 161–183. https://doi.org/10.1080/14794012.2016.1268792

Kunertova, D. (2019). The ethics of burden sharing: When Canada talks about fairness, but actually counts benefits. *Les Ateliers De L'éthique, 13*(3), 4–30. https://doi.org/10.7202/1061216ar

Kwon, G. (1998). Retests on the theory of collective action: The Olson and Zeckhauser model and its elaboration. *Economics & Politics, 10*(1), 37–62. https://doi.org/10.1111/1468-0343.00037

Lipson, C. (1991). Why are some international agreements informal? *International Organization, 45*(4), 495–538.

Männik, E. (2004). Small states: Invited to NATO—Able to contribute? *Defense & Security Analysis, 20*(1), 21–37. https://doi.org/10.1080/1475179042000195483

Marton, P., & Hynek, N. (2012). What makes ISAF S/tick: An investigation of the politics of coalition burden-sharing. *Defence Studies, 12*(4), 539–571. https://doi.org/10.1080/14702436.2012.746862

Massie, J. (2014). Public contestation and policy resistance: Canada's oversized military commitment to Afghanistan. *Foreign Policy Analysis, 12*(1), 47–65. https://doi.org/10.1111/fpa.12047

Massie, J., & Zyla, B. (2018). Alliance value and status enhancement: Canada's disproportionate military burden sharing in Afghanistan: Canada's military burden. *Politics & Policy, 46*(2), 320–344. https://doi.org/10.1111/polp.12247

Milner, H. (1997). *Interests, institutions, and information: Domestic politics and international relations*. Princeton University Press.

Moravcsik, A. (1997). Taking preferences seriously: A liberal theory of international politics. *International Organization, 51*(4), 513–553. https://doi.org/10.1162/002081897550447

Olson, M. (1971). *The logic of collective action: Public goods and the theory of groups*. Harvard University Press.

Olson, M., & Zeckhauser, R. (1966). An economic theory of alliances. *The Review of Economics and Statistics, 48*(3), 266. https://doi.org/10.2307/1927082

Powell, R. (1999). *In the shadow of power: States and strategies in international politics*. Princeton University Press.

PRS Group. (2019). *International country risk guide*. https://www.prsgroup.com/explore-ourproducts/international-country-risk-guide/

Putnam, R. (1988). Diplomacy and domestic politics: The logic of two-level games. *International Organization, 42*(3), 427–460.

Ringsmose, J. (2010). NATO burden-sharing redux: Continuity and change after the cold war. *Contemporary Security Policy, 31*(2), 319–338. https://doi.org/10.1080/13523260.2010.491391

Russett, B., & Oneal, J. (2001). *Triangulating peace: Democracy, interdependence, and international organizations*. Norton.

Saideman, S. (2016). *Nato in Afghanistan—Fighting together, fighting alone*. Princeton University Press.

Saideman, S., & Auerswald, D. (2012). Comparing caveats: Understanding the sources of national restrictions upon NATO's mission in Afghanistan: Comparing caveats. *International Studies Quarterly, 56*(1), 67–84. https://doi.org/10.1111/j.1468-2478.2011.00700.x

Schimmelfennig, F. (1998). NATO enlargement: A constructivist explanation. *Security Studies, 8*(2–3), 198–234. https://doi.org/10.1080/09636419808429378

Schimmelfennig, F. (2001). The community trap: Liberal norms, rhetorical action, and the Eastern enlargement of the European Union. *International Organization, 55*(1), 47–80. https://doi.org/10.1162/002081801551414

Schimmelfennig, F. (2005). Strategic calculation and international socialization: Membership incentives, party constellations, and sustained compliance in Central and Eastern Europe. *International Organization, 59*(4). https://doi.org/10.1017/S0020818305050290

Tago, A. (2014). Too many problems at home to help you: Domestic disincentives for military coalition participation. *International Area Studies Review, 17*(3), 262–278. https://doi.org/10.1177/2233865914544227

Tonelson, A. (2000). NATO burden-sharing: Promises, promises. *Journal of Strategic Studies, 23*(3), 29–58. https://doi.org/10.1080/01402390008437799

Vaubel, R. (2006). Principal-agent problems in international organizations. *The Review of International Organizations, 1*(2), 125–138. https://doi.org/10.1007/s11558-006-8340-z

Zarakol, A. (2014). What made the modern world hang together: Socialisation or stigmatisation? *International Theory, 6*(2), 311–332. https://doi.org/10.1017/S1752971914000141

Zyla, B. (2009). NATO and post-cold war burden-sharing: Canada "the laggard?" *International Journal: Canada's Journal of Global Policy Analysis, 64*(2), 337–359. https://doi.org/10.1177/002070200906400203

Zyla, B. (2015). Sharing the burden?: NATO and its second-tier powers. *University of Toronto Press*. https://doi.org/10.3138/9781442668386

CHAPTER 7

Support for a Risk Management Model of Institutional Burdens

Introduction

This book supports a diversification of burden study research along with the inclusion of new explanatory factors and improved threat measures in models in order to question the utility and functionality of the 2% spending target for partners. The importance of risks and additional information through DSA are included as factors. This chapter presents three distinct studies of burden sharing using descriptive data, quantitative analytical methods and text–based analysis guided by several theoretical approches. The first set of analyses employs the classic measure of burden sharing, military spending. It explores spending across NATO's history and in the post-enlargement era since the creation of the Partnership for Peace, after 1993. A number of theoretical arguments are tested but there is no attempt to test every argument presented; this book seeks to build the literature and facilitate new research programs. The second set of models analyses if states participate in a new operation using an econometric technique permitting the identification of middle powers in the club from the specification of a subsets of constraints shaping the variation in their contributions to operations. Middle powers should have more variation around the average likelihood they participate as they are affected by constraints at home. Finally, a comparative examination of

A. L. Kimball, *Beyond 2%—NATO Partners, Institutions & Burden Management*, Canada and International Affairs,
https://doi.org/10.1007/978-3-031-22158-3_7

the agreements founding NATO COE mobilizing constructivist logical discursive arguments and agreement design aspects from RIT is offered.

Managing Risks Model of Institutional Burden Sharing: Military Spending

The first set of models uses original and publicly available data to study burdens alongside risks and threats. A comparison set of models using different SIPRI measures of military spending as the dependent variable to ensure a comparability to a plurality of research employing this measure is offered.[1]

This section describes each model. The data used were previously detailed. Data sources are identified in an appendix list. Some data were collected from public sources.[2] Explanatory factors such as threats, US DSA, and aspects of democracy are examined with measures different from previous research. Threats are measured by the inter-capital distance from a partner to Moscow for the first set of models. Data on informational improvements concerning partners were from RAND on US defense and security-related agreements (Kavanagh, 2014). Demands for social goods are operationalized using a proxy measure used elsewhere in the literature, i.e., infant mortality rates. This measure is widely available and correlated with social policy spending after 1970 over 7 (Abouharb & Kimball, 2007). The security agreement data were author updated while the infant mortality rate data is updated by USAID annually. The political and economic risk data are from PRS Group. Political risk has a strong relationship with NATO membership offers after the cold war (Kimball, 2021b). Arms importation data are from SIPRI while the COE data represent an original data collection effort as a measure of burden and contribution not included elsewhere. Each model includes a lag of the previous year's military spending as a control variable. The models using a longer temporal period examine between 1,000 and 1,100 cases depending on the variables included, whereas the number of cases for the shorter time period falls to around 570 cases; both samples are large enough for quantitative analysis. It is worth noting for the 1950–1990 period the estimated number of cases is 600 as it is NATO members excluding Iceland–the sample size increases starting in 1994, in particular, when each post-Cold War entrant state joined the PFP. Cases in the second population include PFP states and NATO partners from 1994 until 2019. This sample permits an examination of burden sharing since enlargement. The formulas below offer the expected effect of the independent variables on military spending, as does Table 7.1.

Models 1 to 3 (1950–2019) annual military spending OR military spending as % of GDP/capita by year = $\alpha + \beta_1$ **threats** + β_2 **information** (US DSA) + $\beta_{3.1}$ **'democracy'** + $\beta_{3.2}$ **'demands for social policy'** + β_4 military spending$_{(t\text{-}1)}$ + ε_i.

Models 4 and 5 (1994–2019) annual military spending OR military spending as % of GDP/capita = $\alpha + \beta_1$ **threats** + β_2 **information** (US DSA) + β_3 **social policy demands** – $\beta_{4,5}$ 'political risk' + $\beta_{6\text{-}8}$ SIPRI arms importations (from US, NATO, global partners) + β_9 COE+ β_{10} military spending$_{(t\text{-}1)}$ + ε_i.

Table 7.2 presents results for specifications covering the longest temporal period and most cases. The first models test military spending as a percent of GDP (the 2% goal). Threat measures, based on geography, do not influence military spending despite a link with NATO membership offers to entrants after the cold war (Kimball, 2021b). The cumulative number of DSA with the US increases spending supporting rationalist claims about informational improvement through hand tying and constraints. The informational and constraint arguments receive greater support than threat-based measures. Demands for social policy, as measured by infant mortality rates, are positively associated with military spending. The cumulative number of US DSA decreases military spending when not controlling for the lag of spending, then it has a positive relationship. The second specification of model 1 accounts for arms imports from the US and partners. Arms transfers from partners increased military spending though US arms imports are associated with increased spending in some specifications. Results remain stable, arms importations (from the US or NATO partners) increased military spending even after accounting for lagged spending (in 1B). The second set of models uses a mild transformation of the dependent variable from a percentage into a ratio (to reduce the standard deviation relative to the mean). Model 2A includes three measures of threat coded annually: 1. number of partners whose security increased through enlargement, 2. if a partner state's inter capital distance is closer to Russia than the median member accounting for enlargement, and 3. kilometers of border exposed; none are significantly related to defense spending. The second threat measure was retained for analyses after 1990 due to its performance in previous research (Kimball, 2021b). Results show a strong positive relationship between US DSA and military spending. Arms importations from the US and NATO positively

Table 7.1 Analyses and expected directions of the risk management model of burden sharing

Time period	*1949–2019*			*1990–2019*		
	(DV) Military spending ('collective defense')	**Expectation**	**IV**	**(DV) Contribution - crisis managment (NATO operations)**	**IV**	**Expectation**
Realism	Threat	+	intercapital distance to Moscow, author	threat	distance to crisis/conflict region for partner, author	+
	Top four contributor increase spending t-1	+	US, Germany, France, UK	state is a top 4 contributor to NATO	US, Germany, France, UK	+
	cold war NATO partners	–	partners previous to 1999			
	post cold war NATO partner	+	partners joining after 1998			
---				economic risk	PRS Group, 2019	mitigated
Liberalism	demands for social goods	–	IMR (Abouharb & Kimball, 2007)	demands for social goods	IMR (Abouharb & Kimball, 2007)	+
	'corruption'	+	V-dem, see appendix	new COE sponsor/host	original data	-

Time period	*1949–2019*			*1990–2019*		
				national elections	V-dem, see appendix	-
				government seat % in legislature	Comparative Party Manefesto Data	+
RIT	side payments by US	+	Kavanagh, 2014	side payments by US	Kavanagh, 2014	+
				political risk	PRS Group, 2019	+
				contributions by top 4 states to OP	US, Germany, France, UK	+
				number of new Ops/year	UN & EU Ops, author	-

Source author's creation

Table 7.2 NATO partner military spending, models 1 & 2, 1950–2019

	Expectation	*M1A*	*M1B*	*support*	*M2A*	*M2B*	*M2C*	*support*
DV		*mil. spending as % GDP*			*mil. spending as % GDP as a ratio*			
# of states secured by partner	+ (prop1)	− 0.0195	− 0.0218	no	0.00034	–	− 0.00022	no
(S.E.)		(0.0420)	(0.0408)		(0.0002)		(0.0004)	
Intercapital distance to Moscow under median	− (prop1a)	–	–		0.00039	− 0.0033	–	
					(0.0009)	(0.0044)		
Russian exposure	+ (prop 1a)				0.00031	–	–	
					(0.0002)			
DSA cumulative count	+ (prop 2)	0.0076*	0.0075	partial	0.000048**	0.00003	− 0.00007	partial
		(0.0045)	(0.0047)		(7.71 e-06)	(0.000026)	(0.0005)	
Arms imports from the US (proxy defense link)	+ (prop 2)	–	0.0005		–	0.000011**	5.03 e-06	**yes**
			(0.00031)			(0.00000273)	(3.07 e-06)	
Corruption	− (prop 3c)	–	–		–	–	–	
Political risk	− (prop 3a)	–	–		–	–	–	
Economic risk	− (prop 3b)	–	–		–	–	–	
Democracy	+ (prop 5)	–	–		–	–	–	
Infant mortality rate	+ (prop 5)	0.0321**	0.0273**	**yes**	0.00037**	0.0003**	0.0003**	**yes**
		(0.0074)	(0.0070)		(0.000024)	(0.000084)	(0.00007)	
Arms imports from NATO ptrs (proxy link)	+ (prop 2)	–	0.0097*	**yes**	–	–	9.70 e-06*	**yes**

	Expectation	*M1A*	*M1B*	*support*	*M2A*	*M2B*	*M2C*	*support*
			(0.00058)				(5.83 e-06)	
Lag of military expenditures	control	0.00005**	0.000047**		–	–	4.97 e-07**	
		(0.00002)	(0.00002)				(2.13 e-06)	
Constant		1.8377**	1.8002**		0.0151**	0.01550**	0.0180**	
		(0.7345)	(0.7179)		(0.00083)	(0.0058)	(0.0072)	
#		1076	1076		1097	1094	1076	
R-square		0.3686	0.3961		0.2204	0.2826	0.3961	
Error details		country	country		year	country	country	

Source author's creation, Standard error in parentheses, $*p > .10$; $**p > .05$

influence military spending. However, once the previous year's spending is included, then the role of partner arms transfers is more important than US arms transfers (1B & 3F). The influence of NATO partner arms transfers on partner spending is absent from previous analyses, another contribution. That notwithstanding demands for social goods and aspects of the informational argument retain support across models.

Table 7.3 presents data since 1949 using the logarithm of military expenditures as the dependent variable (Model 3 and its variations) permitting a comparison to previous research. As a technical note, such models permit clustering upon either year or country. Otherwise one can specify the calculation of robust standard errors. (Robust standard errors adjust the model-based standard errors using the empirical variability of the model residuals that are the difference between observed outcome and the outcome predicted by the statistical model.) All represent techniques to correct for the possibility of a non-random error distribution across time/cases based on knowledge about the data composition. Country clustering is selected because the theoretical model points to the importance of national differences, so statistically significant findings appear despite a comparatively 'constrained' test of propositions. Threat measures obtain stronger support when using this dependent variable indicating how one measures burden is consequential to results and inferences drawn. US support via DSA cumulatively influencing military spending, after accounting for imports from the US and NATO allies, demonstrates the role of the US influencing partner spending. A comparison of the coefficients indicates the influence of DSA is larger than arms imports and it reduces once the previous year's military spending is added. Corruption, as an alternative measure of risk, does not effect on military spending, nor does democracy, such findings are not surprising given members should not have much variation in democracy or corruption due to shared liberal democratic governance according to the Washington Treaty. The table below offers replica models with a shortened period of analysis.

Since the post-cold war (models 4 & 5) and creation of the PFP, there remains a relationship between arms imports from US, NATO partners and global partners about spending after accounting for earlier spending. Political risk is negatively related to spending, while economic risk increases military spending, yet in the same model the effects change. The relationship between risk and military spending requires more research. The fact inter-capital distance, as a measure is correlated with spending,

Table 7.3 NATO partner military spending, model 3, 1950–2019

	Expectation	*M3A*	*M3B*	*M3C*	*M3D*	*M3E*	*support*
DV		*logarithm of mil. spending*					
# of states secured by partner	+ (prop1)	– 0.0352**	–	–	–	–	no
(S.E.)		(0.0123)					
Intercapital distance to Moscow under median ('threat')	– (prop1a)	– 0.5520**	– 0.7388**	– 0.4560**	– 0.05287	– 0.5291	**yes**
		(0.1003)	(0.3859)	(0.0583)	(0.3615)	(0.3800)	
DSA by year	+ (prop 2)	–	0.0219**	– 0.0012	– 0.0037	– 0.0036	partial
			(0.0122)	(0.0033	(0.0084)	(0.0044)	
DSA cumulative count	+ (prop 2)	0.0172**	0.0176**	0.0066**	–	–	**yes**
		(0.0012)	(0.0046)	(0.0011)			
Arms imports from the US (proxy defense link)	+ (prop 2)	0.0014**	0.0014**	0.0009**	0.0004**	0.0004**	**yes**
		(0.0001)	(0.0003)	(0.0001)	(0.0002)	(0.0002)	
Corruption	– (prop 3c)	0.2542	– 0.0874	0.0444	–	–	
		(0.2870)	(1.2007)	(0.2783)			
Democracy	+ (prop 5)	–	–	–	– 0.0120	–	
					(1.083)		
Infant mortality rate	+ (prop 5)	0.0023	0.0039	0.0025*	– 0.0036	– 0.0035	partial
		(0.0018)	(0.0043)	(0.0016)	(0.0084)	(0.0054)	
Arms imports from NATO ptrs (proxy defense links)	+ (prop 2)	0.0014**	0.0014**	0.0090**	0.0023*	0.0023**	**yes**
		(0.0001)	(0.0003)	(0.0001)	(0.0007)	(0.0007)	
Lag of military expenditures	control	–	–	0.00005**	0.00007**	0.00007**	
				(2.2 e-06)	(7.19 e-06)	(6.97 e-06)	

(continued)

Table 7.3 (continued)

	Expectation	*M3A*	*M3B*	*M3C*	*M3D*	*M3E*	*support*
Constant		7.2827**	7.0609**	7.1971**	7.4781**	7.4677**	
		(0.1309)	(0.4843)	(0.0793)	(0.8813)	(0.2600)	
Standard error type		robust		robust			
#		1033	1033	1016	1016	1016	
R-square		0.5919	0.5916	0.6821	0.6962	0.6962	
Clustering			country		country	country	

Source author's creation, Standard error in parentheses, $^{*}p > .10$; $^{**}p > .05$

Table 7.4 NATO partner military spending, models 4 & 5, **1993–2019**

	Expectation	*M4A*	*M4B*	*M4C*	*M4D*	*support*	*M5A*	*M5B*	*support*
DV		*logarithm of mil. spending*					*mil. spending as % GDP (as a ratio)*		
# of states secured by nearest new partner	+ (prop1)	–	– 0.0711**	– 0.0653**	– 0.0582**	no	0.0003**	–	yes
(S.E.)			(0.0339)	(0.0336)	(0.0334)		(0.0001)		
Intercapital distance to Moscow under median ('threat')	– (prop1a)	– 0.2287	–	–	–		–	–	
		(0.3244)							
DSA by year	+ (prop 2)	– 0.0034	0.0091	– 0.0078	–		0.0002	–	
		(0.0104)	(0.0100)	(0.0100)			(0.0002)		
DSA, cumulative count	+ (prop 2)	–	–	–	0.0010		–	– 0.00003	
					(0.0044)			(0.00016)	
Arms imports from the US (proxy defense link)	+ (prop 2)	0.0007**	0.0006**	0.0018**	0.0007**	**yes**	5.93 e-06**	6.6 e-06**	**yes**
		(0.00032)	(0.0003)	(0.0007)	(0.0003)		(2.66 e-06)	(2.5 e-06)	
Political risk	– (prop 3a)	– 0.0087*	– 0.0026	–	0.0320**	**yes-P3d**	0.00002	–	
		(0.0053)	(0.0054)		(0.0111)		(0.00002)		
Economic risk	+ (prop 3b)	–	–	0.0084**	– 0.0753**	**yes-P3d**	–	–	

(continued)

Table 7.4 (continued)

	Expectation	*M4A*	*M4B*	*M4C*	*M4D*	*support*	*M5A*	*M5B*	*support*
				(0.0108)	(0.0179)				
Democracy	+ (prop 5)	–	–	–	–		–	–	
Infant mortality rate	+ (prop 5)	– 0.0218	– 0.0160	– 0.0164	– 0.0207		0.0003**	0.0003**	**yes**
		(0.0158)	(0.0170)	(0.0167)	(0.0192)		(0.0001)	(0.0001)	
Arms imports from NATO ptrs (proxy defense links)	+ (prop 2)	0.0020**	0.0019**	0.0019**	0.0022**	**yes**	9.71 e-06**	9.68 e-06**	**yes**
		(0.0007)	(0.0007)	(0.0007)	(0.0008)		(4.71 e-06)	(4.1 e-06)	
Arms imports from global partners (proxy defense links)	+ (prop 2)	0.0057**	0.0058**	0.0057**	–	**yes**	0.00001	–	
		(0.0022)	(0.0020)	(0.0003)			(9.52 e-06)		
Years since COE established		–	–	–	–		–	– 0.0002	
								(0.0002)	
Lag of military expenditures	control	0.00006**	0.00006**	0.00006**	0.0006**		1.15 e-06**	2.2 e-07**	
		(9.04 e-06)	(0.00001)	(0.00001)	(0.0001)		(7.18 e-08)	(1.24 e-07)	
Constant		7.5739**	7.9296**	7.9169**	7.8583**		0.0109**	0.0142**	
		(0.3146)	(0.4324)	(0.4338)	(0.5536)		(0.0035)	(0.0029)	
#		552	552	552	564		578	578	
R-square		0.7367	0.7536	0.7553	0.7526		0.1924	0.1989	

	Expectation	*M4A*	*M4B*	*M4C*	*M4D*	*support*	*M5A*	*M5B*	*support*
Clustering		country	country	country	county		country	country	

Source author's creation, Standard errors in parentheses, $*p > .10$; $**p > .05$

but gives way to the number of current partners secured through a new partner indicates in the post-cold war distance mattered less than perceptions of the territory at risk, in a holistic view. Model 5 uses the same dependent variable as model 2 truncating the time period and adds risk variables. In alterative versions of model 5, US DSA were dominated by US arms importations though the direct correlation is less than 0.2. Also, including and excluding, previous year military spending permits a comparison of R-square to determine how much variation in the dependent variable is explained through inclusion. The R-square is larger for models using the logarithm of military spending, than the percentage target (though over 35% of variance can be explained in the percent target) with the included specifications. The R-squares from the logarithm of military spending models indicate an impressive 2/3 to ¾ of the variation explained through the models—and less than 10% is explained by the previous year's military spending. The last model includes information on COE hosting behavior.

Appendix materials (Appendix B) offer readers instructions to develop figures illustrating implications from estimated models. With regression models, the calculations are the sum of the effects of the parameter or coefficient results (βs) multiplied by the average for continuous OR the mode for binary variables plus the constant (α) of military spending. Illustrative figures from model results are presented from the next set of models because joint predicted probabilities are more complicated to compute in multiple equation binary choice models than estimated effects from regression models. Many statistical programs offer hard-wired commands for marginal effects after running a regression, and such options are not available for most simultaneous equation models.

Modeling Middle/Second Level NATO Partners—Participation in a New Operation

The second set of models inserts itself in the literature on middle powers in II dominated by qualitative studies (Zyla, 2015, 2016); this section offers an improved model linking the econometric specification to middle power arguments. This analysis uses a statistical technique to identify the members shouldering/middle/burdens within the data to examine the variation in the likelihood a partner contributes. If the argument is supported, then a group of states only distinguishable by larger variation in the likelihood they participate in an operation is identifiable.[3] Members with the least military capabilities and most capabilities should offer average probabilities of participating with little variation, i.e., persistent.

The heteroskedastic probit is an econometric solution to identifying 'middle power' behavior within NATO. If the claim is correct—then middle powers have larger variation in behavior due to them systematically accepting punctual participation as missions grew and mandates changed. So, the errors around the prediction of their likelihood of participating in a new operation should be non-uniform per the standard probit assumption. (Recalling in statistics, a sequence of random data is persistent (i.e., homoscedastic) if all have the same limited variance; also known as homoscedastic variance.) However, middle powers have larger variation around the average likelihood they participate distinguishing them from others over time. Few statistical models (even in recent research) systematically consider heterogeneity across partners econometrically though much research points to partner differences affecting participation behavior. Measures of risks and security threats, identifying constraints shaping the variance around average behavior, are integrated along US DSA and enlargement progression to develop the model. These analyses use a new dependent variable, if a NATO partner participates in a new crisis/conflict operation. The data are coded from troop allocations indicated in public sources collected for this research. Crisis and conflict operations are NATO's activities at crisis management.

Table 7.5 illustrates the chronological overlap of EU and NATO operations identifying years with multiple new missions. NATO activities appear first then EU missions, there were multiple years when European partners choose from over two missions. Years of NATO enlargement are indicated in bold, recalling the foreign policy action is the partner choice to participate in a new NATO operation.[4]

Kimball and Lewis (2010, 2011) identified the variety of activities undertaken by II[5] in response to crises. They include: peace making (a third party helps the belligerents to work effectively together to develop a viable peace agreement) and peace building (any activity conducted at different levels (elite, intermediate, grassroots), designed to encourage non-hostile attitudes and the strengthening of cooperative relationships across common lines-activities include negotiations, workshops, and local peace commissions); peace keeping and peace enforcement (large-scale military interventions in a third country with the stated objective of maintaining or restoring local, regional or international peace and security by ending violent conflict); mediation and conflict management;

Table 7.5 Timeline overlap of NATO & EU Operations since 1990

Year	*NATO Ops*	*NATO Ops*	*EU Ops*	*Location*	*EU Ops*	*Location*	*New Ops*
1990							0
1991	Sourthern Guard						1
1992	Maritime Monitor						1
1993							0
1994	Deny Flight						1
1995	IFOR						1
1996	SFOR						1
1997							0
1998							0
1999	Allied FOR I (Albania) Essential Harvest	AFOR II KFOR					4
2000							0
2001	Amber Fox Active Endeavour	Eagle Assist					3
2002							0
2003	ISAF		EU Concordia (fYRM)		EU Artemis	DR Congo	3
2004	NTMI (Iraq) *Peace Support*		ALTHEA (B-H)				
			EUFORII (Sarejevo)		EUFORI (Sarejevo)		4
2005							0
2006			EUFOR (DR Congo)				1
2007			EUPOL	DR Congo			1
2008			EUFOR	CAR/Chad	ATALANTA - EUNAVFOR (Somalia)		2
2009	Ocean Shield		EUMM (Georgia)				3
2010			EUTM-Somalia				1

(continued)

Table 7.5 (continued)

Year	*NATO Ops*	*NATO Ops*	*EU Ops*	*Location*	*EU Ops*	*Location*	*New Ops*
2011							0
2012	Active Fence						1
2013			EUTM (Mali)		EUSEC (DR Congo)		2
2014			EUFOR	CAR			1
2015			EUMAM-CAR				1
2016	Sea Guardian		EUTM - CAR				2
2017							0
2018	NMI (Iraq)						1
2019							0
2020			EUNAVOR MED				1

Source author's creation

conflict prevention and rule of law; peace observation and monitoring; and disarmament, demobilization, and reintegration of conflicting parties (i.e., DDR). Disarmament is the collection, inspection and disposal of small arms, ammunition, explosive devices and heavy weapons in the hands of combatants, as well as weapons used by civilians. Demobilization is the process through which combatants leave military life and return to civilian life. Disarmament is a prerequisite for this process, allowing ex-combatants to receive the various benefits intended to facilitate reintegration into society. Reintegration (or reinsertion) consists of assistance measures (financial compensation, vocational training programs and income-generating activities) to promote the socio-economic reintegration of ex-combatants. The tables update previous compilations (Kimball & Lewis, 2010, 2011).

An examination of IO behavior in Table 7.6 from 1990 to 2020 shows NATO acts in crises and conflicts after IO or states failed to improve the situation, e.g., Kosovo, Bosnia-Herzegovina. These tables offer historical cases with ongoing operations bringing the data a step further. Of 163 crisis (Table 7.6) and conflict (Table 7.7) interventions by the UN, NATO, EU, OSCE, ASEAN, African Union and Economic Community of Western African States (ECOWAS) since 1949, *NATO acts in less*

Table 7.6 IO activities in crises, 34 ongoing of 99 total in bold; *original data*

***Ongoing** activities = 33*		***total** IO activities = 99*	
Country	**IO**	**Name**	**Ongoing (mandate start–end)**
Albania	OSCE	OSCE Presence in Albania	**1 (1997)**
	NATO	AFOR I & II	0 (1999)
Angola	UN	MONUA	0 (1997–1999)
	UN	UNAVEM I	0 (1989–1991)
	UN	UNAVEM II	0 (1993–1995)
	UN	UNAVEM III	0 (1995–1997)
Armenia	OSCE	Office in Yerevan	0 (2000–2017)
Azerbaïdjan	OSCE	Office in Bakou	0 (1999–2015)
	OSCE	Office in Minsk	0 (2003–2010)
	OSCE	Advisory and Monitoring Gr in Belaus	0 (1998–2002)
Bosnia-Herzegovina	NATO	DENY FLIGHT	0 (1993–1995)
	UN	UNMIBH	0 (1995–2002)
	NATO	SFOR	0 (1996–2004)
	EU	EUPMBH (police mission)	0 (2004–2012)
	EU	EUFOR-ALTHEA	**1 (2004)**
	UN	UNPROFOR	0 (1992–1995)
	OSCE	OSCE Mission in B-H	**1 (1995)**
Burundi	UN	BINUB (political)	**1 (2007)**
	UN	ONUB	0 (2004–2006)
	African Union	AMIB	0 (2003–2004)
Cambodia	UN	UNTAC	0 (1992–1993)
	UN	UNAMIC	0 (1991–1992)
Columbia	UN	UNVMC	**1 (2017)**
Croatia	UN	UNPSG	0 (jan 1998–oct 1998)
	UN	UNTAES	0 (1996–1998)

Ongoing *activities = 33*		***total*** *IO activities = 99*	
	UN	UNMOP	0 (1996–2002)
	UN	UNCRO	0 (1995–1996)
	UN	UNPROFOR	0 (1992–1995)
	OSCE	Office in Zagreb	**1 (2008)**
	OSCE	Mission to Croatia	0 (1996–2007)
Cyprus	UN	UNFICYP	**1 (1964)**
Egypt	UN	MFO	**1 (1981)**
El Salvador	UN	ONUSAL	0 (1991–1995)
Estonia	OSCE	Mission to Estonia	0 (1993–2001)
	OSCE	Representative to Military Penssioner commision	0 (1994–2006)
Georgia	OSCE	Mission to Georgia	0 (1992–2008)
Guatamala	UN	MINUGUA	0 (1997)
Haïti	UN	MINUSTAH	0 (2004–2017)
	UN	BINUH	**1 (2019)**
	UN	MINUJUSTH	0 (2017–2019)
	UN	MIPONUH	0 (1997–2000)
	UN	UNTMIH	0 (1997)
	UN	UNSMIH	0 (1998–1997)
	UN	UNMIH	0 (1993–1996)
Indonesia	EU/ASEAN	MSA	0 (2005–2006)
Iraq	UN	UNIKOM	0 (1991–2003)
	UN	UNAMI	**1 (2003)**
	NATO	NMI	**1 (2018)**
	NATO	NTM-I	0 (2004–2011)

(continued)

Table 7.6 (continued)

Ongoing *activities = 33*		***total*** *IO activities = 99*	
Jamaica	**UN**	**Jamaica Violence Prevention, Peace and Sustainable Development (JVPPSD) Programme**	**0 (2008–2011)**
Kazakhstan	OSCE	Program office in Nur-Sultan	**1 (1998)**
Kosovo	UN	UNMIK	**1 (1999)**
	NATO	IFOR	0 (1995–1996)
	NATO	KFOR	**1 (1999)**
	EU	EULEX-Kosovo	**1 (2008)**
	OSCE	Mission to Kosovo	**1 (1999)**
	OSCE	Mission of Long Duration Kosovo	0 (1992–1993)
	OSCE	Kosovo verification mission	0 (1998–1999)
Kuwait	UN	UNIKOM	0 (1991–2003)
Kyrgyzstan	OSCE	Program office in Bishkek	**1 (1998)**
Latvia	OSCE	Mission to Latvia	0 (1993–2001)
	OSCE	Skrunda Radar station	0 (1995–1999)
Moldova	OSCE	Mission to Moldova	**1 (1993)**
Montenegro	OSCE	Mission to Montenegro	**1 (2005)**
	OSCE	Mission of Long Duration Sanjak	0 (1992–1993)
Maroc	UN	MINURSO	**1 (1991)**
	UN	ONUMOZ	0 (1992–1994)
Niger	UN/AU/ECOWAS	Mission conjointe ONU/UA/CEDEAO à Niamey (development)	**1 (2009)**
North Macedonia	OSCE	Mission to Skopje	**1 (1992)**
	UN	UNPREDEP	0 (1995–1999)
	NATO	ESSENTIAL HARVEST	0 (2001)
	NATO	AMBER FOX	0 (2001–2002)

Ongoing *activities = 33*		***total*** *IO activities = 99*	
	EU	Concordia fYROM	0 (2003)
Papua New Guinea	UN	UN Bougainville Programme & Nation building through crisis prevention and recovery (development)	**1 (2008)**
Russia	OSCE	Assistance Group to Chechnya	0 (1995–1998)
Rwanda	UN	UNOMUR	0 (1993–1994)
Senegal	UN	UNOWAS	**1 (2002)**
Serbia	OSCE	Mission to Serbia	**1 (2001)**
	OSCE	Mission of Long Duration Vojvodina	0 (1992–1993)
	OSCE	Personal Representative for Peace in B-H	0 (1995–2015)
Sierra Leone	OSCE	UNOMSIL	0 (1999–2005)
Syria	NATO	ACTIVE FENCE (air)	**1 (2012)**
Tadjikistan	OSCE	Program Office in Dushanbe	**1 (1994)**
	UN	UNMOT	0 (1994–2000)
Turkménistan	OSCE	Centre in Ashagabat	**1 (1998)**
Uganda	UN	UNOMUR	0 (1993–1994)
Ukraine	OSCE	Mission to Ukraine	0 (1994–1999)
	OSCE	Special Monitoring Mission to Ukraine	**1 (2014)**
	OSCE	Project Co-ordinator in Ukraine	**1 (1994)**
	OSCE	Observer mission at Russian Checkpoints in Gukovo & Donetsk	0 (2014–2021)
US	NATO	EAGLE ASSIST	0 (2001)
Uzbeckistan	OSCE	Project Co-ordinator in Uzbeckistan	**1 (2006)**
	OSCE	Liason office in Central Asia	0 (1995–2000)
Yemen	UN	UNMHA	**1 (2019)**
Med Sea	NATO	SOUTHERN GUARD	0 (1991)

(continued)

Table 7.6 (continued)

Ongoing *activities = 33*		***total*** *IO activities = 99*	
Adriatic Sea	NATO	MARITIME MONITOR	0 (1992–1993)
Med Sea	NATO	ACTIVE ENDEAVOR	0 (2001–2016)
Med Sea	NATO	SEA GUARDIAN	**1 (2016)**
Med Sea	EU	EUNAVFOR MED	**1 (2020)**
Total active			34
Total			99

Source author's creation

Table 7.7 IO activities in conflicts since 1948, 21 ongoing of 64 total in bold; *original data*

***Ongoing** conflicts (from 1949) with IO activities: 21*

Country	**Nature (Inter/Intrastate)**	**OI**	**Name**	**Period**
Afghanistan	Inter	UN	UNGOMAP	1988–1990
	Intra	UN	UNAMA	2002-until March 2023
	Intra	UN	ISAF	2001–2003
		NATO	ISAF	2003–2014
		NATO	RESOLUTE SUPPORT	2015–2021
		EU	EUPOL	2007–2016
Central Africa	Intra	UN	MINURCA	1998–2000
		UN	BONUCA	2000–2010
		UN	BINUCA	2010–2014
		UN	MINUSCA	2014–2022
		African Union	MISCA	2013–2014
		ECOWAS	MICOPAX	2008–2013
		ECOWAS	FOMUC	2002–2008
		EU	EUFOR	**2004–**
Chad		UN	UNOSOG	1994
DR Congo	Intra	UN	ONUC	1960–1964
		UN	MONUC	1999–2010
		UN	MONUSCO	**2010–**
		EU	Artimus	2003
		EU	EUPOL	2007–2014
		EU	EUSEC	2005–2016
East Timor	Inter	UN	UNTAET	1999–2002
		UN	UNMISET	2002–2005
		UN	UNMIT	2006–2012
Ethiopia		UN	UNMEE	1999–2010
Georgia - S. Ossetia	Inter	CTSO	JPKF	**1994–**
Georgia - Abkhasia		CTSO	CPKF	**1994–**
		UN	UNOMIG	1993–2009

(continued)

Table 7.7 (continued)

***Ongoing** conflicts (from 1949) with IO activities: 21*				
		EU	EUMM	**2008–**
India		UN	UNMOGIP	**1949–**
Israël	Intra	UN	UNTSO	**1948–**
		UN	UNDOF	**1974–**
	Inter	UN	UNIFIL mandat +	**2006–**
Ivory Coast	Intra	UN	UNOCI	2009–2017
Kazakhstan		CSTO	peacekeeping	2022
Lebanon	Intra	UN	UNIFIL	**1978–**
Liberia	Intra	UN	UNOMIL	1993–1997
		UN	UNMIL	2003–2018
Libya		UN	UNSMIL	**2011–**
Mali		UN	MINUSMA	**2013–**
		EU	EUTM	**2013–**
Mexico	Intra	EU	PRODESIS	2004–2008
Nepal	Intra	UN	MINUNEP	2007–2010
Pakistan		UN	UNGOMAP	1988–1990
		UN	UNMOGIP	**1949–**
Rwanda		UN	UNAMIR	1993–1996
Sierra Leone	Intra	UN	UNOMSIL	1998–1999
		UN	MINUSIL	1999–2005
		UN	BINUSIL	2005–2008
		UN	UNIPSIL	2008–2014
Somalia	Intra	UN	UNOSOM I	1992–1993
		UN	UNOSOM II	1993–1995
		EU	EUNAFOR	2007–2008
Somalia-Horn *of Africa*		EU	OP ATALANTA (EUNAVFOR)	**2008–**
		African Union	AMISOM	2007–2022
		African Union	ATMIS	**2022–**
		UN	UNSOS	**2015–**
		UN	UNSOM	**2013–**

(continued)

Table 7.7 (continued)

Ongoing *conflicts (from 1949) with IO activities: 21*				
Somalia-Horn *of Africa*		NATO	OCEAN SHIELD	**2009–**
Sudan	Intra	UN	UNMIS	2005–2011
		UN	UNMISS	**2011–**
		UN	UNISFA	**2011–**
		UN	UNITAMS	**2020–**
		African Union/UN	UNAMID	2007–2020
Total **active**				21
Total				64

Source author's creation

than 12%. Currently, Mali, Somalia, Bosnia-Herzegovina, North Macedonia and Kosovo invite missions from multiple IO, while the only II in Ukraine since 1994 is the OSCE. From 1990–2020, Afghanistan, Burundi, Croatia, Central African Republic, Democratic Republic of the Congo, Georgia, Iraq and Sudan invited multiple IO to manage conflicts and/or crises. The UN acts in 28 of 55 current conflicts and crisis. The EU leads missions in four conflict areas and three crises in 2022. The OSCE leads 15 of 26 crisis interventions (55%). The UN leads missions in eight conflict and six crisis environments. NATO is involved in two crisis operations (located in states-Kosovo, Iraq (KFOR & NMI)) and three regional ops (Air Police, ACTIVE ENDEAVOR, SEA GUARDIAN) for 5 of the 55 (9%).[6] Enhanced Forward Presence is a NATO mission within partners exposed to territorial threats—in response to the Ukraine crisis.

This research explores members' differences analytically. It considers threats facing individual partners and constraints distinguishing the chances they participate in a new club operation. Examining how partners collaborate to provide the common goods of the institution, i.e., collective defense, cooperative security and crisis management beyond quantitative models of military spending (i.e., the 'collective defense target'), this book offers probabilistic choice models of partner participation in a new operation (i.e., crisis management) accounting for differences in capacity, COE investment (i.e., cooperative security) and threats. This portion of the research brings together the quantitative analytical with qualitative descriptive literatures on burden sharing with that on middle powers.

The literature on middle powers (henceforth, MP) identifies a discursive and substantive group of states distinguished by certain behaviors (Cooper, 2016; de Sá Guimarães & de Almeida, 2017; Jongryn, 2015; Jordaan, 2003; Patience, 2018; Shin, 2016; Ungerer, 2007),

> Middle powers (however defined) obviously cannot do some of the things that great powers can do. On the other hand, they *can* do things that smaller powers can *not* do…In sum, having middling capabilities, determines, not what middle powers will do, but what, in principle, they *can* do (Stairs in (Booth, 1998, p. 275), emphasis in original)

The Canadian Prime Minister Mackenzie King in 1943 demanded MP representation in the post-war institutions "on a functional basis which will admit (…) those countries large or small which have the greatest contribution to make to the particular object in question," (Holbraad, 1984, p. 57). Having failed to make the MP status recognized at the UN, "'middle power' became essentially a self-elected post for many states," (Neack et al., 1995, p. 225). The mixture of perception and political context internalized by scholars within those states creating a research program to support this explanation of foreign policy behavior. However, the absence of theoretical development in MP studies creates ideographic discussions of the foreign policies of self-identified MPs (Neack, 1993; Neack et al., 1995). Some argue "from the outset 'middle power theory' is not a theoretical framework nor a methodological approach," (Neack et al., 1995, p. 224) contending states take on roles because they are understood as those of MP. Moreover, "a great deal of scholarship on middle powers has been atheoretical and descriptive… is methodologically unsophisticated," (Neack et al., 1995, p. 227). Canada, Australia, South Korea, India, Brazil, South Africa, Malaysia, Indonesia and Mexico are some attributed MP status by scholars (Burges, 2013; Carr, 2014; Chapnick, 2000; Macdonald & Paltiel, 2016). Zyla refers to both MPs and second-tier 'powers' within NATO (2015, 2016).

MP behavioral claims refer, not only to the choice of behavior, but also to the regularity with which they engage in such behaviors. MP, as second-tier partners, maintain a steady 'contribution' to collective defense on average, yet be willing to step-up and over contribute during a crisis/conflict (Dorussen et al., 2009). This suggests a model accounting for not only the choice an actor makes but the variation around said choice so a subclass of binary outcome probabilistic models is employed, i.e., the heteroskedastic probit. The variation in the contribution behavior of MPs is larger compared to top and bottom contributors. To motivate the linkage between the claims and the econometric model, an example by Clark and Nordstrom (2005) is mobilized. Those authors shared an interest in how 'constraints' affect foreign policy choice. In particular, how domestic political institutions influence decisions to use force by different types of democratic states examining nature of the executive as essential to foreign policy choice (Clark & Nordstrom, 2005, p. 256). This research examines the factors influencing the chances a state participates in a new NATO operation. The models analyze if threats, informational advantages, hosting a NATO COE and 'free-riding' influence decisions to participate. It tests factors examined in the military spending models indicating consistency even while changing dependent variables and reducing time periods. Finally, the functional capacity to study MP claims using a theoretically motivated econometric technique offers another contribution of the book.

The following section offers the motivation for the econometric model estimated drawn from expected utility theory, also known as decision theory (Bueno de Mesquita, 1980; Bueno de Mesquita & Lalman, 1992), where actors pick the option maximizing their utility.[7] Readers not familiar with formal motivations for empirical models are encouraged to consult fundamental contributions (Bueno de Mesquita, 2005; Bueno de Mesquita et al., 1999; Evans et al., 1993; Milner, 1997; A. Smith, 1995, 1996). This model is articulated around an actor's expected utility from implementing a foreign policy action (participating in a conflict/crisis operation) with some probability of success but at a cost associated with the internal constraints on implementing the policy action for the actor (Linde, 2020). If costs are zero, then the actor decides across outcomes based on their utility and the chances of success. On the other hand, if costs, measured as constraints matter, they affect policy choice. Novice readers are invited to advance 2.5 pages after the following block detailing the expected utility model in linkage to the econometric model.

In an expected utility model for the decision of an actor, A, its expected utility, ω, for foreign policy action, i, would be a function of her utility (u) for the foreign policy action, the probability it succeeds (p), and costs associated (C) with the constraints on implementing the policy (Clark & Nordstrom, 2005, p. 257), here constraints are based on military capacity and risk. It is assumed actors are neutral with respect to their contributions.

$$\omega_{A,i} = ui^* p_i + [(1 - u_i)^* (1 - p_i)] - C \qquad (7.1)$$

Since an actor is trying the maximize $\omega_{A,i}$ when the costs of pursuing policy i increase, then her expected utility for the policy falls. In the absence of constraints, C, the actor chooses policy i if the first term is larger than the second. Here, it is assumed the effect of C depends only on the existence of C, as there is no account for how any variability in C or the willingness of an actor under certain conditions to disregard C might affect behavior.

Suppose, actors differ concerning how much they are constrained by those constraints, C. Imagine actors differ with respect to their orientation toward 'the crisis,' δ, where some actors will be prone to contribute and others less likely to contribute for unknown reasons. And, furthermore, those constraints affect actors differently depending on their orientation toward the crisis itself, δ ($0 < \delta_A < +\infty$). Thus,

$$\omega_{A,i} = ui^* p_i + [(1 - u_i)^* (1 - p_i)] - (C/\delta_A) \qquad (7.2)$$

The probability of any action is

$$Pr(i) = Pr[(ui^* p_i + [(1 - u_i)^* (1 - p_i)]) > (C/\delta_A)] \qquad (7.3)$$

When actors are oriented toward a crisis $\delta > 1$, the effects of constraints are overwhelmed by their willingness to engage. In contrast, when actors are indifferent with respect to a crisis, $\delta = 1$, then 'domestic' constraints act as actual constraints on policy choice. However, if actors are averse to a crisis then $\delta < 1$ and the effects of constraints inhibit her capacity to implement policy, i, then it will be observed with significant coefficients. The last term represents action costs over 'willingness/constraints to act'—in the presence of constraints it will be less than one and increase costs, thus affecting the probability a state participates. It is important to note standard statistical treatments assume $\delta = 1$, or the model is homoscedastic estimating, i.e., a probit (which assumes $\delta = 1$) and, thus, do not control for how constraints affect foreign policy choice. If the process is heteroskedastic then, the probit produces incorrect estimates affecting the model's inferences.[8]

Thus, constraints affect the average of the probability actors contribute in a crisis. However, if constraints within MPs affect the average chance a partner participates because MPs will, otherwise, behave consistently. The econometric model subsequently is:

$$Pr(i) = \Phi(C'\beta/\delta) + \varepsilon \tag{7.4}$$

where the β parameter represents the effect of constraints, *C*, on the mean of the probability actors respond to crisis, *i*, ε is a normally distributed error terms and δ represents the actor's orientation toward crisis. Thus, a probit estimated with a modification of parameterizing δ as a function of constraints so $\delta = e^{z'y}$:

$$Pr(i) = \Phi(C'\beta/e^{z'y}) + \varepsilon \tag{7.5}$$

The equation can be estimated with a heteroskedastic probit;[9] likelihood function is

$$\mathrm{Ln}\, L = \sum_{i=1}^{n} y_i \ln\, \Phi(X'\beta/\sigma) + (1 - y_i)\ln[1 - \Phi(X'\beta/\sigma)] \tag{7.6}$$

which is similar to formula 7.4. The parameterization of σ in the heteroskedastic model is the same as the parameterization of δ above, as $e^{z'y}$, so one can model the effects of constraints on the variance in *Pr(i)*, i.e., the probability a state participates in a crisis/conflict operation. If the variance term does not equal 1, the estimated of β will shift as well, demonstrating non-consistency among the errors of the probit producing possibly both inconsistent and/or inefficient estimates.

The vector or set of constraints *(C)* shaping the variance in the likelihood a partner participates a given crisis, *Pr(i)*, is influenced by factors differentiating club members institutionally and along willingness and capacity to contribute. For example, partners may forego troop allocations to a new a crisis/conflict operation, if they are hosting/sponsoring a COE (e.g., investing in another club asset—budget trade-offs), undergoing national elections or seeking to free-ride. The top four alliance contributors have increased variation in the chances they participate compared to others. The final factor separates the most powerful and weakest partners, systematically due to contribution consistency by powerful partners (no variation around the average chances they participate) and the rare, but substantial, jumps in the probability of participation by the smallest partners (based on willingness). If the constraints on partners have no effect then, the coefficients will not be significant and the model collapses into a standard probability choice model, a probit, where the likelihood a partner participates in a mission are calculated based on the factors identified in the probability stage of the model. This would indicate MP are not distinguishable from great powers or small states concerning the chances they participate in a new operation.

The set of factors shaping a partner's average likelihood of participating in a crisis/conflict operation include threats, informational improvement, the opportunities for contributions, military spending and arms imports by the US. The probit could offer biased predictions if the constraints 'identified' are significant, resulting in either over or under predicting the probability a partner participates. That being said, comparing the model results (a.k.a. coefficients) offers only partial insight as the predicted probabilities are conditioned (i.e., divided) by the set of factors included in the variance portion if factors are significant (the case concerning three factors) and the mean/mode of the estimated factor in the model exceeds 1, as is the case with one factor. The result offers visual evidence of a potential for over and under estimations with econometric models excluding important factors when correcting the estimation procedure for the effects of constraints.

Partner participation in operations receives special attention in the burden sharing literature. It is measured herein by troop allocations as a binary indicator of operation participation. Having previously presented original data on operations by II, the analyses focuses on state-level participation in NATO operations covering 55 past and ongoing missions drawn from the 163 intervention activities since 1949 by all IO. Each model examines about 760 cases at the state-level. Since 1949, an average of two activities per year are launched by II. The sample includes the 12 current missions by NATO and the EU as well as completed missions by both; if a NATO partner contributed to the policy action *(i)*, i.e., the dependent variable. There are 34 operations included over three decades. It is notable multiple operations (as many as four) started in the same year, creating opportunities for trade-offs by constrained European partners. Years with multiple missions were 1999, 2001, 2003, 2004, 2008, 2009, 2013 and 2016. The set of Constraints *(C)* affecting the inconsistency around the average partner contribution is influenced by whether it has a **COE involvement, national elections and top contributing status**. A partner's decision to participate in an operation is a result of military spending, threats, the number of operation opportunities, arms imports by the US and the effects of the informational advantage acquired through US bilateral DSA. The factors newly tested include original threat measures, information, COE sponsorship and if trade-offs increase with operation numbers.

$$\begin{aligned}\text{Mean P}\big(\text{Contribute to a new Op}\big) = {} & \alpha + \beta_1 \text{threats} \\ & + \beta_2 \text{information improvement (via US DSA)} \\ & + \beta_3 \text{arms imports from the US} \\ & - \beta_4 \text{COE sponsorship} \\ & \pm \beta_5 \text{arms imports from NATO partners} \\ & + \beta_6 \text{number of new Ops} + \varepsilon_{\text{I}} \qquad (7.7)\end{aligned}$$

$$\begin{aligned}\text{Variance P}\big(\text{Contribute to a new Op}\big) = {} & \beta_1 \text{Top four contributor} \\ & - \beta_2 \text{COE sponsor/host} \\ & - \beta_3 \text{election government seat percentage} \\ & - \beta_4 \text{'exploitation'} + \varepsilon_{\text{I}} \qquad (7.8)\end{aligned}$$

Table 7.8 offers probit and heteroskedastic probit models in comparison. The models offer support arguments proposed about threats and informational advantages, while the figures illustrate the difference in predicted probabilities between the probit and its counterpart that accounts for factors differentiating partners shaping the consistency of the average probability a partner participates. The risk management model of burden sharing proposes states examine signals reducing uncertainty, such as those from bilateral US DSA. The analyses of military spending and state participation in a new NATO operation support the informational advantages accrued with US DSA—partners with more DSA spend more on their respective militaries and are likely participate. Therefore, figures are plotted across the number of DSA per year signed by a partner.

Table 7.8 presents results comparing the heteroskedastic to the probit model. One of NATO's central mandates is crisis management, so if a partner participates in a NATO crisis/conflict operation offers another measure for testing NATO burden sharing. The model examines arguments drawn from theoretical approaches—threats, informational advantage, the effects of COE hosting, and the exploitation claim. Two probits are offered in support of claims. Threats, measured by inter-capital distance from a partner's national to the capital of the conflict/crisis country, decrease the chances a state participates. The number of operations per year increases the likelihood of participation. When constraints

Table 7.8 Probit and heteroskedastic probit, P(participation in new NATO operation) from 1990; ***new model & dependent variable***

		Probit		*Het Probit*	*Probit*		*Het Probit*	*Probit*	*Het Probit*
		M1.a	M1.b	M1	M1.a	M1.b	M2	M2	M3
P (Contri-bution to new Op)									
'threat' (geographic exposure)	(–)	– 0.0000729**	– 0.0000752**	– 0.0000617**	– 0.0000893**	– 0.0000681**	– 0.0000608***	– 0.000079**	–0.000016**
		(0.000024)	(0.0000243)	(0.0000232)	(0.000023)	(0.0000235)	(0.0000193)	(0.0000243)	(0.00000232)
Informational improvement (US DSA)	(+)	0.0011400	0.0012835	0.06566**	0.0797696**	0.0565819**	0.0441936*	0.0560917*	0.0656176**
		(0.00086)	(0.0008689)	(0.029955)	(0.0263301)	(0.0286633)	(0.0241383)	(0.0285844)	(0.0299038)
Arms imports - US	(+)	0.00096**	0.0007313**	0.0010962**	0.0010661**	0.0009755**	0.000766**	0.0009491**	0.010945**
		(0.000242)	(0.002696)	(0.0002406)	(0.0002315)	(0.0002359)	(0.0002145)	(0.0002369)	(0.0002405)
Arms imports - (non-US) NATO partners	(+)	–	0.0007998**	–	–	–	–	–	–0.001214
			(0.0004131)			–			(0.0056098)
N of new Ops	(+)	0.4062536**	0.4147983**	0.375653**	0.3941698**	0.4095201**	0.2959806**	0.4168779**	0.3752833**

		Probit		*Het Probit*	*Probit*		*Het Probit*	*Probit*	*Het Probit*
		(0.04921)	(0.049689)	(0.05466)	(0.0491426)	(0.0499372)	(0.0522245)	(0.0501933)	(0.0546709)
COE sponsor/host	(–)	– 0.9888126**	– 1.021489**	–	–	– 0.9465984**	–	– 0.9218418**	–
		(0.193412)	(0.195637)			(0.190259)		(0.1954109_)	
military spending	(+)	0.000000177**	0.000000126**	0.0000005	0.00000129**	0.00000143**	0.000000327	0.00000136**	0.0000000511
		(0.000000498)	(0.000000564)	(0.000000640)	(0.00000456)	(0.000000638)	(0.000000553)	(0.00000064)	(0.0000000656)
Constant		– 1.5073**	– 1.55477**	– 1.576651**	– 1.62732**	– 1.490187**	– 1.172728**	– 1.269159**	-1.576452**
		(0.13796)	(0.141455)	(0.1639)	(0.138544)	(0.1421288)	(0.1974494)	(0.1822484)	(0.1634065)
Variance P (Contribution to new Op)									
% electoral seats obtained by government		n/a	n/a	0.0072292	n/a	n/a	0.0505219	n/a	0.0033322
				(0.31094)			(0.3220535)		(0.3112236)
Top 4 NATO contributor	(+)	n/a	n/a	0.5337891*	n/a	n/a	0.3523678	n/a	0.5254296*

(continued)

Table 7.8 (continued)

		Probit		*Het Probit*	*Probit*		*Het Probit*	*Probit*	*Het Probit*
				(0.293379)			(0.03081068)		(0.02926331)
COE sponsor/host	(–)	n/a	n/a	– 0.6003489**	n/a	n/a	– 0.613061**	n/a	-0.5975421**
				(0.1389208)			(0.1477743)		(0.1394969)
'exploitation'	(–)	n/a	n/a	–	n/a	n/a	– 0.0309516**	n/a	–
							(0.012612)		
LR chi-square		136.4**	139.96**		111.19**	145.64**		149.23**	
Pseudo R-square		0.1872	0.1921		0.1526	0.1999		0.2048	
test sigma-squared = 0		n/a	n/a	20.29			26.68	n/a	19.69
Prob chi-square		n/a	n/a	0.0001**			0.0000**	n/a	0.0002**
N		759	759	759	759	759	759	759	759

Source author's creation, Standard error in parentheses, $^{*}p > .10$; $^{**}p > .05$

are included in the heteroskedastic model, then the effect of military spending is unrelated to whether a partner participates in an operation. One implication of that compared finding is the incorrect modeling technique can lead to type I or type II errors, in this case it would be a false positive relationship, relationship based on the probit model. It is likely the measure for top four contributor absorbs a portion of that variation as it is in the expected direction but unstable. COE hosting/sponsorship negatively influences the chances a state participates in a new operation. Arms imports from the US and NATO partners increase the chances a partner participates until the constraints are specified, then only US arms imports increase that probability. Finally, the informational advantages of US DSA increase the likelihood a partner participates as well in the constrained models and in the probit. These models support claims on exploitation and the strong substitution effect of hosting/sponsoring a COE. Once the exploitation measure is added, the influences of the informational advantage through US DSA are reduced but still significant though being a top contributor no longer affects the likelihood of participation. Both findings suggest further study, with alternative measures, is needed. The significance of factors in the variance portion and the test of sigma-squared[10] indicate the constrained models outperform the probit in both cases. The probit may over predict or under predict relative to the constrained model, therefore figures are helpful. Those below illustrate and discuss the over and under predictions. As is practice, figures vary an independent variable on the X axis across a continuum with the outcome, this factor should have a significant relationship with the chances a partner participates in a new operation.

The following figures are predicted probabilities plotted across increases in the number of bilateral DSA which vary from 0–13 in a given year. The probabilities are calculated using the averages for continuous variables and the mode for binary indicators, then evaluate on the normal distribution. Figure 7.1 illustrates the refinement from the heteroskedastic model compared to the probit. There is a level of DSA links (around 6 to 8) where a partner's chances of participating in a new operation converges near 100% and, moreover, that relationship offers a different linearity relative to the probit predictions on the same sample. In comparison, the probit under predicts the chances a state participates restraining it to less than 60%, while increasing the information in the model controlling for COE host/sponsorship, being a top contributor and the number

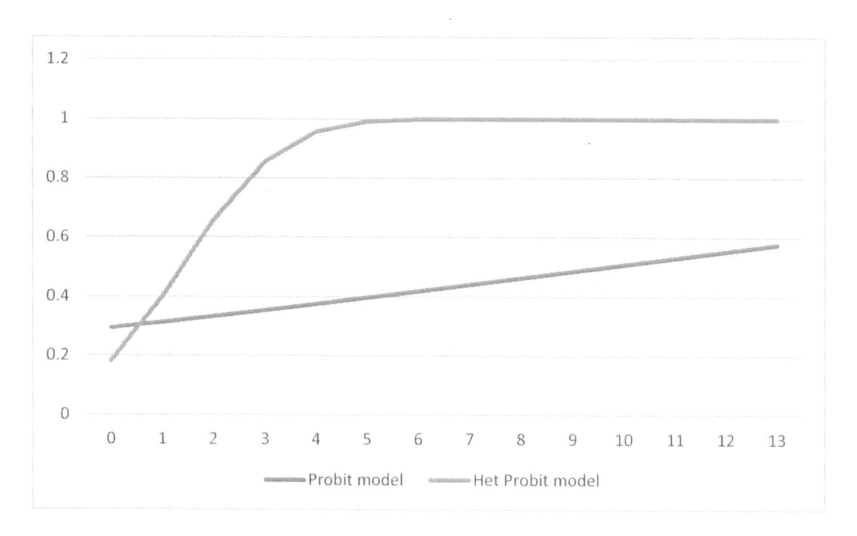

Fig. 7.1 Probit versus Heteroskedastic probit P(participation in new NATO operation) at mean/mode as US DSA rise

of partners having security increased through enlargement offer distinct measures to differentiate the models.

This Fig. 7.2 doubles the number of potential operations to four offering choices and trade-offs. Again, the probit under predicts the chances a partner participates as DSA increase. It illustrates the effects of increasing choice to multiple operations are much larger than in the constrained model. Probabilities for the model with factors set to averages/modes are included for comparison.

The final Fig. 7.3 in the series for model one offers comparisons of increasing various factors one standard deviation above the mean for military spending, US arms imports and exposure to Russia. Recalling these figures are drawing from the effects across all cases in the sample, and this sketch case of a partner with increased risks and US arms' imports could be Lithuania, for example. The challenges for small entrants to NATO joining after the Cold War have been examined by others (Männik, 2004; Marton & Eichler, 2013). The illustration indicates military spending and US arms imports offers greater effects than geostrategic concerns. One explanation is exploitation, whereby small partners are incentivized to not contribute, yet still receive the collective good. This exploitation

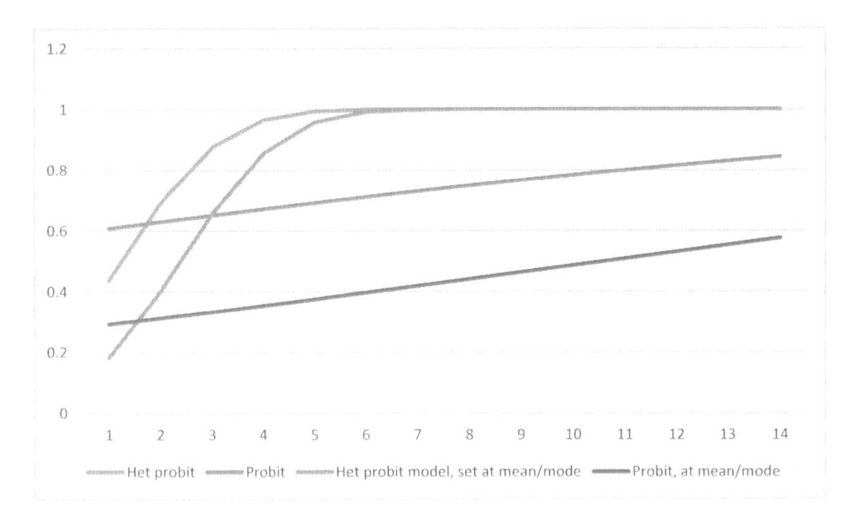

Fig. 7.2 Comparison of P(participation in new NATO operation) when four new Ops in a year, as US DSA rise

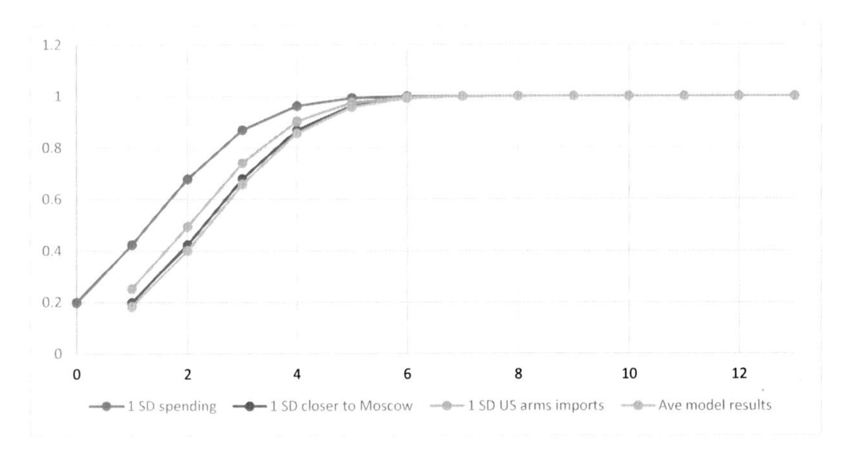

Fig. 7.3 Comparing heteroskedastic probit P(participation in new NATO operation) as DSA rise, plus a SD: threat exposure, military spending & US arms imports

argument, free-riding, is invoked in discourse and research as a central distributional issue for bargaining over burdens.

The exploitation claim, measured by how many partners' geographic security increased through each new partner joining, is supported by the analysis. States which increase the security of others in the club, by increasing the buffer between national capitals and Moscow, are less likely to exhibit inconsistency in the chances they participate since they should rarely contribute due to limited capacity. Moreover, the probit over predicts relative to its counterpart offering a probability at the high end of about one in two while the heteroskedastic model corrects to a likelihood of one in four.

This figure draws attention to the effects of COE hosting/sponsoring on participation a new operation. There is a strong negative relationship supporting resource allocation substitution arguments, recalling the US hosts two COE; the data measure burdens distinctly from previous research. The effect of sponsoring/hosting a new COE on the consistency of the likelihood a partner participates in an operation is substantial. Once the constraints of hosting a COE are accounted for, then the chances a partner contributes are much lower (less than 10%) while the standard model would over predict an implication of 50% probability.

The final figure of this model series illustrates how being a top four contributor affects the probability a partner contributes to a mission.

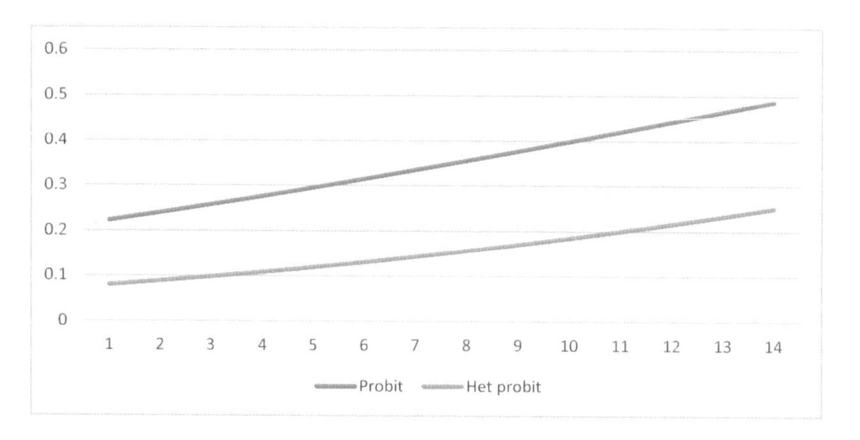

Fig. 7.4 Model 2-Probit versus heteroskedastic probit on P(participation in new NATO operation) as US DSA rise

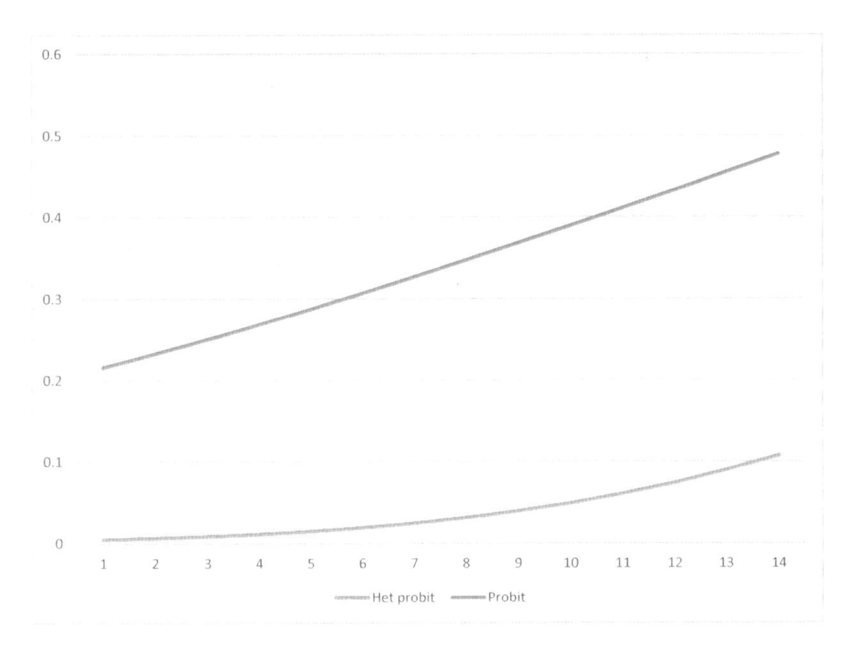

Fig. 7.5 Model 2-Comparing the effects of COE host/sponsorship on P(participation in new NATO operation) as US DSA rise

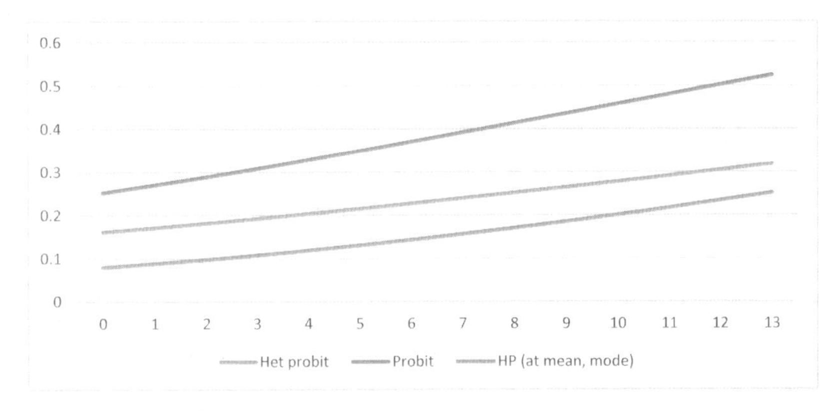

Fig. 7.6 Model 2-Top four contributor effect on P(participation in new NATO operation) as US DSA rise

Again, the standard model over predicts the probabilities relative to heteroskedastic counterpart offering a probability of almost one in two a partner participates when adjusted in the constrained model it reduces to less than one in three.[11]

The statistical models offer support partner constraints influence the variance in the chances a partner contributes to a new operation. Those constraints are COE sponsorship or hosting, being a top four contributor and seeking to free-ride through exploiting larger partners. The strong negative effects of COE hosting/sponsoring on the likelihood a state participates in an operation offer support to the argument they remain unexplored in the burden sharing literature and deserve in-depth study provided in the next section.

NATO—Manager of Stability: The Club in a Global System

The section tackles NATO, as an autonomous actor, with institutional assets and capacities contributing to defense, cooperative security and managing crises/conflicts compared to the UN and EU. Its relative role in II activities historically and globally was presented in Tables 7.5 through 7.7. The book discussed the institutions NATO designed to manage future uncertainty, internal and external, i.e., PFP as the pre-entry club (adds 20 states discussed earlier in the book) and, now, the sponsoring nation framework for intra-club goods (Kimball, 2019), known as NATO Centres of Excellence are examined in-depth. Institutional design differences between NATO and other 'security' actors affect the credibility and types of resources it offers. Institutional investments in identity-building and operational integration, training and exercising with partners results in a specialized defense product. "IOs are called to intervene where and when the big states fail…(and) are thus actors whose agency is granted and the powers delegated by states to carry out mandates," (Kimball, 2021a, p. 343). Moreover, the quantitative models offer a strong relationship between NATO COE hosting/sponsorship and not participating in a new NATO operation indicating a substitution decision for states concerning the sharing of punctual club burdens versus long-term cooperative security investment. COE represent NATO's forward-looking transition to the future; how partners will cooperate functionally and operationally over 28 mandates given an increasingly complex defense and security context. While the PFP and COE are NATO-specific institutions, the research rarely discusses NATO's multiple institutions with demands for troop allocations by non-US European partners. When there are multiple operations, partners are forced to choose.

European troop allocations to NATO versus other II operations from the 2013 to 2020 are presented in Fig. 7.7. Cold war partners illustrate curvilinear troop allocations to NATO starting at 20% dropping to as low as 8% then rebounding to 12%. Their shifting contributions to NATO operations are explained by increased troops to EU operations in Fig. 7.8; substitution behavior across II. European cold war partners shifted troops from NATO operations to EU and UN operations over the years pointing to the importance of considering trade-offs across operations under multiple demands with shifting risks. The observation is that much burden-sharing research does not consider how European states allocate between NATO operations relative to those under the auspices of other IO points to the circumscribing of the burden concept. The support for substitution arguments indicates enlargement's facilitation of post-cold war allies replacing those cold war partner troops in operations when one examines the data in appendix detailing how burdens shifted (see, appendix Table A.1).

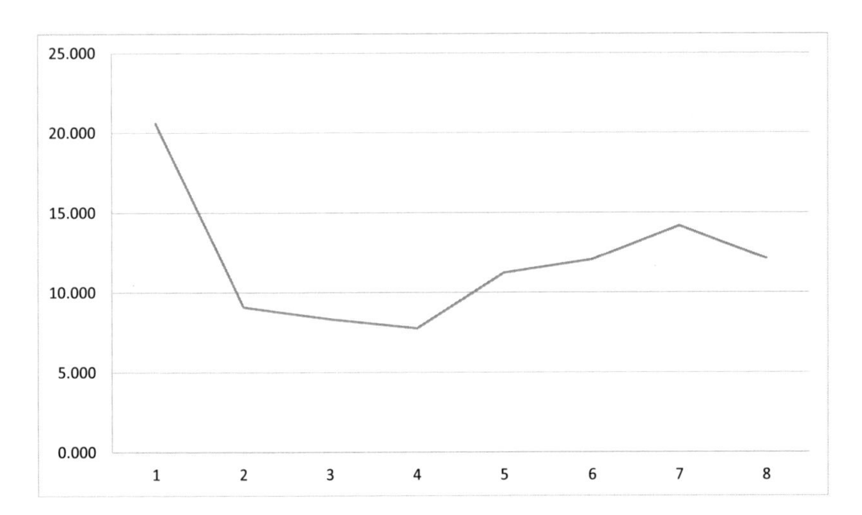

Fig. 7.7 European partner troop allocations—NATO operations, percent from 2013–2020 (*Source* The Military Balance, 2014–2021 [London: International Institute for Strategic Studies])

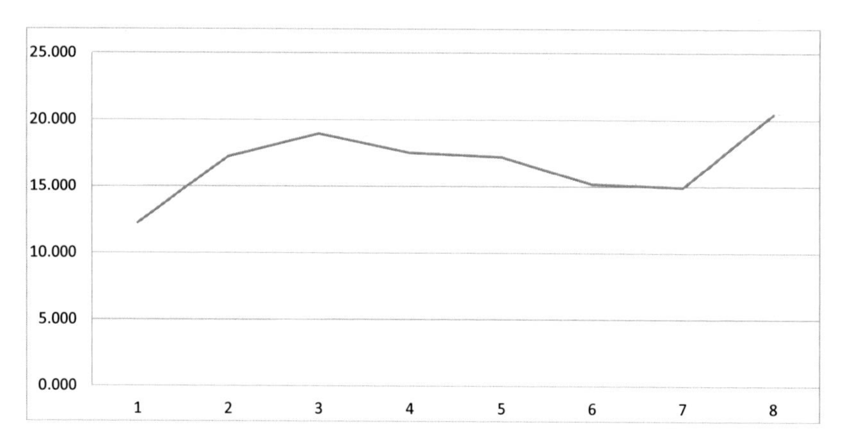

Fig. 7.8 European partner troop allocations—EU & UN operations, percent from 2013–2020 (*Source* The Military Balance, 2014–2021 [London: International Institute for Strategic Studies])

Centres of Excellence—Redistributing NATO Burdens: Comparing Two COE

Another way (European) NATO partners increased burdens was by hosting and sponsoring COE permitting the club to externalize some burdens associated with uncertainty about the future state of the world, defense and security risks and threats, and alliance transformation. The COE concept developed "because of command structure reforms and reductions in personnel warrant and demands for cost-effectiveness and a leaner organization. Since the COE concept is not at the expense of NATO personnel warrants, it is thus cost effective for NATO as an institution, and for the alliance," (Lobo, 2012, p. 62). The emergence of COE permitted partners to slice burdens differently. "Added value stresses that there should be added value only and no duplication, a principle stressing that a mandatory purpose for COE is to provide improvement to NATO capabilities rather than competition," (Lobo, 2012, p. 35).

Following 9/11, NATO underwent structural modifications to the military command (see, "NATO Military Command Structure" 14 May 03 MC 224/1). NATO established Allied Command Transformation (ACT) as the hub to manage, coordinate (doctrinal, operational, functional) alliance transformation by helping prepare and sustain club operations and capabilities, and assist in the transformation of partner capabilities (Lindley-French, 2015; Lobo, 2012). This transformation is how NATO will meet the collective defense and cooperative security challenges of the future. ACT directs various subcommands and NATO schools to facilitate and advocate improved military capabilities, maintain relevance and adapt to the changing environment. It also accredits COE, reviews them and recommends necessary steps to regain re-accreditation (though no COE lost accreditation). Finally, "ACT's responsibility to identify areas of military activity where there are gaps in expertise that an existing COE should target, or where a new COE might be appropriate," (Lobo, 2012, p. 36). The COE institutional innovation redistributes burdens across sponsors, hosts, and partners ensuring a minimal level of the collective good. They are also forums of information exchange, socialization, debate, consultation and outreach for stakeholders both internal and external. They are locations where partners develop discursive arguments and research expertise to legitimize courses of action. States collaborate on future defense and security policy actions. Partner participation contributes to the overall quality of the good, while offering individual level benefits (creating partial excludability).

The COE concept was released by the Military Command before the end of 2003 (04 Dec 03 MCM-236–06). Sponsoring and contributing nations fund COE activities with a cost-share formula agreed upon when the COE is established. The generalized cost-share formula equals the number of officers assigned by participants at a COE/(total of NATO COE assigned officers x total NATO COE budget). Contribution to operational budgets in most COE was around 20,000–25,000 Euros per officer per year in 2016 (Simion, 2016). They operate at 'no cost to NATO' by not drawing from NATO Common Funding. They are part of a wider framework of supporting NATO command arrangements but retain a level of autonomy. They must be accredited on at least three of the four pillars of Command Transformation among *enhancing education & training; assisting in doctrine development; testing and validating concepts through experimentation;* and *supporting analyses and lessons learned processes* (see "NATO COE Accreditation Criteria," 11 June 04 IMSM-0416–04). COE Steering Committees collaborate with Supreme Allied Command Transformation (hereafter, SACT) and may be asked to do a number of activities, (17 May 04 MC 58/1 "Terms of Reference for SACT"). Partners commit to the mutual support of each other's educational activities and relevant events such as exercises, courses, seminars, and workshops through the exchange of Subject Matter Experts such as lectures, researchers and mentors. The Program of Work (POW) is decided in consultation and collaboration with the COE Steering Committee, the MC, and ACT. Many COE focus on the 'education and training' pillar to socialize and collaborate to enhance. Those COE seeking to offer NATO certified education and training must "proceed for supplementary accreditation, from quality assurance perspective – derived from the EU standards for higher education institutions," (Simion, 2016, p. 95). They "serve as hubs for information and best practices, but may also serve as a matchmaker between private institutions with expertise on one subject matter area and state militaries (and NATO as alliance)," (Lobo, 2012, p. 49). Figure 7.9 offers a map of COE by host location and sponsoring partners.

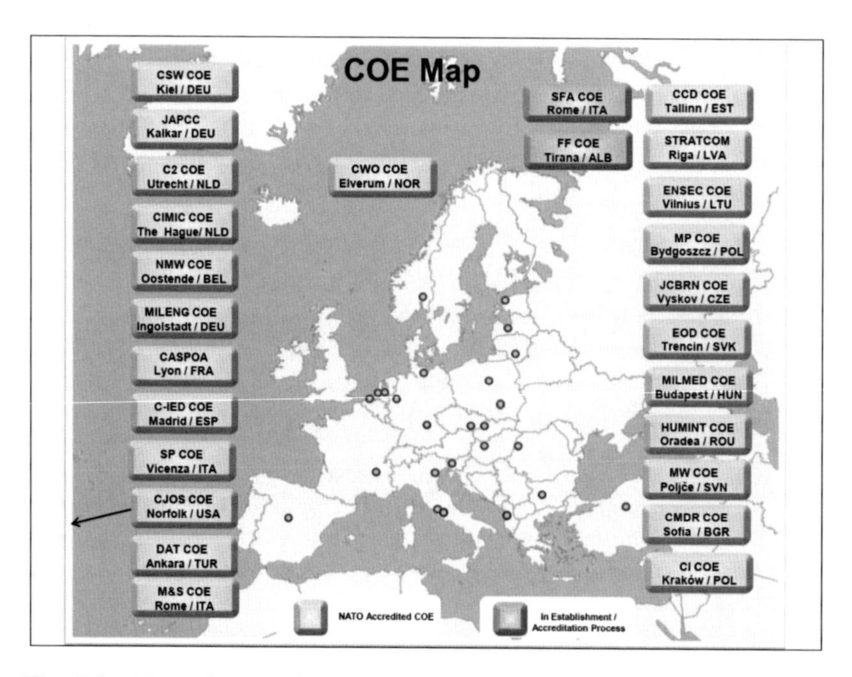

Fig. 7.9 Map of COE locations in 2014 (*Source* NATO Supreme Allied Command Transformation, Introduction to NATO Centres of Excellence, 2014)

The first COE established, accredited and endorsed by the North Atlantic Council in June 2005 was the Joint Air Power Competence Centre (**JAPCC**) in Germany which is one of the cases discussed along with Strategic Communications, **STRATCOM** (2014, Latvia), Joint Chemical, Biological, Radiological, and Nuclear, **JCBRN** (2007, Czech Republic), and Military Medicine, **MILMED** (2014, Hungary). The MOU from MILMED and JCBRN COE are studied from rational institutionalist and constructivist approaches (Czech Republic et al., 2006; Hungary et al., 2014). Each of those COE combine more than six states. The partners and sponsor-host nations obtain a level of agenda-setting power and supporting states promote bilateral and military interests through COE, as well as benefit from training, education, and participation in exercises. Information sharing is accomplished through "COE products (like assessments, reports, papers, etc.) are shared within NATO, and second the degree of information sharing between respective COE involved states and strategic or civil-military partner(s)," (Lobo, 2012, p. 20)). But, also, those individuals posted by COE participants report back home with access to what is produced by experts, scholars and practitioners at a high-value. "COE is also a contribution to the burden sharing within the Alliance; having a NATO-flag on national soil is still something that seems to be considered as valuable, perhaps especially in newer [partners]," (Lobo, 2012, p. 23).

Bringing together Germany, as a host-sponsor with 14 partners, the **JAPCC**'s mandate is to provide decision-makers effective solutions on Air and Space Power challenges, in order to safeguard NATO and the Nations' interests. It is composed of multiple branches: assessment, coordination and engagement; air operations support; command, control, communication; combat air branch; and space branch. COE are considered an outreach tool for NATO as they develop relationships with NATO agencies, NATO schools, Non-NATO nations and external actors (II, governmental organizations, non-governmental organizations, industry & academia), and work with 'Communities of Interest.' "JAPCC, the first accredited NATO COE [2005] and one of the most sponsored by Member Nations holds as primary customers the NATO Headquarters (ACO, ACT, NATO Joint Commands and Air Command) and its national contributors," (Simion, 2016, p. 82). One research respondent offered "COE-JAPCC is open for, and working actively to establish contact with actors outside the traditional chains of command, hereby EU, industry, PFP, etc. The contact varies depending on how deep it goes. It can happen through participation in meetings, give briefs, and directly cooperate in solving specific projects," (Lobo, 2012, p. 48).

With two framework nations supported by eight nations, **STRATCOM** became the 20th accredited COE in 2014 representing the second wave of COE formed a decade after the establishment of the concept. Its tasks include "*doctrine development and harmonization*, conducting *research and experimentation*, identifying *lessons learned* from applied STRATCOM during operations, and *enhancing training and education*," (Simion, 2016, p. 87). Its networking and extension through a logic of defense pluralism is evidenced by its role as, "a debate and research forum for various STRATCOM disciplines: public diplomacy, public affairs, military public affairs, information operations and psychological operations," (Simion, 2016, p. 87). The tasks of STRATCOM are practices and activities influenced centralization and communication mandates. Doctrine development, harmonization, as well as training and education occur in social communities where information centralization, diffusion and learning from takes place. Those practices and interactions represent how partners participate in transformation, outside the central budgeting and collective activities, in distinct locations within hosts producing common goods at extra individual costs.

Comparing MILMED & JCBRN COE MOU In-Depth

The following section examines MILMED COE from 2014 and the JCBRN COE from 2006.

> All COE must act as a catalyst for NATO transformation and open activities to all Alliance members. COE must not duplicate nor compete with current NATO capabilities, but instead offer an area of expertise not already found within the Organization. To this end, all COE must have subject matter experts in their field of specialization. Allied Command Transformation periodically re-assesses COE in order to ensure that they continue to meet those criteria and assure continued NATO accreditation status.[12]

The constructivist approach focuses on the creation of individual identities "through a process of individualization and socialization, an actor voluntary chooses self-imposed and selected roles and rules and where obligations, responsibilities, and commitment are learned and followed, not chosen," (Lobo, 2012, p. 12). COE represent a bottom-up approach as partners drive agenda creation, therefore, some partner coordination is necessary for establishment. Each COE offers role specialization to merit the development of a structure. This ensures COE remain "a common endeavor among states, (to) achieve security through sharing of military resources and mutual reliance," (Lobo, 2012, p. 16). Lobo argues NATO COE call upon four constructivist institutional logics, organized in pairs: logic of defense sovereignty versus logic of defense solidarity (level of integration) and logic of defense exclusiveness versus logic of defense pluralism (level of openness) (2012, p. 4). These represent classic trade-offs between the monopoly over the control of power, policy autonomy and who to include versus exclude in the activities.

Those are also rationalist strategic problems (Koremenos, 2013), e.g., distributional problem, uncertainty over the future and the commitment/enforcement problem. RIT proposes different design features to mitigate strategic problems and facilitate the creation of self-enforcing agreements. Those agreements are designed with an appropriate mix of flexibility, precision and discretion to permit adaptation to differing strategic contexts. COE are co-constructed institutions of collaboration offering sets of representational and ideational practices and behaviors for state partners to follow. Logics of persuasion are linked to COE design and funding. For example, a logic of defense solidarity suggests an assurance game associated with summation and threshold aggregation technologies. In those strategic forms, states focus on summing capacities to a threshold, coordination, and cost-sharing agreements are predicted (Sandler, 2004, pp. 82, 110).

COE offer a generalized cost-sharing structure concerning the individuals allocated to the them by members. They resemble semi-exclusive club goods where sponsors contract but all partners receive a portion of the good transferred to other institutional actors, i.e., ACT. The pooling of capacities appears in MOU cost-sharing formulas and detailed troop allocations (Koremenos, 2008) presented in MOU annex. COE support national capabilities by ensuring governments meet "national pledges to meet agreed shortcomings over an agreed timetable, this guideline seeks realistic and attainable targets that tasks, and consequently commits, states individually or with other allies to specific capability improvements," (Lobo, 2012, p. 59). Other pragmatic benefits of COE include international and NATO-wide visibility, building multi and bilateral relations between partners, learning best-practices and sharing lessons from post-deployment, 'inherent interoperability'; social practices to naturalize and reproduce in the community. Moreover, for hosts the COE can facilitate.

> enabling national vision, pushing specific interests into the COE's services and products, with potential impact at the Alliance's level; promotion and development of national projects and programmes with a consistent support of the COE; sharing costs – possibility to reduce investment costs by gaining similar results with other Nations being part of the same activities; ensuring an entry point into the entire COEs network and, the associated communities of interest, international organizations, academia, and industry, sometimes difficult to establish in a purely National or NATO environment. (Simion, 2016, p. 89)

Drawing from the MOU of the functional operation of JCBRN COE hosted and sponsored by the Czech Republic with eleven partner states and Allied Command Transformation in 2006 and the establishment of the MILMED COE MOU with eight partners in 2014, the next portion examines constructivist claims alongside rational institutionalist predictions using MOU agreement texts. The MOUs were signed by National Level Representatives; these are intra-NATO discussions.

JCBRN—Functional Relationship MOU, 2006

The **JCBRN** supports alliance transformation and interoperability through developing doctrine and standards, offering education and training, studying lessons learned and assisting partners in individual JCBRN efforts including "validation through experimentation. The initial core mission of the JCBRN Defence COE diversified since 2014 following the acceptance, implementation, and provision of reach back and operational planning support capabilities to NATO," (Simion, 2016, p. 83). The reach back element is presented as "a power asset, because you have this reach back system. In an operation you suddenly stumble over something chemical, biological or radioactive, and instead of having expertise on all areas in every operation, you can have an expert system where you report back to a COE where experts eventually send staff to the operation theatre," (Lobo, 2012, p. 55). The 2006 functional Operation MOU clarifies there is no command relationship between the COE and SACT and is part of a "wider framework... it supports and complements SACT's efforts by providing CBRN defence expertise to NATO's military transformation with first priority," (Czech Republic et al., 2006, Sect. III.2–3). Its tasks are detailed:

> a. Provide competent and timely advice to NATO on CBRN defence issues, to include support to the development of a NATO CBRN reach back capability;
> b. *Test and validate* CBRN defence-related NATO concepts and doctrines through experimentation;
> c. Assist in CBRN *defence doctrine development* by leveraging knowledge and *lessons learned*;
> d. Contribute to the NATO *standardisation* in the field of CBRN defence;
> e. Provide *training and education* for military and civilian personnel on all aspects of CBRN defence;
> f. *Network* with the relevant CBRN organisations and subject matter experts;
> g. Adhere to established HQ SACT support requirements, guidance and directives, as may be developed and instituted in support of overall COE Network efficiency and effectiveness; and
> h. Adhere to all NATO regulations and standards that are appropriate to the function of the JCBRN Defence COE. (Hungary et al., 2014, Sect. IV.2)

The tasks not only invoke COE accreditation criteria (b, c, e) indicating a logic of defense solidarity but also mention networking and calling upon various expertise (f.); a call for defense pluralism. The MOU details project submission to the COE by SACT, entitled coordination,

> The SC will decide on the JCBRN Defence COE annual POW. For coordination of all NATO requirements in the POW, HQ SACT will provide the NATO requests for services or products to the JCBRN Defence COE. A HQ SACT representative will be invited to participate in the relevant SC meetings on a non-voting basis to advise the SC on the POW with regard to the NATO requirements and priorities. (Czech Republic et al., 2006, Sect. V)

And instructs, “HQ SACT and the JCBRN Defence COE will, *on a continuous basis, coordinate the execution of the POW*. Emergent NATO requests will be forwarded to the JCBRN Defence COE by HQ SACT for appropriate consideration.” Because of uncertainty concerning future preferences, the MOU offers section XI, clause 2 on withdrawal supporting RIT arguments and indicates the MOU remains in effect until “such time as the Participants decide otherwise in writing or if the accreditation of the JCBRN Defence COE is revoked or if HQ SACT withdraws from this MOU or if the JCBRN Defence COE Operation MOU ceases to be in effect.” The MOU specifies, “any dispute regarding the interpretation or implementation of this MOU or any of its TAs will be settled *only by consultation* among the Participants,” (Czech Republic et al., 2006, Sect. XI.2). Amendments are possible with mutual written consent of parties. Expansion of the COE is details “joining of a new Participant will be accomplished through a Note of Joining (NOJ) signed by the new Participant and all the current Participants. It will come into effect with the last signature thereto but not before the corresponding NOJ to the JCBRN Defence COE Operation MOU comes into effect,” (Czech Republic et al., 2006, Sect. XI.1).

Not only does the functional operation MOU structural design suggest a reliance on emphasizing the accreditation criteria along with the institution’s mandate, the costs for joining by other members is low consistent with self-enforcement, resembling an assurance game so partners should not free-ride per collective action arguments (Sandler, 2004). Though some may not be able to fulfill COE personnel mandates because of national constraints,[13] considered an involuntary defection from an international level promise (Putnam, 1988). The Operational MOU linking COE participants focus on as second-level concerns, i.e., funding, personnel commitments and aspects of power allocation across participants.

MILMED-Establishment MOU, 2014

An establishment MOU focuses on identifying the commonality of the project and outlining its link relative to transformation goals. This MOU transmits the rationale and justification for investing in the specialized collective good. It serves the purpose of preparing for the follow-on Operational MOU and signals a new collaboration to interested stakeholders. Hungary is the sponsor-majority-host of the MILMED COE with eight partners per Sect. 7.2, "the purpose of this MOU is to establish the NATO MILMED COE in Budapest, Hungary and establish arrangements for its operation, funding, manning, equipment, and infrastructure, as well as for its administrative and logistical support" (Hungary et al., 2014) This COE's central goal is "to further develop and improve medical support to NATO operations, based on expertise resulted from innovation, experience, and sharing best practices," (Simion, 2016, p. 84).

The mission is stated in Sect. 3.1 as Medical *Training and Evaluation* leading to certification; Medical *Lessons Learned* focusing on tactical aspects; *Standards Development* and custodianship; and Deployment related health surveillance. It details the chair of the SC (i.e., Steering Committee) is from a Framework Nation and distinct from that country's national representative to ensure the chair's neutrality. Section 4.2 details, "decisions of the SC will be taken by the consensus of the representatives. SC decisions can be taken by other means of communication than a meeting, as agreed by SC, but no decision will be taken under silence procedure in this case" (Hungary et al., 2014). On personnel allocations, "the internal structure of the NATO MILMED COE, manning and position allocations are outlined in Annex A. The SC may, with the written consent of the Participant or Participants concerned, temporarily reallocate any person provided that they bear no effect on either the cost share (Hungary et al., 2014, Sect. 9.2) or the execution of the current budget." Sect. 4.8 references the follow-on functional Operational relationship MOU between ACT and the COE. The COE personnel responsibilities are included identifying 52 positions allocated across partners with identified qualifications. The smallest COE had 4 posts and the largest 95 for allocation by partners (Simion, 2016, p. 88).

> If a Participant is not able to fulfill its obligations for more than one year as regards assignment of personnel or contributing to the budget, its rights in the decision-making will be suspended until the SC determines that those obligations are fulfilled. If that Participant is not able to fulfil its obligations for more than two years, this will be considered as the withdrawal from this MOU by the Participant automatically. (Hungary et al., 2014, Sect. 16.4)

That notwithstanding annexes D and E detail items provided, "administrative expenses, travel costs, POW related project-specific expenses, hospitality costs, information and PR services and POW related project-specific lab equipment and furnishing," Resources committed by Hungary include offices, administrative support, access to dining and recreational facilities and medical support,

> provide free of charge on-base first aid, out-base regular sick call hours, on call emergency care, stabilization and preparation of injured for further evacuation to higher level medical treatment facilities, within military medical service system. NATO MILMED COE Personnel and their dependents have access to Hungarian medical facilities in accordance with the legal regulations of Hungary and applicable international agreements relevant for the treatment of foreigners. (Hungary et al., 2014, Annex E.3.1-2)

Finally, German assets offered to the Health Surveillance Capacity Section include offices, administrative and medical support and access to dining facilities at the same rates as German personnel. On dispute adjudication, they are resolved through consultations and "will not be referred to any national or international tribunal or any other third party for settlement," (Hungary et al., 2014, Sect. 17) ensuring an absence of third party intervention.

States may join a COE and there is a margin of maneuver for bargaining sunk costs, "prior to the signing of the NOJ, the amount of the budgetary funds initially required from the new Participants to offset previous investments will be negotiated and determined between the new Participants and the existing Participants, and laid down in the NOJ," (Hungary et al., 2014, Sect. 15.2). Budgeting aspects are in Sect. 9 and the cost-sharing formula is in Sect. 9.2 and, even if states cannot fill the positions, Sect. 9.5 statess each remains, "responsible for its share of costs associated with assigned but unfilled positions," (Hungary et al., 2014). Amendments occur upon written consent of participants and, "in the event of one or more Participants joining or withdrawing from this MOU or changing their personnel contribution, the existing or remaining Participants will consider any necessary amendments to this MOU," (Hungary et al., 2014, Sect. 18.1). The institutional design aspects highlight agreement flexibility while ensuring it self-enforces with detailed allocation criteria. The logic of defense solidarity is discursively presented in clauses discussing incidental failure of allocation personnel and the POW is developed in collaboration with ACT and the MC.

Calls for defense pluralism include inviting collaboration with stakeholders in academia, industry, NGOs, governments, etc., while ensuring the common goods are distributed through NATO. Participating states access bilateral goods, creating some excludability, as partners pay a low-entry cost contribute. States cannot access those goods without sending qualified personnel to the COE and financing it.

COE are expert hubs available for NATO to ask for collaboration in aspects of mission planning, exercise, execution, sustainment, analysis, as well as doctrine and standards development across diverse partners. Such activities are community practices contributing toward NATO identity-building a socialized community constructivists contend (Gheciu, 2005; Zehfuss, 2001). COE are both information centralizers and diffusers to NATO partners and beyond in their network capacity to assist in alliance transformation. COE founding documents reflect specialization, concerns about resource pooling and long-term collaboration recognizing the importance of continued capability transformation and interoperability improvements to enhance the operational effectiveness. COE specialization fits many into crisis management (CMDR, CIMIC) evidencing the alliance shifting burdens to meet future security challenges. The discursive logics deployed in founding documents and an examination of COE institutional design identified convergence on the logics of defense pluralism and solidary in the texts. Further research could examine how discourses and representational practices are adopted and co-constructed at the national level through the #WeAreNATO media campaign. This is where common doctrine, standards and interoperability enter as well as communication and convergence upon mandate interpretation by partners.

COE are security communities co-constructed by partners, hosts and ACT. They are also rationally designed institutions. Referring to Table 5.1, several design aspects are linked to strategic problems including agreement **flexibility, centralization** and lower **membership costs** than the NATO club. 'Uncertainty about the state of the world' contributes to **flexibility** observed in a) amendments, b) capacity to invite new members (i.e., NOJ process) and c) yearly budgeting and personnel allocation cycles. 'Uncertainty about the state of the world' also contributes to the **centralization** of information (Koremenos, 2008) and its redistribution which is precisely the *mandates* of COE. 'Enforcement' should not be an issue as one observes lower membership cost and voluntary 'commitment' to allocations suggesting there is little 'uncertainty about the future preferences' of partners. Another element of flexibility is partners can withdrawal with notice (Koremenos & Nau, 2010). Partners can also be ejected for failing to fulfill financial and personnel allocations for more than one year without explanation; ensuring *obligations* are met. Finally, the **centralization** aspects of the COE are essential given the heterogeneity of members and the potential for increasing partner numbers. The **scope of issues** is controlled and managed directly by ACT, the accrediting institution of COE, and described with a level of *precision* in founding documents, i.e., MOU. The delegation of power **(i.e., internal control)** within the COE as are the procedures for its POW to emerge in collaboration with ACT suggesting the COE lacks *discretion* to act independently from ACT's requests evidencing a continued informal influence of the US (as the hub and command of ACT) in the absence of direct COE membership by the country. The MOU also direct partners of the COE to **resolve disputes internally** in saying there will be no **external delegation of dispute resolution** (Koremenos, 2013). Taken together COE design aspects stated in MOU address the strategic problems of 1. Commitment, 2. Enforcement, 3. Uncertainty about the future state of the world and 4. Uncertainty about future preferences. The documents include precision on the obligations, delegation of power, discuss aspects of centralization and limit the discretion of action of the COE. The mechanisms to mitigate strategic problems include flexibility, centralization, limiting the scope of issues, membership costs and ensuring internal control of power and dispute adjudication with preventing the external delegation of dispute resolution. Four strategic problems are mitigated with six different mechanisms identified within the agreements. The agreements also discuss cost-sharing, personnel commitments, obligations and activities explicitly so partners are aware of expectations for participation. Their operation at zero cost to NATO's budget line is not equivalent to stating they do not contribute to NATO's mandates of collective defense, cooperative security and crisis management. These diverse institutions deserve more attention by scholars.

Conclusions—Triangulating Methods, Models and Measures

This chapter offered three analyses of burdens. The first set explored factors related to military spending for a majority of partners since 1949. This set of models is comparable to the subgroup of the literature on most partners examining military spending. This book goes *Beyond 2%* with the presentation of studies advancing research. The second set of models, offered a new dependent variable, with a dichotomous indicator of if a partner participated in a new NATO operation after 1990 identifying a strong substitution relationship with a partner hosting/sponsoring a new COE. The second set of analyses captured burden sharing examining participation in a new NATO operation including information about the institutional innovations developed since 2003 to ensure the alliance readiness for transformation at NO COST to the club, the COE. COE offer an environment to examine rational institutional claims about self-enforcing design alongside primary documents for the discursive arguments brought by critical approaches. COE mandates, as described in respective founding Memoranda of Understanding (MOU), were linked to COE accreditation language and rational institutionalist design mechanisms were identified offering complementary viewpoints for examining agreement content. Employing a triangulation of methods and dependent variables permitted a study of the burden complexity from different theoretical approaches. The availability of the collected and centralized data offers extension potential for the project.

The last section offers a comparison of the establishment and operational relationship MOU for two COE. It discusses rational strategic problems and identified relevant MOU provisions aiming to mitigate issues. Discursive language was examined in relation to convergence with COE mandates. COE are institutional motors of alliance transformation organizing around future defense and security concerns developing agendas with retrospective and prospective mandates. They create subgroups of specialized management and collective international expertise called upon by the club, if needed in crisis or conflict situations. They are also interaction locations and social communities worthy of more comparative and systematic study.

In synthesis, the propositions offered by theories and operationalized offered consistent effects on burden sharing. Direct threats reduced military spending and the chances partners participated in a new NATO operation, while the information provided through contracting US DSA increased spending and the chances a state participated in an operation. Risk management is related to NATO offers and Table 7.4 tests the effects of political and economic risk on military spending supporting the claim political risk increased spending while economic risk decreased spending. Other authors discussed those trade-offs (Bueno de Mesquita & Lalman,

1992; O'Neill, 2001; Snider, 2005) on decision-making at length; results supported rationalist claims. The exploitation argument was supported as geographic closeness to Russia reduced chances of participation in an operation. Descriptive data illustrated cold war European partners practiced troop substitution from 2013 to 2020. The effects of multiple operations and hosting/sponsoring COE were significant.

COE host/sponsorship significantly reduced the chances a partner participates in a new operation. COE hosting and sponsorship is a substantial political, economic and collaborative effort. Those institutions do not draw from the NATO budgets and their funding falls upon members-participants; this project offered comparative examinations of the founding texts of two COE as a starting point for future research.[14]

This chapter mobilized theories and methods, examined different dependent variables and offered original evidence to study burden sharing in a social science research framework. The remaining chapter discusses contributions, future plans, implications, as well as offers final conclusions.

Policy Pop Out 4

Support for the risk management model of institutional burden sharing

For the policymaker	*Support for the risk management model of institutional burden sharing*
What aspects of the background information does the reader/recipient need to know? What does the reader 'know' compared to what they 'do not know'?	Political risks across partners due to differing geography and internal constraints should be considered systematically as well as factors explaining differences in burden sharing. Shifting to a logic of allocations linked to the functioning and participation in operations by partners is a next step. There must be a reflection about partner management of risks while burden bargaining in the production of NATO's common club goods. This will require arguments on the appropriateness of changing the metric and the consequences for failing to adapt to changed norms/practices. The more partners participate in revised and transparent revision of the allocation process, then the increasingly legitimate it becomes for the club to adopt. The risk management model is supported by the book's studies and includes a number of untested factors in previous research. The inclusion of COE in burden allocations and their contributions to cooperative security and crisis management merits increased study by defense spending and bargaining researchers.

(continued)

(continued)

For the policymaker	*Support for the risk management model of institutional burden sharing*
What is their position on the matter? Who else is affected by the issue?	A majority of partners should favor reconceptualizing burdens as most do not meet the 2% goal. The effects of this change will reach across the military, government ministries and defense industry stakeholders. Those affected should be in favor as it will highlight contributions and allocations unrecognized. This will bring needed attention to the diplomatic, political activities and individual partner contributions rather than a myopic focus on defense spending. The findings of the analyses offer support and the data on COE point to a set of institutions that, for the most part, remain neglected by scholars.
What are the costs and/or risks associated with this decision?	Given the current political target is not widely met and debated widely by partners, politicians and scholars, the risk of having a worse process than the status quo is low. This will add interlocutors increasing bargaining costs resulting in some short-term inefficiencies because of increased transaction and 'perceived' opportunity costs but resulting outcomes will be understood as more fair and transparent. Those are important democratic norms which underlie the entire community and Atlantic alliance institution.

(continued)

(continued)

For the policymaker	*Support for the risk management model of institutional burden sharing*
What advantages and disadvantages should the reader know about who is to make the decision?	While a major advantage is increases in fairness and transparency concerning how NATO's is supported, the disadvantages arise from how to determine comparative value of participation across parts/operations/activities of the institution. A holistic approach is time-consuming in its creation however, once institutionalized, efficiencies from increased coordination and learning will be gained. A step-by-step process to reach such a holistic approach will help manage partners expectations, as well as allowing actual under-contributing partners to show their good faith throughout a modified and improved process.
What other evaluation criteria must the recipient use?	Recasting burden models to be diverse and inclusive requires rethinking evaluation fairness/just participation criteria across the categories of club assets to ensure functioning. This will highlight the contributions of those in the middle to lower end of the allocations. If evaluation criteria are jointly considered legitimate and the alliance manages to convey messages to partners to participate with active intent then, this process will contribute to advancing burden bargaining efficiency and regularizing transparency in future rounds of missions/activities club force generation during crises as well as facilitating a collaborative process during the Alliance's annual common and military budget negotiations.

Notes

1. GDP/capita had no relationship to NATO membership offers in recent research and the EU is arguably the institution most concerned with economic health of partner states.

2. Thanks go to F. Chaves Correa, E. Douguet & M. Philaire for data collection, drafting pop outs and comments, CRSH 95–2019-1000.
3. Heteroskedasticity occurs when the standard deviations of a predicted variable, monitored over different values of an independent variable or as related to prior time periods, are non-constant. See appendix Figs. (A.2 and A.3).
4. The data exclude hybrid operations with other II, e.g., combined mission with the EU and ASEAN in Indonesia, MSA (2005–6) and the EU legal mission in Mexico (PRODESIS, 2004–8).
5. The legal foundations of II interventions for the UN, NATO, EU, ASEAN, OSCE, African Union, Organization of American States, and the CSTO (Russia's Collective Security Treaty Organization) are discussed (Kimball & Lewis, 2010).
6. Operations in the Mediterranean Sea extend from Gibraltar to Turkey, appendix Fig. (A.4).
7. For a general introduction, see Briggs, R. A., "Normative Theories of Rational Choice: Expected Utility," The Stanford Encyclopedia of Philosophy (Fall 2019 Edition), Edward N. Zalta (ed.), https://plato.stanford.edu/archives/fall2019/entries/rationality-normative-utility/, last access 28 June 2022.
8. Due to inefficient standard errors possibly creating type I or type II errors biasing predictions.
9. The heteroskedastic probit employed in IR (Clark and Nordstrom 2005) accounts for (1) consistency or inconsistency of beliefs or preferences or (2) uncertainty or ambivalence about some outcome. IR applications employ it to examine consistency/inconsistency about preferences for conflict; a discrete outcome event is observed, i.e., conflict, contribution.
10. A significant test indicates the null hypothesis sigma-squared is equal to zero is rejected indicating this is the correct model.
11. Data for examining the effects political risk are in the appendix for scholars.
12. https://c2coe.org/about-coes/, last access 28 June 2022.
13. See Table 2 (Lobo, 2012, p. 37).
14. This is among few studies examining primary documents; there is a case study citing the HUMINT MOU authored by a Romanian defense researcher also head of training and education at said COE (Simion, 2016). Another study offered a survey of COE using institutionalist approaches but mobilized a small set of interviewees to respond to questions about how COE are linked to alliance transformation (Lobo, 2012).

References

Abouharb, M. R., & Kimball, A. L. (2007). A new dataset on infant mortality rates, 1816–2002. *Journal of Peace Research, 44*(6), 743–754. https://doi.org/10.1177/0022343307082071

Booth, K. (Ed.). (1998). *Statecraft and security: The cold war and beyond*. Cambridge University Press.

Bueno de Mesquita, B. (Ed.). (2005). *The logic of political survival* (1. paperback ed). MIT Press.

Bueno de Mesquita, B. (1980). An expected utility theory of international conflict. *American Political Science Review, 74*(4), 917–931. https://doi.org/10.2307/1954313

Bueno de Mesquita, B., & Lalman, D. (1992). *War and reason: Domestic and international imperatives*. Yale University Press.

Bueno de Mesquita, B., Morrow, J., Siverson, R., & Smith, A. (1999). An institutional explanation of the democratic peace. *American Political Science Review, 93*(4), 791–807. https://doi.org/10.2307/2586113

Burges, S. (2013). Mistaking Brazil for a middle power. *Journal of Iberian and Latin American Research, 19*(2), 286–302. https://doi.org/10.1080/13260219.2013.853358

Carr, A. (2014). Is Australia a middle power? A systemic impact approach. *Australian Journal of International Affairs, 68*(1), 70–84. https://doi.org/10.1080/10357718.2013.840264

Chapnick, A. (2000). The Canadian middle power myth. *International Journal, 55*(2), 188. https://doi.org/10.2307/40203476

Clark, D., & Nordstrom, T. (2005). Democratic variants and democratic variance: How domestic constraints shape interstate conflict. *The Journal of Politics, 67*(1), 250–270. https://doi.org/10.1111/j.1468-2508.2005.00316.x

Cooper, A. (2016). *Niche diplomacy: Middle powers after the cold war*. Palgrave Macmillan Limited. https://public.ebookcentral.proquest.com/choice/publicfullrecord.aspx?p=5645087

Czech Republic, Germany, Hellenic Republic, Romania, Slovak Republic, Republic of Slovenia, United Kingdom of Great Britain and Northern Ireland, & Allied Command Transformation. (2006). *MOU concerning the functional relationship regarding the joint chemical, biological, radiological, and nuclear defence centre of excellence*.

de Sá Guimarães, F., & de Almeida, M. (2017). From middle powers to entrepreneurial powers in world politics: Brazil's successes and failures in international crises. *Latin American Politics and Society, 59*(4), 26–46. https://doi.org/10.1111/laps.12032

Dorussen, H., Kirchner, E., & Sperling, J. (2009). Sharing the burden of collective security in the European Union. *International Organization, 63*(4), 789–810. https://doi.org/10.1017/S0020818309990105

Evans, P., Jacobson, H. K., & Putnam, R. (Eds.). (1993). *Double-edged diplomacy: International bargaining and domestic politics*. University of California Press.

Gheciu, A. (2005). Security institutions as agents of socialization? NATO and the "New Europe." *International Organization, 59*(4), 973–1012.

Hungary, Belgium, Czech Republic, French Republic, Republic of Germany, Italian Republic, Netherlands, Poland, Romania, Slovak Republic, United Kingdom of Great Britain and North Ireland, & United States of America. (2014). *MOU concerning the establishment, administration, and operation of a COE for military medicine*.

Holbraad, C. (1984). Middle powers in international politics. *Palgrave Macmillan UK*. https://doi.org/10.1007/978-1-349-06865-4

Jongryn, M. (Ed.). (2015). *MIKTA, middle powers, and new dynamics of global governance: The G20's evolving agenda* (1st edition). Palgrave Macmillan.

Jordaan, E. (2003). The concept of a middle power in international relations: Distinguishing between emerging and traditional middle powers. *Politikon, 30*(1), 165–181. https://doi.org/10.1080/0258934032000147282

Kavanagh, J. (2014). *U.S. Security-Related Agreements in Force Since 1955: Introducing a New Database*. RAND Corporation.

Kimball, A. & Lewis. (2010). Le rôle accru des organisations internationales dans les conflits contemporains. In *Conflits dans le monde 2010b*. Presses Université Laval.

Kimball, A. & Lewis. (2011). La délégation à l'épreuve du terrain: Les difficiles interventions militaires et civiles des organisations internationales dans les conflits et les crises. In *Conflits dans le monde, 2011*. Presses Université Laval.

Kimball, A. (2019). Knocking on NATO: Strategic and institutional challenges risk the future of Europe's seven-decade long cold peace. *The School of Public Policy Publications, 12*. https://doi.org/10.11575/SPPP.V12I0.68129

Kimball, A. (2021a). L'OTAN peut-elle encore avoir un rôle multilatéral? In *L'après COVID-19: Quel multilatéralisme face aux enjeux globaux? Regards croisés: Union européenne – Amérique du nord – Chine* (pp. 343–356). Bruylant-Larcier.

Kimball, A. (2021b). Managing risks, side payments, and multi-institutional enlargement: The role of US defence, big four investment agreements and candidate risks on NATO and EU enlargement. *European Politics and Society, 22*(5), 696–715. https://doi.org/10.1080/23745118.2020.1820152

Koremenos & Nau. (2010). Exit, no exit. *Duke Journal of Comparative & International Law, 21*(1), 81–120.

Koremenos, B. (2008). When, what, and why do states choose to delegate? *Law & Contemporary Problems, 71*(1), 151–192.

Koremenos, B. (2013). The continent of international law. *Journal of Conflict Resolution, 57*(4), 653–681. https://doi.org/10.1177/0022002712448904

Linde, J. (2020). *Expected utility and political decision making*. Linde, Oxford Research Encyclopedia of Politics. Oxford University Press. https://doi.org/10.1093/acrefore/9780190228637.013.885

Lindley-French, J. (2015). *The North Atlantic Treaty Organization: The enduring alliance* (2nd edition). Routledge.

Lobo, S. (2012). *NATO transformation and centers of excellence: Analyzing rationale and roles*. University of Oslo. http://urn.nb.no/URN:NBN:no-32044

Macdonald, L., & Paltiel, J. (2016). Middle power or muddling power? Canada's relations with emerging markets. *Canadian Foreign Policy Journal, 22*(1), 1–11. https://doi.org/10.1080/11926422.2016.1144626

Männik, E. (2004). Small states: Invited to NATO—able to contribute?. *Defense & Security Analysis, 20*(1), 21–37. https://doi.org/10.1080/1475179042000195483

Marton, P., & Eichler, J. (2013). Between willing and reluctant entrapment: CEE countries in NATO's non-European missions. *Communist and Post-Communist Studies, 46*(3), 351–362. https://doi.org/10.1016/j.postcomstud.2013.06.002

Milner, H. (1997). *Interests, institutions, and information: Domestic politics and international relations*. Princeton University Press.

Neack, L., Hey, J., & Haney, P. (1995). *Foreign policy analysis: Continuity and change in its second generation*. Prentice Hall.

Neack, L. (1993). Delineating state groups through cluster analysis. *The Social Science Journal, 30*(4), 347–371. https://doi.org/10.1016/0362-3319(93)90014-M

O'Neill, B. (2001). Risk aversion in international relations theory. *International Studies Quarterly, 45*(4), 617–640.

Patience, A. (2018). Australian foreign policy in Asia. *Springer International Publishing*. https://doi.org/10.1007/978-3-319-69347-7

Putnam, R. (1988). Diplomacy and domestic politics: The logic of two-level games. *International Organization, 42*(3), 427–460.

Sandler, T. (2004). *Global collective action* (1st edition). Cambridge University Press. https://doi.org/10.1017/CBO9780511617119

Shin, S. (2016). South Korea's elusive middle powermanship: Regional or global player? *The Pacific Review, 29*(2), 187–209. https://doi.org/10.1080/09512748.2015.1013494

Simion, E. (2016). *NATO centres of excellence and the transformation of the North-Atlantic alliance*. University of Oradea. https://nbn-resolving.org/urn:nbn:de:0168-ssoar-73403-8

Smith, A. (1995). Alliance formation and war. *International Studies Quarterly, 39*(4), 405. https://doi.org/10.2307/2600800

Smith, A. (1996). To intervene or not to intervene: A biased decision. *Journal of Conflict Resolution, 40*(1), 16–40. https://doi.org/10.1177/0022002796040001003

Snider, L. (2005). Political risk: The institutional dimension. *International Interactions, 31*(3), 203–222. https://doi.org/10.1080/03050620500294176

Ungerer, C. (2007). The "Middle power" concept in Australian foreign policy. *Australian Journal of Politics & History, 53*(4), 538–551. https://doi.org/10.1111/j.1467-8497.2007.00473.x

Zehfuss, M. (2001). Constructivism and identity: A dangerous liaison. *European Journal of International Relations, 7*(3), 315–348. https://doi.org/10.1177/1354066101007003002

Zyla, B. (2015). Sharing the burden?: NATO and its second-tier powers. *University of Toronto Press*. https://doi.org/10.3138/9781442668386

Zyla, B. (2016). Who is keeping the peace and who is free-riding? NATO middle powers and burden sharing, 1995–2001. *International Politics, 53*(3), 303–323. https://doi.org/10.1057/ip.2016.2

CHAPTER 8

Contributions, Future Plans, Implications and Conclusions

Contributions of the Book

This research project is articulated around five burden sharing arguments. Many arguments receive full, and several, partial support. The analysis of original data supported past and recent arguments with an approach across levels-of-analysis permitting a cross-sectional look partner allocations/acceptance of burdens accounting for the effects of information and threats. It offers analytical and descriptive evidence exploring COE as social communities from a constructivist perspective while being self-enforcing due to precise, yet flexible institutional design.

This book advances our understanding of NATO burden sharing along multiple dimensions. First, it offered a comparison of the literature and descriptive analysis of methods used and outcome variables examined. The literature, for the most part, is limited to single-method analyses and shorter time periods. This research inserts into the 11% of research examining all partners and all years. Second, it employs conceptual indicators reflecting burdens as they are operationally shared through participation in NATO operations. This improves conceptualization by identifying burden categories to measure and to understand national military expenditures; the classic measure fails to capture the burden diversity in the institution and partner allocations given individual risks and threats across theaters and activities. A literature review and expansion

A. L. Kimball, *Beyond 2%—NATO Partners, Institutions & Burden Management*, Canada and International Affairs,
https://doi.org/10.1007/978-3-031-22158-3_8

of burden conceptualization are complemented by an improved model of risk management in burden sharing.

Third, the results of the military spending models for partners show US DSA and arms transfers inside NATO, from the US and global partners increase spending. Concerning the target of 2%, US DSA and arms importations remain significant. Military spending by partners is affected by geostrategic considerations. Propositions one (threat), two (US DSA as information) and five (on public policy efforts on social spending, measured as infant mortality rate) are supported while the proposition 3d on risk trade-offs also had support, indicating the importance of political and economic risks when examining military spending. Together results supported the risk management model of institutional burden sharing.

The arguments and models presented indicate some factors should not be omitted studying burdens. Results indicate 'spending as a percent of GDP' is not well explained by the factors offered from theories. Those theories serve as the building blocks for advancing the comparative knowledge of findings as anchors of common understanding for the motivations of actor behavior. Informational and collective action perspectives do better at explaining long-term trends, while individual benefits relative to threat perceptions claims offer stronger explanations for spending over past decades. Evidence indicates partners shifted resources to changing threat vectors based on geography and their individual exposure to threats. Partners re-allocated burdens within the alliance; post-cold war partners moved resources toward proximate threats after 2012 letting mid-tier cold war partners increase support to long-term activities. Burden sharing research focusing on activities or a limited time period cannot observe this behavior because it occurs within the alliance across operations.

Across the quantitative models and COE comparisons, the management of risks and threats influencing burden sharing measured as military spending and participation in a new NATO operation as functional measures of burden allocations remain important. This research calls for an expansion of conceptualization, operationalization and evaluation of burdens. Concerning future defense and security risks to the club, NATO innovated when it created the COE, externally financed by ACT and 'controlled' voluntary participatory institutions that are rationally designed to be self-enforcing and endure with provisions mitigating the uncertainties associated with strategic problems. The documents founding those institutions offer constructivist discursive logics of behavior for states, specifically logics of defense pluralism and defense solidarity. State partners manage club and individual risks to defense and security to improve information about candidate defense 'credibility/quality' with institutional innovations. The club itself designed the PFP and COE as forums to advance socialization across partners, candidates and global NATO partners. The risk management model focuses on the intersections of shifting partner versus club threats and risks over time and analyzing the influence of enlargement on burden sharing systematically using novel data and drawing from RIT, which remains outside mainstream IR theories in many classrooms.

The risk management model advances our understanding of institutional burden sharing by testing the same claims across two measures of burdens and two distinct time periods. It highlighted in importance of reliable measures of threats and risks as well as the signaling effects of US DSA on reducing uncertainty yet not homogenously across partners. This motivated an original argument that differences across partners in terms of constraints on capacity or action can distinguish middle powers/second-tier states. This novel theoretical-econometric link was examined in a heteroskedastic probit model offering support for the contention an improved theoretical—econometric linkage is required in quantitative burden sharing analyses.

Future Plans

If anything, this book's arguments and evidence require a shake-up and fresh thinking/measures about risks, threats, geostrategy and institutional enlargement concerning burden sharing negotiations and evaluations of partner contribution 'credibility'. Scholars studying allocations to II should collaborate in the development holistic indices including aspects of burdens while improving theoretical and quantitative models and measures. Another concern is the absence of data in the early years of the alliance forcing a reliance on proxies to increase sample size to study behavior over an extended time period. The absence of budget data from foreign affairs to NATO gives an incomplete picture of the support, personnel and allocations by non-defense and military ministries to the institution; the myopia of a focus on defense contributions has limited scholars and decision-makers in their understanding of how the institution provides its complex club goods. Scholars have access to civilian budget shares, military spending data and troop/personnel allocations to

HQ/operations when they are made available and/or archived by the institution. There is little effort to centralize allocation and burden share data—a contribution of the digital appendix.

The effects of COE received little attention in research despite their explicit role and clear criteria to support future transformation at *no cost to the club's current cost-sharing* negotiations for the past 15 years. They are social communities of information and knowledge transfer per constructivists with mechanisms for rational institutionalist to mitigate the strategic problems preventing cooperation such as enforcement and uncertainty concerns. A half-dozen mechanisms are deployed in the agreement to counter issues and facilitate self-enforcing participation. Moreover, the explicit cost-sharing aspects and relations to NATO's other budgeting are important theoretically, financially and functionally though they escaped most burden research. There is rich material for future research on defense cooperation, bargaining, community creation and reproduction, organizational learning and institutional design with dozens of COE agreements to examine across over two dozen specialties.

A holistic burden sharing process index requires greater transparency by all partners and a shift in norms about budget secrecy concerning defense and security. The broader conceptualization asks states for transparency in what they allocate to NATO across aspects of the institution. And what they provide to NATO, e.g., fixed assets, trainings at military schools for partners, integration in national units, etc. Some partners invested in the 2% concept politically and discursively, e.g., the US, but changing and broadening the discussion is consistent with US requests for partners to contribute more. An improved and transparent process benefits the club and, many, partners individually though some will be identified as weaker links. This offers an opportunity to improve club and national defense and security by supporting those partners as opposed to stigmatizing them for failure to comply with the 'politically negotiated' collective targets (Zarakol, 2014).

It also requires a recognition some partners are at higher risk and require greater club assets in support. Some countries are less 'security providers' than 'security demanders' of the club. This explains the comparative ease with which Finland and Sweden moved through the NATO membership process in 2022 as they are categorized as 'security providers' (Archik et al., 2022). Casting partners as defense/security 'providers or demanders' is not a consideration in most research and deserves future development analytically and empirically. This research brought two factors: diverse measures of threats and informational improvements from US DSA to identify 'security demanders' in the club in relationship to both military spending and participation in a new club operation. This is why impending enlargement is an opportune moment to reconceptualize burden sharing across the institution in terms of what partners allocate to the club across domains, ministries and budgets nationally.

Implications

The addition of Finland and Sweden to NATO constrains Russia's mobility of action to some extent in the north because they bring monitoring capacity in the North Sea, near Kaliningrad, Arctic awareness and agility with deployment capacity. They reduce Russian informational domination in maritime areas contributing to the '360-degree approach' the alliance describes in the 2022 Strategic Concept.[1] The duo offers a level of existing interoperability with the club due to participation in operations, exercises, trainings, etc., as European partners to NATO. This is important for NATO defense planning as is the fact they have well-trained land forces and significant deployment capabilities in air and at sea. There will be requests on their assets as well as what they should procure in the short-term to support the club's collective defense, collective security and crisis management missions. Their close relationship outside the alliance could push them to jointly undertake club tasks. Geostrategic aspects of their joining could also coax a reluctant Denmark to increase allocations and participation. They will negotiate the size of the role and burden contribution they want in the alliance because the bargaining situation is favorable given how much existing non-cold war partners have invested in supporting Ukraine against Russian invasion. This is also a moment for them to publicly signal their 'credible commitment to the alliance' as NATO Common Budget share comparisons represent how partners annually slice one portion of the burden. Together they may take on as much 8–12% of the Common Budget or restrain themselves to around 4–6% (similar to Dutch contributions but at the low end) outside the top-third of contributors and behind Poland. The Danes contribute less financially to the alliance because they offer a geostrategic location valuable to the club (Blankenship, 2021). By comparison in 2019, the thirteen post-cold war partners, together, contributed 7.511% to the common budget (Kimball, 2019, p. 21). By implication, some will benefit from reductions, which will be determined after the last partner ratifies and deposits their accession protocols at HQ and budget negotiations start for 2023.

Conclusions

NATO's adaptability, as an institution, and capacity, as an actor, are reasons it is called upon to contribute to cooperative security and crisis management by other II and states beyond the collective defense mandate of its partners. As an institution, it adapted to different strategic contexts and increasingly complex threats vectors after 9/11 while maintaining a level of deterrence from Russia (until it entered the territory of PFP member Georgia in 2008). Russia meddled in the affairs of Moldova—in the maintenance the Transnistrian conflict ergo simultaneously destabilizing a portion border with Ukraine. A multifront invasion of Ukraine by Russia in February 2022 does not indicate the failure of NATO deterrence. It reveals information about Russian territorial aims in Ukraine and the surrounding region—which increase security risks for multiple partners. Partners donated military equipment, ammunitions and associated aid so the next cycle of procurement defense and security requests will be made to replace assets—this convergence favors an argument for recasting burden sharing and allocations across the club.

The data and analyses offered contend burden sharing studies must account for risks, threats and the effects of US DSA providing information about partner quality. Improved measures of threats and original data are contributed. The risk management model of burden sharing can be applied to other II. Institutions are created to reduce the continual transaction costs of interacting by regularizing behavior and creating shared expectations. Well-designed institutions may self-enforce, but there remains burden to share across partners to support an institution financially and with personnel. This book is a call for rethinking how partners examine burdens and how the institution should study and legitimize partner contributions across different environments to the maintenance of the institution and the completion of its operations. The entry of Finland and Sweden will shift burdens and permit a fortuitous opening for a deeper look at club needs versus partner needs in resupplying partner government after the extensive contributions to Ukraine in 2022. The arguments, data and tools in this book offer a perspective for opening discussions, reconceptualizing burdens and advancing alliance cohesion and unity through the adoption of a holistic and transparent burden process under the guidance evidence-based and multiple method analyses.

Notes

1. https://www.thestar.com/opinion/contributors/2022/07/17/natos-new-strategic-concept-is-a-dangerous-plan-to-preserve-western-power-through-global-militarism.html, last access 26 July 2022.

References

Archik, K., Bowen, A., & Belkin, P. (2022). *NATO: Finland and Sweden Seek Membership* (No. IN11949; Congressional Research Service). US Congress. https://crsreports.congress.gov/product/pdf/IN/IN11949

Blankenship, B. (2021). The price of protection: Explaining success and failure of US alliance burden-sharing pressure. *Security Studies, 30*(5), 691–724. https://doi.org/10.1080/09636412.2021.2018624

Kimball, A. (2019). Knocking on NATO: Strategic and institutional challenges risk the future of Europe's seven-decade long cold peace. *The School of Public Policy Publications, 12*. https://doi.org/10.11575/SPPP.V12I0.68129

Zarakol, A. (2014). What made the modern world hang together: Socialisation or stigmatisation? *International Theory, 6*(2), 311–332. https://doi.org/10.1017/S1752971914000141

Appendix A

Tasks to Delegate in International Agreements

Executive functions

- Figurehead (a ceremonial role) to executive authority to a secretary general (limited to unconstrained)
- Secretariat or administrative duties
- Financial administration
- Representing the group in interactions with states or IOs
- Deciding and participating in the process by which new members may join
- Granting exceptions under the escape clause
- Overseeing negotiating partner withdrawal

Reducing uncertainty

- Collection of information
- Collation of information
- Analysis of information

A. L. Kimball, *Beyond 2%—NATO Partners, Institutions & Burden Management*, Canada and International Affairs,
https://doi.org/10.1007/978-3-031-22158-3

- Diffusion of information
- Monitoring compliance
- Soft procedures encouraging compliance, ex., review meetings, self-reporting, etc.
- Overseeing complaints and punishments for noncompliance

Rules, roles and rights

- Making rules/laws in addition to those stipulated agreement
- Role in amending and/or implementing agreement
- Voting rules/decisions made by another body
- Presiding over, setting the agenda, or overseeing reports—another body's meetings
- Role in dispute resolution—internal body
- Redistributing or 'assigning new' property rights
- Addressing new, non-redistributive issues arising from club goods
- Rights of residual control

Appendix B

Predicted Values of Dependent Variable in a Regression Model

Novice readers should refer to Brannick's Regression Basics, detailing "scores on a dependent variable can be thought of as the sum of two parts: (1) a linear function of an independent variable, and (2) random error. In symbols, we have:

$$Y_i = \alpha + \beta X_i + \varepsilon_i \tag{A.1}$$

where Y_i is a score on the dependent variable for the *i*th person, $\alpha + \beta X_i$ describes a line or linear function relating X to Y, and ε_i is an error. Note that there is a separate score for each X, Y, and error (these are variables), but only one value of α and β, which are population parameters.

The portion of the equation denoted by $\alpha + \beta X_i$ defines a line. The symbol X represents the independent variable. The symbol α represents the Y intercept, that is, the value that Y takes when X is zero. The symbol β describes the slope of a line. It denotes the number of units that Y changes when X changes 1 unit. If the slope is 2, then when X increases 1 unit, Y increases 2 units. If the slope is −0.25, then as X increases 1

A. L. Kimball, *Beyond 2%—NATO Partners, Institutions & Burden Management*, Canada and International Affairs,
https://doi.org/10.1007/978-3-031-22158-3

unit, Y decreases 0.25 units. Equation A.1 is expressed as parameters. We usually have to estimate the parameters.

The equation for estimates rather than parameters is:

$$Y_i = a + bX_i + e_i \quad \text{(A.2)}$$

If we take out the error part of Eq. A.2, we have a straight line that we can use to predict values of Y from values of X, which is one of the main uses of regression. It looks like this:

$$Y' = a + bX \quad \text{(A.3)}$$

Equation A.3 says that the predicted value of Y is equal to a linear function of X. The slope of a line (b) is sometimes defined as rise over run. If Y is the vertical axis, then rise refers to change in Y. If X is the horizontal axis, then run refers to change in X. Therefore, rise over run is the ratio of change in Y to change in X. This means exactly the same thing as the number of units that Y changes when X changes 1 unit (e.g., $2/1 = 2$, $10/12 = 0.833$, $-5/20 = -0.25$). Slope means rise over run.

The idea of a linear transformation is that one variable is mapped onto another in a 1-to-1 fashion. A linear transformation allows you to multiply (or divide) the original variable and then to add (or subtract) a constant. In junior high school, you were probably shown the transformation Y = mX + b, but we use Y = a + bX instead." (Brannick, M).

Brannick, M. (no date) Department of Psychology, University of South Florida. Source: http://faculty.cas.usf.edu/mbrannick/regression/regbas.html. Accessed 15 June 2022.

Appendix C

See Table A.1.

Table A.1 Non-French NATO partner contributions: Ops Serval & Barkhane

	2013	*2014*	*2015*	*2016*	*2017*	*2018*	*2019*	*2020*
Serval	0	0	0	0	0	0	0	0
Barkhane	0	0	2	0	0	235	295	295
Total	0	0	2	0	0	235	295	295

Source International Institute of Strategic Studies. The Military Balance. London: ISIS, 2014–2021

A. L. Kimball, *Beyond 2%—NATO Partners, Institutions & Burden Management*, Canada and International Affairs,
https://doi.org/10.1007/978-3-031-22158-3

Appendix D

Data References and Public Data Sources

Abouharb, M. R., & Kimball, A. (2007). A new dataset on infant mortality, 1816–2002. *Journal of Peace Research*, *44*(6), 745–756.

Bennett, D. S. & Stam, A. (2000). EUGene: A conceptual manual. *International Interactions*, *26*,179–204. http://eugenesoftware.org. V3.212.

European Union Naval Force. Operation ATALANTA. Key facts and figures. https://eunavfor.eu/key-facts-and-figures/. Accessed 9 July 2021.

International Institute of Strategic Studies. (2014). The Military Balance 2014. London: ISIS.

International Institute of Strategic Studies. (2015). The Military Balance 2015. London: ISIS.

International Institute of Strategic Studies. (2016). The Military Balance 2016. London: ISIS.

International Institute of Strategic Studies. (2017). The Military Balance 2017. London: ISIS.

International Institute of Strategic Studies. (2018). The Military Balance 2018. London: ISIS.

International Institute of Strategic Studies. (2019). The Military Balance 2019. London: ISIS.

International Institute of Strategic Studies. (2020). The Military Balance 2020. London: ISIS.

A. L. Kimball, *Beyond 2%—NATO Partners, Institutions & Burden Management*, Canada and International Affairs,
https://doi.org/10.1007/978-3-031-22158-3

International Institute of Strategic Studies. (2021). The Military Balance 2021. London: ISIS.

Map Distance Calculator. (2021). https://www.calcmaps.com/map-distance/. Accessed 15 September 2021.

Military OneSource. (2021). US Military Installations. https://installations.mil itaryonesource.mil/. Accessed 15 September 2021.

Ministry of Defence of France. Dossier de reference. https://www.defense.gouv.fr/operations/territoire-national/france-metropolitaine/operation-sentinelle/dossier-de-reference. Accessed 9 July 2021.

Ministry of Defence of France. Find the press kit. https://www.defense.gouv.fr/operations/afrique/bande-sahelo-saharienne/operation-barkhane/dossier-de-reference/operation-barkhane. Accessed 30 June 2021.

Ministry of Defence of Italy. National Contingent. 19 June 2015. https://www.difesa.it/EN/Operations/InternationalOperations/NATO_Support_to_Tur key/Pagine/National_Contingent.aspx. Accessed 9 July 2021.

Ministry of Defence of the Netherlands. Operation Active Fence (Patriot Mission Turkey). https://english.defensie.nl/topics/historical-missions/mis sion-overview/2013/patriot-mission-in-turkey. Accessed 9July 2021.

Ministry of Foreign Affairs of France. France's action in the Sahel. April 2020. https://www.diplomatie.gouv.fr/en/french-foreign-policy/security-disarm ament-and-non-proliferation/terrorism-france-s-international-action/article/france-s-action-in-the-sahel. Accessed 9 July 2021.

Multinational Force & Observers. Origins. https://mfo.org/origins. Accessed 8 July 2021.

NATO. (2021). Centres of Excellence. https://www.nato.int/cps/en/natohq/topics_68372.htm. Last accessed 15 September 2021.

NATO. Defence Expenditure of NATO Countries (2014–2021). https://www.nato.int/cps/en/natohq/news_184844.htm?selectedLocale=en. Accessed 28 June 2021.

Partnership for Peace. (2021). PFP training centers. https://www.act.nato.int/ptecs. Accessed 15 September 2021.

PRS Group. (2019). https://epub.prsgroup.com/list-of-all-variable-definitions, 1994 to 2016. Accessed 25 February 2019.

Stockholm International Peace Research Institute. (2019). Arms transfers, (1994–2019). https://www.sipri.org/databases/armstransfers. Accessed 15 September 2021.

Stockholm International Peace Research Institute. (2019). Military expenditures, (1949–2019). https://www.sipri.org/databases/milex. Accessed 15 September 2021.

V-Dem. (2021). "Varieties of democracy and corruption" dataset. https://www.v-dem.net/en/data/data/v-dem-dataset-v111/. Accessed 15 September 2021.

Appendix E

See Fig. A.1.

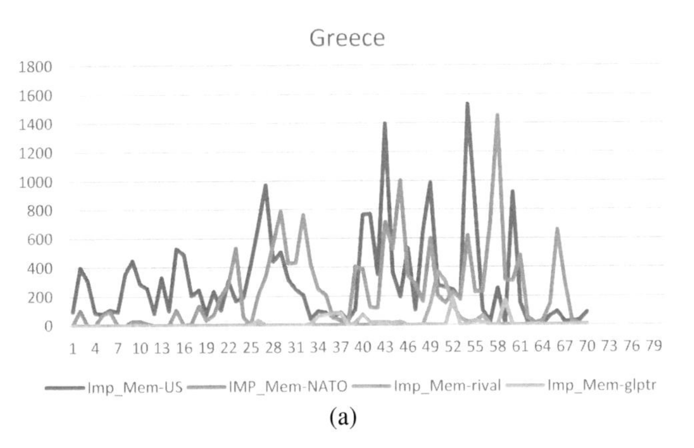

(a)

Fig. A.1 Panels a to g.: Arms transfers to partner from the US (blue), NATO partners (orange), Russia, global (yellow), 1993–2019 (Color figure online) (*Source* SIPRI. 2019. Arms transfers, [1994–2019] https://www.sipri.org/databases/armstransfers)

A. L. Kimball, *Beyond 2%—NATO Partners, Institutions & Burden Management*, Canada and International Affairs,
https://doi.org/10.1007/978-3-031-22158-3

Fig. A.1 (continued)

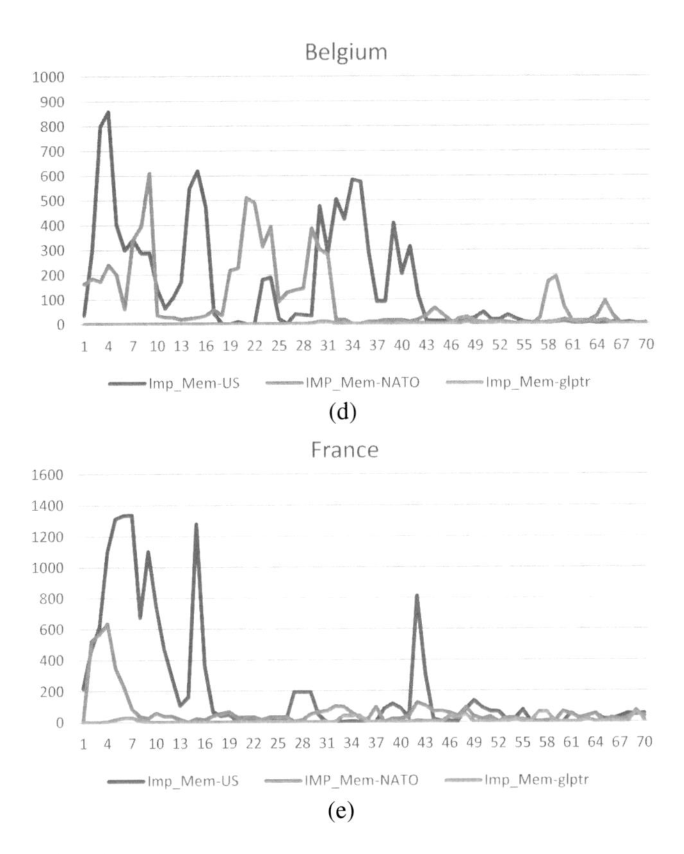

Fig. A.1 (continued)

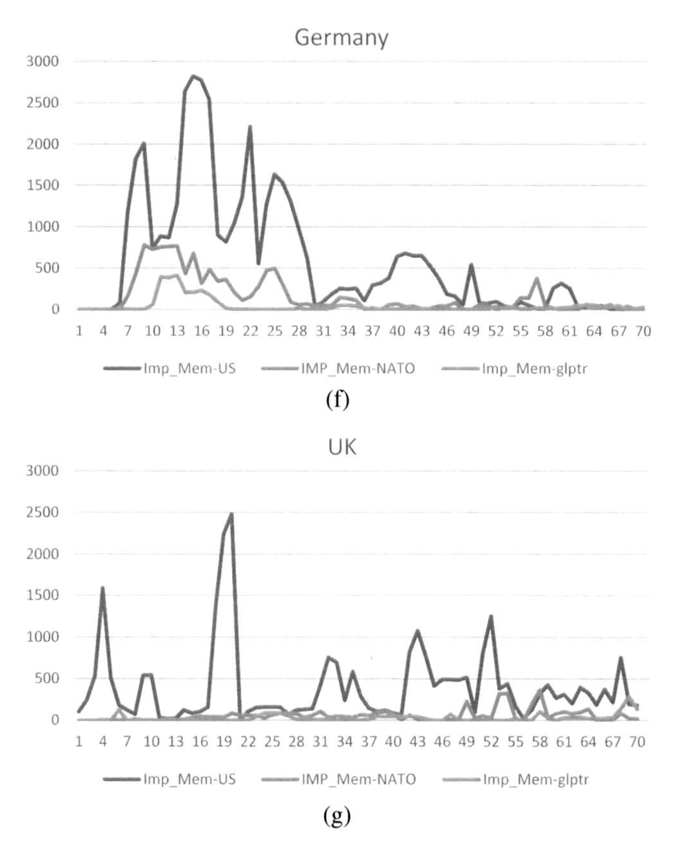

(f)

(g)

Fig. A.1 (continued)

Appendix F

See Table A.2.

Table A.2 Operations 2013–2020

Recording Unit	*Logic for inclusion*	*Operations and efforts*
NATO	Those under NATO command. Forces in location under national control are coded as National Commitments	International Security Assistance Force (ISAF), Operation RESOLUTE SUPPORT, Kosovo Force (KFOR), Air Policing, Standing NATO Maritime Groups (SNMG), Operation OCEAN SHIELD, Operation ACTIVE FENCE, Training Mission-Iraq (NTM-I), Enhanced Forward Presence (EFP), and tailored Forward Presence
EU	Those under EU command	Operation ALTHEA, EU Training Mission Mali, EU Training Mission *République Centrafricaine*, EU Naval Forces Mediterranean (EUNAVFORMED), EU Training Mission Somalia, Operation ATALANTA

(continued)

A. L. Kimball, *Beyond 2%—NATO Partners, Institutions & Burden Management*, Canada and International Affairs,
https://doi.org/10.1007/978-3-031-22158-3

Table A.2 (continued)

Recording Unit	*Logic for inclusion*	*Operations and efforts*
UN	Those under UN command	UNTSO, UNFICYP, UNDOF, UNIFIL, MINURSO, UNMIK, UNSMIL, UNMIL, MINUSTAH, MONUSCO, UNMISS, MINUSMA, MINUSCA, UNMOGIP, UNAMID, UNAMA, UNSOM, UNSOS and the MFO Sinai[1]
French led Coalitions	Those coalitions led by France	Operations Barkane & Serval
U.S. led Coalitions	Those coalitions led by the U.S	Operation Inherent Resolve, Combined Maritime Forces (CMF), and the Joint Military Training Group—Ukraine (JMTG-U)[2]
National Commitments	Garrisons in foreign locations or overseas dependent territories Forces in foreign locations under national control	

Source International Institute of Strategic Studies. The Military Balance. London: ISIS, 2014–2021

[1]UN acronyms used. MFO in the Sinai was coded as UN, despite its unique status due to the inability of the UNSC to reach an agreement on a UN peace support operation to supervise the implementation of the peace treaty between Egypt and Israel. See Multinational Force & Observers, "Origins", https://mfo.org/origins, accessed 8 July 2021.

[2]Turkish troops in Syria under national direction against Da'esh coded with U.S.-led coalition.

Appendix G

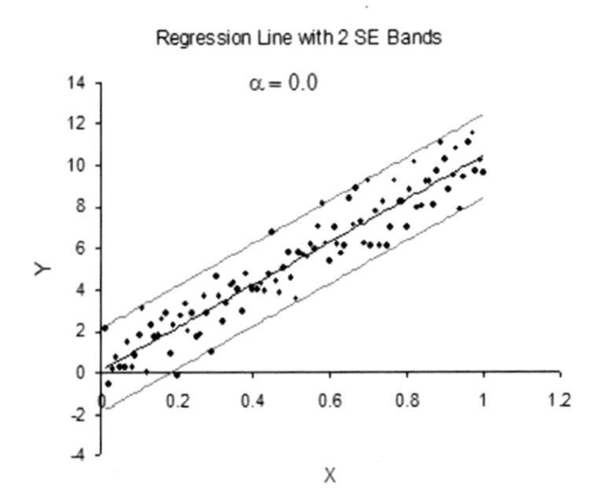

Fig. A.2 Homoskedasticity in the bivariate model (*Source* http://www3.wabash.edu/econometrics/EconometricsBook/chap19.htm. Accessed 15 June 2022)

Fig. A.2 "…depicts a classic picture of a homoscedastic situation with a regression line estimated via OLS in a simple, bivariate model. The vertical spread of the data around the predicted line appears to be fairly constant as X changes".

Fig. A.3 shows "… the vertical spread of the data around the predicted line is clearly increasing as X increases. One of the most difficult parts of handling heteroskedasticity is that it can take many different forms".

A. L. Kimball, *Beyond 2%—NATO Partners, Institutions & Burden Management*, Canada and International Affairs,
https://doi.org/10.1007/978-3-031-22158-3

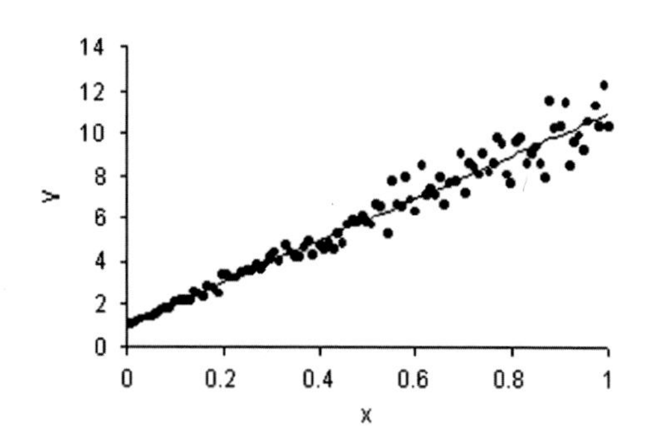

Fig. A.3
Heteroskedasticity in the bivariate model (*Source* http://www3.wabash.edu/econometrics/EconometricsBook/chap19.htm. Accessed 15 June 2022)

Appendix H

See Fig. A.4.

Fig. A.4 Mediterranean Sea Naval Ops area (Gibraltar to Diyarbakir, 4000 km) (*Source* https://www.eu-logos.org/2016/11/15/a-stronger-nato-means-a-stronger-europe-sea-guardian-and-operation-sophia-together/. Accessed 24 October 2022)

A. L. Kimball, *Beyond 2%—NATO Partners, Institutions & Burden Management*, Canada and International Affairs,
https://doi.org/10.1007/978-3-031-22158-3

References

Abbott, K., & Snidal, D. (1998). Why states act through formal international organizations. *Journal of Conflict Resolution, 42*(1), 3–32. https://doi.org/10.1177/0022002798042001001

Abbott, K., & Snidal, D. (2000). Hard and soft law in international governance. *International Organization, 54*(3), 421–456. https://doi.org/10.1162/002081800551280

Abouharb, M. R., & Kimball, A. L. (2007). A new dataset on infant mortality rates, 1816–2002. *Journal of Peace Research, 44*(6), 743–754. https://doi.org/10.1177/0022343307082071

Alley, J. (2021). Reassessing the public goods theory of alliances. *Research & Politics, 8*(1), 205316802110052. https://doi.org/10.1177/20531680211005225

Allison, G. (2018). *Destined for War: Can America and China escape Thucydides's Trap?* (First Mariner Books edition 2018). Mariner Books.

Altfeld, M. (1984). The decision to ally: A theory and test. *Western Political Quarterly, 37*(4), 523–544. https://doi.org/10.1177/106591298403700402

Archik, K., Bowen, A., & Belkin, P. (2022). *NATO: Finland and Sweden Seek Membership* (No. IN11949; Congressional Research Service). US Congress. https://crsreports.congress.gov/product/pdf/IN/IN11949

Arena, P. (2010). Why not guns and butter: Responses to economic turmoil. *Foreign Policy Analysis, 6*(4), 339–348. https://doi.org/10.1111/j.1743-8594.2010.00116.x

A. L. Kimball, *Beyond 2%—NATO Partners, Institutions & Burden Management*, Canada and International Affairs,
https://doi.org/10.1007/978-3-031-22158-3

Arena, P., & Nicoletti, N. P. (2014). Selectorate theory, the democratic peace, and public goods provision. *International Theory, 6*(3), 391–416. https://doi.org/10.1017/S1752971914000347

Asmus, R. (2008). Europe's Eastern promise: Rethinking NATO and EU enlargement. *Foreign Affairs, 87*(1), 95–106.

Badcock, G., & Marks, D. C. (Eds.). (2010). *War, human dignity and nation building: Theological perspectives on Canada's role in Afghanistan*. Cambridge Scholars.

Balzacq, T. (2005). The three faces of securitization: Political agency, audience and context. *European Journal of International Relations, 11*(2), 171–201. https://doi.org/10.1177/1354066105052960

Banka, A. (2022). Neither reckless nor free-riders: Auditing the Baltics as US treaty allies. *Journal of Transatlantic Studies*. https://doi.org/10.1057/s42738-022-00096-3

Barnett, M., & Duvall, R. (2005). Power in international politics. *International Organization, 59*(1), 39–75. https://doi.org/10.1017/S0020818305050010

Barnett, M., & Finnemore, M. (1999). The politics, power, and pathologies of international organizations. *International Organization, 53*(4), 699–732. https://doi.org/10.1162/002081899551048

Beardsley, K., & Schmidt, H. (2012). Following the flag or following the charter? Examining the determinants of UN involvement in international crises, 1945–2021: Following the flag or following the charter? *International Studies Quarterly, 56*(1), 33–49. https://doi.org/10.1111/j.1468-2478.2011.00696.x

Becker, J. (2017). The correlates of transatlantic burden sharing: Revising the agenda for theoretical and policy analysis. *Defense & Security Analysis, 33*(2), 131–157. https://doi.org/10.1080/14751798.2017.1311039

Becker, J. (2021). Rusty guns and buttery soldiers: Unemployment and the domestic origins of defense spending. *European Political Science Review, 13*(3), 307–330. https://doi.org/10.1017/S1755773921000102

Becker, J., & Malesky, E. (2017). The continent or the "Grand large"? Strategic culture and operational burden-sharing in NATO. *International Studies Quarterly, 61*(1), 163–180. https://doi.org/10.1093/isq/sqw039

Béraud-Sudreau, L., & Giegerich, B. (2018). NATO defence spending and European threat perceptions. *Survival, 60*(4), 53–74. https://doi.org/10.1080/00396338.2018.1495429

Bernauer, T., Kalbhenn, A., Koubi, V., & Spilker, G. (2013). Is there a "Depth versus participation" dilemma in international cooperation? *The Review of International Organizations, 8*(4), 477–497. https://doi.org/10.1007/s11558-013-9165-1

Bernhard, M. (2021). Democratic backsliding in Poland and Hungary. *Slavic Review, 80*(3), 585–607. https://doi.org/10.1017/slr.2021.145

Blankenship, B. (2020). Promises under pressure: Statements of reassurance in US alliances. *International Studies Quarterly, 64*(4), 1017–1030. https://doi.org/10.1093/isq/sqaa071

Blankenship, B. (2021). The price of protection: Explaining success and failure of US alliance burden-sharing pressure. *Security Studies, 30*(5), 691–724. https://doi.org/10.1080/09636412.2021.2018624

Bogers, M., Beeres, R., & Bollen, M. (2020). NATO burden sharing research along three paradigms. *Defence and Peace Economics, 1–14*. https://doi.org/10.1080/10242694.2020.1819135

Booth, K. (Ed.). (1998). *Statecraft and security: The cold war and beyond*. Cambridge University Press.

Brunnermeier, M. (2004). Learning to reoptimize consumption at new income levels: A rationale for prospect theory. *Journal of the European Economic Association, 2*(1), 98–114. https://doi.org/10.1162/154247604323015490

Bueno de Mesquita, B. (1980). An expected utility theory of international conflict. *American Political Science Review, 74*(4), 917–931. https://doi.org/10.2307/1954313

Bueno de Mesquita, B. (Ed.). (2005). *The logic of political survival* (1. paperback ed). MIT Press.

Bueno de Mesquita, B., & Lalman, D. (1992). *War and reason: Domestic and international imperatives*. Yale University Press.

Bueno de Mesquita, B., Morrow, J., Siverson, R., & Smith, A. (1999). An institutional explanation of the democratic peace. *American Political Science Review, 93*(4), 791–807. https://doi.org/10.2307/2586113

Burges, S. (2013). Mistaking Brazil for a middle power. *Journal of Iberian and Latin American Research, 19*(2), 286–302. https://doi.org/10.1080/13260219.2013.853358

Buzan, B., Wæver, O., & Wilde, J. de. (1998). *Security: A new framework for analysis*. Lynne Rienner Pub.

Camerer, C. (2003). *Behavioral game theory: Experiments in strategic interaction*. Princeton University Press.

Carr, A. (2014). Is Australia a middle power? A systemic impact approach. *Australian Journal of International Affairs, 68*(1), 70–84. https://doi.org/10.1080/10357718.2013.840264

Chapnick, A. (2000). The Canadian middle power myth. *International Journal, 55*(2), 188. https://doi.org/10.2307/40203476

Checkel, J. (2001). Why comply? Social learning and European identity change. *International Organization, 55*(3), 553–588. https://doi.org/10.1162/00208180152507551

Clark, D., & Nordstrom, T. (2005). Democratic variants and democratic variance: How domestic constraints shape interstate conflict. *The Journal of Politics, 67*(1), 250–270. https://doi.org/10.1111/j.1468-2508.2005.00316.x

Cooper, A. (2016). *Niche diplomacy: Middle powers after the cold war*. Palgrave Macmillan Limited. https://public.ebookcentral.proquest.com/choice/publicfullrecord.aspx?p=5645087

Cortell, A., & Davis, J. (1996). How do international institutions matter? The domestic impact of international rules and norms. *International Studies Quarterly, 40*(4), 451. https://doi.org/10.2307/2600887

Cox, R. (1981). Social forces, states and world orders: Beyond international relations theory. *Millennium: Journal of International Studies, 10*(2), 126–155. https://doi.org/10.1177/03058298810100020501

Czech Republic, Germany, Hellenic Republic, Romania, Slovak Republic, Republic of Slovenia, United Kingdom of Great Britain and Northern Ireland, & Allied Command Transformation. (2006). *MOU concerning the functional relationship regarding the joint chemical, biological, radiological, and nuclear defence centre of excellence*.

Dahl Thruelsen, P. (2009). *International organisations: Their role in conflict management*. Royal Danish Defence College.

Dai, X., Snidal, D., & Sampson, M. (Eds.). (2010). International cooperation theory and international institutions. *Oxford Research Encyclopedia of International Studies*. Oxford University Press. https://doi.org/10.1093/acrefore/9780190846626.013.93

De La Fe, P., & Montolio, D. (2001). Has Spain been free-riding in nato? An econometric approach. *Defence and Peace Economics, 12*(5), 465–485. https://doi.org/10.1080/10430710108404999

de Sá Guimarães, F., & de Almeida, M. (2017). From middle powers to entrepreneurial powers in world politics: Brazil's successes and failures in international crises. *Latin American Politics and Society, 59*(4), 26–46. https://doi.org/10.1111/laps.12032

Dorussen, H., Kirchner, E., & Sperling, J. (2009). Sharing the burden of collective security in the European Union. *International Organization, 63*(4), 789–810. https://doi.org/10.1017/S0020818309990105

Douch, M., & Solomon, B. (2014). Middle powers and the demand for military expenditures. *Defence and Peace Economics, 25*(6), 605–618. https://doi.org/10.1080/10242694.2013.861652

Drake, P., & McCubbins, M. (Eds.). (1998). *The origins of liberty: Political and economic liberalization in the modern world*. Princeton University Press.

Dvorak, J., & Pernica, B. (2021). To free or not to free (ride): A comparative analysis of the NATO burden-sharing in the Czech Republic and Lithuania—Another insight into the issues of military performance in the Central and

Eastern Europe. *Defense & Security Analysis, 37*(2), 164–176. https://doi.org/10.1080/14751798.2021.1919345
Egel, D., Grissom, A., Godges, J., Kavanagh, J., & Shatz, H. (2016). *Economic benefits of U.S. overseas security commitments could far outweigh costs*. RAND Corporation. https://doi.org/10.7249/RB9912
Evans, P., Jacobson, H. K., & Putnam, R. (Eds.). (1993). *Double-edged diplomacy: International bargaining and domestic politics*. University of California Press.
Fang, S., & Stone, R. (2012). International organizations as policy advisors. *International Organization, 66*(4), 537–569. https://doi.org/10.1017/S0020818312000276
Finnemore, M., & Sikkink, K. (1998). International norm dynamics and political change. *International Organization, 52*(4), 887–917.
Friedrichs, J., Mihov, J., & Popova, M. (2005). Synergies and tradeoffs in international cooperation: Broadening, widening, and deepening. *EIoP, 9*(13). https://ssrn.com/abstract=827224
Fuhrmann, M., & Sechser, T. (2014). Signaling alliance commitments: Hand-tying and sunk costs in extended nuclear deterrence. *American Journal of Political Science, 58*(4), 919–935.
Gheciu, A. (2005). Security institutions as agents of socialization? NATO and the "New Europe." *International Organization, 59*(4), 973–1012.
Goldstein, A. (1995). Discounting the free ride: Alliances and security in the postwar world. *International Organization, 49*(1), 39–71. https://doi.org/10.1017/S0020818300001570
Graham, E. (2014). International organizations as collective agents: Fragmentation and the limits of principal control at the World Health Organization. *European Journal of International Relations, 20*(2), 366–390. https://doi.org/10.1177/1354066113476116
Haesebrouck, T. (2017). NATO burden sharing in Libya: A fuzzy set qualitative comparative analysis. *Journal of Conflict Resolution, 61*(10), 2235–2261. https://doi.org/10.1177/0022002715626248
Hartley, K. (2020). NATO at 70: A political economy perspective. *Springer International Publishing*. https://doi.org/10.1007/978-3-030-54395-2
Hartley, K., & Sandler, T. (1999). NATO burden-sharing: Past and future. *Journal of Peace Research, 36*(6), 665–680. https://doi.org/10.1177/0022343399036006004
Hawkins, D., Lake, D., Neilson, D., & Tierney, M. (2006). *Delegation and agency in international organizations*. Cambridge University Press. http://site.ebrary.com/id/10150378
Heath, C., & Staudenmayer, N. (2000). Coordination neglect: How lay theories of organizing complicate coordination in organizations. *Research in*

Organizational Behavior, 22, 153–191. https://doi.org/10.1016/S0191-3085(00)22005-4

Heinen-Bogers, M. (2022). *Burden sharing in security organizations: Broadening the burden sharing debate*. Tilburg University.

Hirshleifer, J. (1983). From weakest-link to best-shot: The voluntary provision of public goods. *Public Choice, 41*(3), 371–386. https://doi.org/10.1007/BF00141070

Holbraad, C. (1984). Middle powers in international politics. *Palgrave Macmillan UK*. https://doi.org/10.1007/978-1-349-06865-4

Hungary, Belgium, Czech Republic, French Republic, Republic of Germany, Italian Republic, Netherlands, Poland, Romania, Slovak Republic, United Kingdom of Great Britain and North Ireland, & United States of America. (2014). *MOU concerning the establishment, administration, and operation of a COE for military medicine*.

Jakobsen, J. (2018). Is European NATO *really* free-riding? Patterns of material and non-material burden-sharing after the Cold War. *European Security, 27*(4), 490–514. https://doi.org/10.1080/09662839.2018.1515072

Johnston, A. I. (2001). Treating international institutions as social environments. *International Studies Quarterly, 45*(4), 487–515. https://doi.org/10.1111/0020-8833.00212

Jongryn, M. (Ed.). (2015). *MIKTA, middle powers, and new dynamics of global governance: The G20's evolving agenda* (1st edition). Palgrave Macmillan.

Jordaan, E. (2003). The concept of a middle power in international relations: Distinguishing between emerging and traditional middle powers. *Politikon, 30*(1), 165–181. https://doi.org/10.1080/0258934032000147282

Kaplan, L. (2004). *NATO divided, NATO united: The evolution of an alliance*. Praeger.

Katchanovski, I. (2011). Puzzles of EU and NATO accession of post-communist countries. *Perspectives on European Politics and Society, 12*(3), 304–319. https://doi.org/10.1080/15705854.2011.596308

Kavanagh, J. (2014). *U.S. security-related agreements in force since 1955: Introducing a new database*. RAND Corporation.

Keohane, R. (2005). *After hegemony: Cooperation and discord in the world political economy* (1st Princeton classic edition). Princeton University Press.

Khanna, J., & Sandler, T. (1997). Conscription, peace-keeping, and foreign assistance: NATO burden sharing in the post-cold war era. *Defence and Peace Economics, 8*(1), 101–121. https://doi.org/10.1080/10430719708404871

Kim, W., & Sandler, T. (2020). NATO at 70: Pledges, free riding, and benefit-burden concordance. *Defence and Peace Economics, 31*(4), 400–413. https://doi.org/10.1080/10242694.2019.1640937

Kimball, A. (2006). Alliance formation and conflict initiation: The missing link. *Journal of Peace Research, 43*(4), 371–389. https://doi.org/10.1177/0022343306064816

Kimball, A. (2010a). Political survival, policy distribution, and alliance formation. *Journal of Peace Research, 47*(4), 407–419. https://doi.org/10.1177/0022343310368346

Kimball, A. (2015). What Canada could learn from U.S. defence procurement: Issues, best practices and recommendations. *The School of Public Policy Publications, 8*. https://doi.org/10.11575/SPPP.V8I0.42517

Kimball, A. (2017). Examining informal defence and security arrangements' legalization: Canada–US agreements 1955–2005. *International Journal: Canada's Journal of Global Policy Analysis, 72*(3), 380–400. https://doi.org/10.1177/0020702017723931

Kimball, A. (2019). Knocking on NATO: Strategic and institutional challenges risk the future of Europe's seven-decade long cold peace. *The School of Public Policy Publications, 12*. https://doi.org/10.11575/SPPP.V12I0.68129

Kimball, A. (2021a). L'OTAN peut-elle encore avoir un rôle multilatéral? In *L'après COVID-19: Quel multilatéralisme face aux enjeux globaux? Regards croisés: Union européenne – Amérique du nord – Chine* (pp. 343–356). Bruylant-Larcier.

Kimball, A. (2021b). Managing risks, side payments, and multi-institutional enlargement: The role of US defence, big four investment agreements and candidate risks on NATO and EU enlargement. *European Politics and Society, 22*(5), 696–715. https://doi.org/10.1080/23745118.2020.1820152

Kimball, A. (2022). Deliberative institutional design & U.S. defense and security agreements: Comparing Canadian agreements to those with partners and competitors. *Journal of Transatlantic Studies, 20*(2), 230–250. https://doi.org/10.1057/s42738-022-00098-1

Kimball, A. & Lewis. (2010). Le rôle accru des organisations internationales dans les conflits contemporains. In *Conflits dans le monde 2010*. Presses Université Laval.

Kimball, A. & Lewis. (2011). La délégation à l'épreuve du terrain: Les difficiles interventions militaires et civiles des organisations internationales dans les conflits et les crises. In *Conflits dans le monde, 2011*. Presses Université Laval.

Kimball, A. (2018). "Future uncertainty, strategic defense and North American defense cooperation: Rational institutionalist arguments pragmatically suggest NORAD's adaptation over replacement". In C. Leuprecht, J. Sokolsky, & T. Hughes (Eds.), *North American strategic defense in the 21st Century: Security and sovereignty in an uncertain world* (pp. 122–137). Springer-Verlag International (Collection: Advanced Sciences and Technologies for Security Applications).

King, D., & Narlikar, A. (2003). The new risk regulators? International organisations and globalisation. *The Political Quarterly, 74*(3), 337–348. https://doi.org/10.1111/1467-923X.00543

Koremenos, B. (2008). When, what, and why do states choose to delegate? *Law & Contemporary Problems, 71*(1), 151–192.

Koremenos, B. (2005). Contracting around international uncertainty. *The American Political Science Review, 99*(4), 549–565.

Koremenos, B. (2013). The continent of international law. *Journal of Conflict Resolution, 57*(4), 653–681. https://doi.org/10.1177/0022002712448904

Koremenos, B., Lipson, C., & Snidal, D. (2001). The rational design of international institutions. *International Organization, 55*(4), 761–799. https://doi.org/10.1162/002081801317193592

Koremenos & Nau. (2010). Exit, no exit. *Duke Journal of Comparative & International Law, 21*(1), 81–120.

Kratochwil, F., & Ruggie, J. (1986). International organization: A state of the art on an art of the state. *International Organization, 40*(4), 753–775. https://doi.org/10.1017/S0020818300027363

Krekó, P., & Enyedi, Z. (2018). Orbán's laboratory of illiberalism. *Journal of Democracy, 29*(3), 39–51. https://doi.org/10.1353/jod.2018.0043

Kunertova, D. (2017). The Canadian politics of fair-share: The first burden-sharing debates about NATO. *Journal of Transatlantic Studies, 15*(2), 161–183. https://doi.org/10.1080/14794012.2016.1268792

Kunertova, D. (2019). The ethics of burden sharing: When Canada talks about fairness, but actually counts benefits. *Les Ateliers De L'éthique, 13*(3), 4–30. https://doi.org/10.7202/1061216ar

Kupchan, C. (1988). NATO and the Persian Gulf: Examining intra-alliance behavior. *International Organization, 42*(2), 317–346. https://doi.org/10.1017/S0020818300032835

Kwon, G. (1998). Retests on the theory of collective action: The Olson and Zeckhauser model and its elaboration. *Economics & Politics, 10*(1), 37–62. https://doi.org/10.1111/1468-0343.00037

Levy, J. (1997). Prospect theory, rational choice, and international relations. *International Studies Quarterly, 41*(1), 87–112.

Linde, J. (2020). *Expected utility and political decision making*. Linde, Oxford Research Encyclopedia of Politics. Oxford University Press. https://doi.org/10.1093/acrefore/9780190228637.013.885

Lindley-French, J. (2015). *The North Atlantic Treaty Organization: The enduring alliance* (2nd edition). Routledge.

Lipson, C. (1991). Why are some international agreements informal? *International Organization, 45*(4), 495–538.

Liu, T.-Y., Su, C.-W., Tao, R., & Cong, H. (2019). Better is the neighbor? *Defence and Peace Economics, 30*(6), 706–718. https://doi.org/10.1080/10242694.2017.1422321

Lobo, S. (2012). *NATO transformation and centers of excellence: Analyzing rationale and roles*. University of Oslo. http://urn.nb.no/URN:NBN:no-32044

Macdonald, L., & Paltiel, J. (2016). Middle power or muddling power? Canada's relations with emerging markets. *Canadian Foreign Policy Journal, 22*(1), 1–11. https://doi.org/10.1080/11926422.2016.1144626

Männik, E. (2004). Small states: Invited to NATO—able to contribute? *Defense & Security Analysis, 20*(1), 21–37. https://doi.org/10.1080/1475179042000195483

Martin, L. (2000). *Democratic commitments: Legislatures and international cooperation*. Princeton University Press.

Marton, P., & Eichler, J. (2013). Between willing and reluctant entrapment: CEE countries in NATO's non-European missions. *Communist and Post-Communist Studies, 46*(3), 351–362. https://doi.org/10.1016/j.postcomstud.2013.06.002

Marton, P., & Hynek, N. (2012). What makes ISAF S/tick: An investigation of the politics of coalition burden-sharing. *Defence Studies, 12*(4), 539–571. https://doi.org/10.1080/14702436.2012.746862

Massie, J. (2014). Public contestation and policy resistance: Canada's oversized military commitment to Afghanistan. *Foreign Policy Analysis, 12*(1), 47–65. https://doi.org/10.1111/fpa.12047

Massie, J., & Zyla, B. (2018). Alliance value and status enhancement: Canada's disproportionate military burden sharing in Afghanistan: Canada's military burden. *Politics & Policy, 46*(2), 320–344. https://doi.org/10.1111/polp.12247

Mattern, J. B., & Zarakol, A. (2016). Hierarchies in world politics. *International Organization, 70*(3), 623–654. https://doi.org/10.1017/S0020818316000126

McFaul, M. (2002). The fourth wave of democracy and dictatorship: Noncooperative transitions in the postcommunist world. *World Politics, 54*(2), 212–244. https://doi.org/10.1353/wp.2002.0004

Milner, H. (1997). *Interests, institutions, and information: Domestic politics and international relations*. Princeton University Press.

Moravcsik, A. (1997). Taking preferences seriously: A liberal theory of international politics. *International Organization, 51*(4), 513–553. https://doi.org/10.1162/002081897550447

Morgenthau, H. (1973). *Politics among nations: The struggle for power and peace* (5th edition). Knopf.

Morrow, J. (1991). Alliances and asymmetry: An alternative to the capability aggregation model of alliances. *American Journal of Political Science, 35*(4), 904. https://doi.org/10.2307/2111499

Munoz Mosquera, A. (2014). NATO legal cornerstones: "Memorandum of understanding (MOU)": A philosophical and empirical approach (Part I), *NATO Legal Gazette, 34*, 55–69. http://www.act.nato.int/images/stories/media/doclibrary/legal_gazette_34a.pdf

Munoz Mosquera, A. (2016). Memorandum of Understanding (MOU): A philosophical and empirical approach (Part II), *NATO Legal Gazette, 37,* 48–61.

Neack, L. (1993). Delineating state groups through cluster analysis. *The Social Science Journal, 30*(4), 347–371. https://doi.org/10.1016/0362-3319(93)90014-M

Neack, L., Hey, J., & Haney, P. (1995). *Foreign policy analysis: Continuity and change in its second generation*. Prentice Hall.

North, D. C. (1990). *Institutions, institutional change, and economic performance*. Cambridge University Press.

Olson, M. (1971). *The logic of collective action: Public goods and the theory of groups*. Harvard University Press.

Olson, M., & Zeckhauser, R. (1966). An economic theory of alliances. *The Review of Economics and Statistics, 48*(3), 266. https://doi.org/10.2307/1927082

Oma, I. M. (2012). Explaining states' burden-sharing behaviour within NATO. *Cooperation and Conflict, 47*(4), 562–573.

O'Neill, B. (2001). Risk aversion in international relations theory. *International Studies Quarterly, 45*(4), 617–640.

Palmer, G., & Morgan, T. C. (2006). *A theory of foreign policy*. Princeton University Press.

Panke, D. (2020). States in international organizations: Promoting regional positions in international politics? *International Journal: Canada's Journal of Global Policy Analysis, 75*(4), 629–651. https://doi.org/10.1177/0020702020965267

Patience, A. (2018). Australian foreign policy in Asia. *Springer International Publishing*. https://doi.org/10.1007/978-3-319-69347-7

Powell, R. (1991). Absolute and relative gains in international relations theory. *American Political Science Review, 85*(4), 1303–1320. https://doi.org/10.2307/1963947

Powell, R. (1999). *In the shadow of power: States and strategies in international politics*. Princeton University Press.

Putnam, R. (1988). Diplomacy and domestic politics: The logic of two-level games. *International Organization, 42*(3), 427–460.

Reiter, D. (2001). Why NATO enlargement does not spread democracy. *International Security, 25*(4), 41–67. https://doi.org/10.1162/01622880151091899

Richter, A. (2021). NATO in the age of Trump: Alliance defense spending during the Trump presidency. *Comparative Strategy, 40*(3), 285–304. https://doi.org/10.1080/01495933.2021.1912511

Ringsmose, J. (2010). NATO burden-sharing redux: Continuity and change after the cold war. *Contemporary Security Policy, 31*(2), 319–338. https://doi.org/10.1080/13523260.2010.491391

Root, H. (1989). Tying the King's hands: Credible commitments and royal fiscal policy during the old regime. *Rationality and Society, 1*(2), 240–258. https://doi.org/10.1177/1043463189001002005

Russett, B., & Oneal, J. (2001). *Triangulating peace: Democracy, interdependence, and international organizations*. Norton.

Saideman, S. (2016). *Nato in Afghanistan—Fighting together, fighting alone*. Princeton University Press.

Saideman, S., & Auerswald, D. (2012). Comparing caveats: Understanding the sources of national restrictions upon NATO's mission in Afghanistan: Comparing caveats. *International Studies Quarterly, 56*(1), 67–84. https://doi.org/10.1111/j.1468-2478.2011.00700.x

Sandler, T. (1977). Impurity of defense: An application to the economics of alliances. *Kyklos, 30*(3), 443–460. https://doi.org/10.1111/j.1467-6435.1977.tb02203.x

Sandler, T. (2004). *Global collective action* (1st edition). Cambridge University Press. https://doi.org/10.1017/CBO9780511617119

Sandler, T., & Hartley, K. (2001). Economics of alliances: The lessons for collective action. *Journal of Economic Literature, 39*(3), 869–896. https://doi.org/10.1257/jel.39.3.869

Schimmelfennig, F. (1998). NATO enlargement: A constructivist explanation. *Security Studies, 8*(2–3), 198–234. https://doi.org/10.1080/09636419808429378

Schimmelfennig, F. (2001). The community trap: Liberal norms, rhetorical action, and the Eastern enlargement of the European Union. *International Organization, 55*(1), 47–80. https://doi.org/10.1162/002081801551414

Schimmelfennig, F. (2005). Strategic calculation and international socialization: Membership incentives, party constellations, and sustained compliance in Central and Eastern Europe. *International Organization, 59*(4). https://doi.org/10.1017/S0020818305050290

Schuette, L. (2021). Why NATO survived Trump: The neglected role of Secretary-General Stoltenberg. *International Affairs, 97*(6), 1863–1881. https://doi.org/10.1093/ia/iiab167

Schwarz, O. (2016). Two steps forward one step back: What shapes the process of EU enlargement in South-Eastern Europe? *Journal of European Integration, 38*(7), 757–773. https://doi.org/10.1080/07036337.2016.1203309

Shin, S. (2016). South Korea's elusive middle powermanship: Regional or global player? *The Pacific Review, 29*(2), 187–209. https://doi.org/10.1080/09512748.2015.1013494

Simion, E. (2016). *NATO centres of excellence and the transformation of the North-Atlantic alliance*. University of Oradea. https://nbn-resolving.org/urn:nbn:de:0168-ssoar-73403-8

Sirici, J., & Coletta, D. (2009). Enduring without an enemy: NATO's realist foundation. *Perspectives, 17*(1), 57–81.

Smith, A. (1995). Alliance formation and war. *International Studies Quarterly, 39*(4), 405. https://doi.org/10.2307/2600800

Smith, A. (1996). To intervene or not to intervene: A biased decision. *Journal of Conflict Resolution, 40*(1), 16–40. https://doi.org/10.1177/0022002796040001003

Smith, M., & Timmins, G. (2000). The EU, NATO, and the extension of institutional order in Europe. *World Affairs, 163*(2), 80–89.

Snider, L. (2005). Political risk: The institutional dimension. *International Interactions, 31*(3), 203–222. https://doi.org/10.1080/03050620500294176

Sperling, J., & Webber, M. (2019). Trump's foreign policy and NATO: Exit and voice. *Review of International Studies, 45*(3), 511–526. https://doi.org/10.1017/S0260210519000123

Stone, R. (2011). *Controlling institutions: International organizations and the global economy*. Cambridge University Press.

Stone, R. (2013). Informal governance in international organizations: Introduction to the special issue. *The Review of International Organizations, 8*(2), 121–136. https://doi.org/10.1007/s11558-013-9168-y

Tago, A. (2014). Too many problems at home to help you: Domestic disincentives for military coalition participation. *International Area Studies Review, 17*(3), 262–278. https://doi.org/10.1177/2233865914544227

Tonelson, A. (2000). NATO burden-sharing: Promises, promises. *Journal of Strategic Studies, 23*(3), 29–58. https://doi.org/10.1080/01402390008437799

Ubriaco, J. (2017). NATO'S Baltic problem: How populism, Russia, and the Baltic can fracture NATO. *Harvard International Review, 38*(1), 13.

Ungerer, C. (2007). The "Middle power" concept in Australian foreign policy. *Australian Journal of Politics & History, 53*(4), 538–551. https://doi.org/10.1111/j.1467-8497.2007.00473.x

Vabulas, F., & Snidal, D. (2013). Organization without delegation: Informal Intergovernmental Organizations (IIGOs) and the spectrum of intergovernmental arrangements. *The Review of International Organizations, 8*(2), 193–220. https://doi.org/10.1007/s11558-012-9161-x

Vaubel, R. (2006). Principal-agent problems in international organizations. *The Review of International Organizations, 1*(2), 125–138. https://doi.org/10.1007/s11558-006-8340-z

Walt, S. (1987). *The origins of alliances*. Cornell University Press.

Waltz, K. (2010). *Theory of international politics* (Reiss). Waveland Press.

Waltz, K. (2018). *Man, the state, and war: A theoretical analysis* (Anniversary Edition). Columbia University Press.

Wendt, A. (1992). Anarchy is what states make of it: The social construction of power politics. *International Organization, 46*(2), 391–425. https://doi.org/10.1017/S0020818300027764

Wendt, A. (2006). *Social Theory of International Politics.* https://doi.org/10.1017/CBO9780511612183

Wiarda, H. (2001). Where does Europe end? The politics of NATO and EU enlargement. *World Affairs, 164*(4), 178–197.

Wolf, R. (2017). Donald Trump's status-driven foreign policy. *Survival, 59*(5), 99–116. https://doi.org/10.1080/00396338.2017.1375260

Zarakol, A. (2014). What made the modern world hang together: Socialisation or stigmatisation? *International Theory, 6*(2), 311–332. https://doi.org/10.1017/S1752971914000141

Zarakol, A. (2018). *A non-Eurocentric approach to sovereignty*. https://doi.org/10.17863/CAM.26865

Zehfuss, M. (2001). Constructivism and identity: A dangerous liaison. *European Journal of International Relations, 7*(3), 315–348. https://doi.org/10.1177/1354066101007003002

Zyla, B. (2009). NATO and post-cold war burden-sharing: Canada "the laggard?" *International Journal: Canada's Journal of Global Policy Analysis, 64*(2), 337–359. https://doi.org/10.1177/002070200906400203

Zyla, B. (2015). Sharing the burden?: NATO and its second-tier powers. *University of Toronto Press*. https://doi.org/10.3138/9781442668386

Zyla, B. (2016). Who is keeping the peace and who is free-riding? NATO middle powers and burden sharing, 1995–2001. *International Politics, 53*(3), 303–323. https://doi.org/10.1057/ip.2016.2

Zyla, B. (2018). Transatlantic burden sharing: Suggesting a new research agenda. *European Security, 27*(4), 515–535. https://doi.org/10.1080/09662839.2018.1552142

Index

A. L. Kimball, *Beyond 2%—NATO Partners, Institutions & Burden Management*, Canada and International Affairs,
https://doi.org/10.1007/978-3-031-22158-3

D